AF326949

LIKE A HEART SO DEARLY NEEDED FOR LIBERATION

LIKE A HEART SO DEARLY NEEDED
FOR LIBERATION

༄༅། །ཐར་འདོད་རྣམས་ལ་སྙིང་ལྟར་གཅེས་པའི་ཉེར་མཁོ་
འགའ་ཞིག་བཞུགས་སོ། ། །

Oral Commentary

by

SERMEY KHENSUR RINPOCHE LOBSANG THARCHIN

on passages selected from the works of
Holy Je Tsong Khapa and his spiritual sons

by

TREHOR KYORBÖN RINPOCHE LOBSANG DARGYE

Transcription and Editing
by
Vincent Montenegro

ORAL COMMENTARY SERIES
MAHAYANA SUTRA AND TANTRA PRESS

Mahayana Sutra and Tantra Press
112 West Second Street
Howell, New Jersey 07731

©2008 by Sermey Khensur Rinpoche Lobsang Tharchin
©2016 Second Printing

All rights reserved.

Library of Congress Cataloging-in-Publication Data

Lobsang Tharchin, Sermey Khensur Rinpoche, 1921-2004.
Like a heart so dearly needed for liberation : oral commentary by Sermey Khensur Rinpoche Lobsang Tharchin on passages selected from the works of Holy Je Tsong Khapa and his two spiritual sons by Trehor Kyorbon Rinpoche Lobsang Dargye / transcription and editing by Vincent Montenegro.
p. cm. -- (Oral commentary series)
Includes bibliographical references.

ISBN 0-918753-22-8

1. Spiritual life--Buddhism. 2. Tshe-dban-nor-bu, Tre-hor Skyor-dpon. Thar 'dod rnams la sñin ltar gces pa'i ñer mkho 'ga' zig. 3. Tson-kha-pa Blo-bzan-grags-pa, 1357-1419. 4. Dignaga, 5th cent. Pramanasamuccaya. I. Montenegro, Vincent, 1954- II. Tshe-dban-nor-bu, Tre-hor Skyor-dpon. Thar 'dod rnams la sñin ltar gces pa'i ñer mkho 'ga' zig. III. Title.
BQ7805.L625 2008
294.3'444--dc22
2008037957

CONTENTS

།སྟོན་པའི་བསྟན་པ་རིགས་པས་ལེགས་པར་གྲུབ།
།དཀོན་མཆོག་གསུམ་ལ་རྩེ་གཅིག་ཡིད་ཆེས་སྐྱེད།
།དེ་དོན་ཚུལ་བཞིན་སྒྲུབ་ལ་བརྩོན་ལྡན་པ།
།སྐྱེས་བུ་གང་དེ་རྟོག་ལྡན་ཡིན་ཞེས་བྱ།

That one is wise who, once establishing the Buddha's
teachings in his mind with logic,
Gains unwavering faith in the Holy Triple Gem
And expends all effort to achieve the goal supreme.

—from Gyaltsab Je's
Clearing the Path to Liberation

NOTE TO THE READER

These teachings were given to a small group of students in the lower teaching room at Rashi Gempil Ling, Howell, New Jersey between 1992 and 1993. As it was customary for Rinpoche to teach from texts in their original Tibetan language and base his commentary on a word for word translation into English, we have retained here the original Tibetan text accompanied by an English translation in accord with that commentary. Wherever necessary, we have used the Wylie system of transliteration, which has been set off in parentheses following appropriate phrases and names.

The text used for this oral commentary is a compilation by Trehor skyor dpon blo bzang dar rgyas entitled *Thar 'dod rnams la snying ltar gces pa'i nyer mkho 'ga' zhig*, consisting primarily of passages from the works of rJe Tsong kha pa blo bzang grags pa and his spiritual sons, rGyal tshab rje dar ma rin chen and mKhas grub rje dge legs bzang po. Transcriptions of Rinpoche's teachings on this text were taken from cassette tapes diligently recorded at the time and digitally remastered by one of his students, Dietrich Gewissler, and offered for the production of this work.

Whatever faults that may have surfaced in the attempt to render Rinpoche's words into written language are strictly the responsibility of the editor.

INTRODUCTION

INTRODUCTION

What is your main goal as a Buddhist practitioner? What is the purpose of your practice? Of course your main goal is to achieve Buddhahood—the status of a Buddha. But do you know anything about Buddha? Do you know anything about a Buddha's qualities? If I were to ask you this you would probably just shrug your shoulders and answer, "I'm not sure." So you're saying that you don't know anything about the qualities of what you are striving after … your main goal?! This is precisely what logic is for. Its principal purpose is to help you gain a clear understanding of the goal you are pursuing, which is the main subject and purpose of this present book.

The root text[1] to which this work is a commentary was composed by the great Indian Buddhist pandit and teacher Dignaga.[2] He was the principal founder of Buddhist logic. The traditional story that has come down to us relates how Dignaga, while composing this text on a piece of slate suddenly had the thought: "Since no one is going to be able to understand what I am writing this is almost useless!" So in frustration he threw the slate up into the sky. However, the slate didn't fall down immediately as one might have expected but continued to fly up and up until it completely vanished only to land later far away on the north side of the Himalayan mountains. At one point, as the slate lay there on the side of that mountain it began to emanate light rays, which struck a place in Tibet known as *Jang Gün Chö* (*'jang dgun chos*)

---

[1] *Compendium of Means of Valid Cognition* (T: *Tshad ma kun btus*; S: *Pramāṇasamuccaya*).

[2] Dignāga (T: *sLob dpon phyogs kyi glang po*), father of Buddhist logic and epistemology who flourished in India around 450 CE.

where, due to the miraculous appearance of this light, the local people decided that they should construct a monastery. This is where monks later went to study logic. As it occasionally happened in earlier days that Dignaga's slate would glisten and shine and emit light rays toward the monastery, they placed some flat stones in the front yard to catch the holy rays and receive the blessings as they reached there. Consequently, long thereafter, when the monks did their prostrations before assembly they prostrated in all directions, since no one knew for sure in which direction those stones lay. If they happened to prostrate in the exact direction of one of those stones they would receive the holy logic wisdom and blessing in their mind like magic. That was their hope anyway.

When Manjushri saw what Dignaga had done he suddenly appeared before him and reprimanded him saying: "You have to write this book nicely and finish it. In the future it will be very useful for beings." So Dignaga proceeded to complete this important brief text. In Tibetan we call this work *Tse Ma Do* (*Tshad ma mdo*) or *Sutra of Valid Cognition. Tse ma* means logic or correct cognition. *Do* means sutra or discourse. The name derives from the fact that Dignaga gathered in it many of the most essential points of logic from his other works.

***

At the very beginning of the text Dignaga pays homage with these lines:

།ཚད་མར་གྱུར་པ་འགྲོ་ལ་ཕན་བཞེད་པ།

།སྟོན་པ་བདེ་གཤེགས་སྐྱོབ་ལ་ཕྱག་འཚལ་ཏེ།

I prostrate to the One who became perfectly correct, whose desire is to benefit beings, to the Teacher, the Sugata, and Protector.

ACHARYA DIGNAGA'S HOMAGE TO BUDDHA

By way of introduction I will give a brief explanation of these lines here and discuss them in more detail later. *Tse ma* means *correct cognition* but in this case refers to a correct, infallible object. *Gyur pa* means *to turn into* or become that. Who was it that turned into an infallible object? Buddha. The words "turned into" imply that he wasn't that way before but was to become that infallible object.

This root text was composed in India at a time when there was an abundance of philosophies representing many different tenets and belief systems. There were eight major groups in all. Buddhist philosophy was a rather late arrival. One of these groups held the belief that their world and all the beings inhabiting it were created by a powerful god (*dbang phyug*). The most famous creator, however, was what is known in Tibetan as *chi tso wo* (*spyi gtso bo*) or the "primordial nature."[3] This nature, according to some, was a permanent, unchanging entity (*rtag pa*). In short, they believed in a self-existent unchanging being (*rtag pa rang byung gi skyes bu*). *Tak pa* is

---

[3] S: *prākṛti*, a fundamental, universal principle that is partless, unchanging, and creator of all.

the quality of being static or unchanging; *rang jung* means arising from itself, self-existent; that is, a being who had no causes but appeared spontaneously as a creator. *Kye bu*, usually translated as person, in this case refers to a great being. So their philosophy held that this great being was both their creator and *mi lu wa* (*mi slu ba*), or an infallible authority.

Buddha, however, was not infallible in the beginning but *turned into* an infallible being later. The case is similar to when we say, for instance, "This material wasn't pure gold before but later became that." There are many such things. Buddha Shakyamuni is being used in the line quoted above, *tse mar gyur pa*, to represent the meaning of someone who though initially not infallible *became* that way. This indicates that Buddha Shakyamuni is not a permanent, unchanging being and as such is at variance with the authorities of the other tenet systems of India of the time. So the words "turns into" highlight a logical reason that has very important significance for us.

At the beginning of his text Dignaga pays homage to the person who later turned into an infallible object—the Buddha. To grasp the logical implications of this statement we have to understand that Buddha was not infallible from the outset but turned into that kind of person later. How did he accomplish this? It required the gathering of many good causes, among them of course being rigorous practice. What was Buddha like before he became infallible? He was just like us. However, our condition, our color, our ability have not changed as did Buddha's. He changed himself through having worked unbelievably hard over a long period of time so that he eventually became an infallible authority. Before changing, Buddha was no different from us. If we examine this carefully we will realize that if we do just as Buddha did and practice in the same manner we too can achieve Buddhahood exactly as he did. There are no obstacles if we do it nicely. Since there is no permanent obstacle we can remove each and every obstacle one by one as did Buddha. At some point we ourselves can turn into an infallible object, become perfectly valid as well.

How then did he achieve this? In the homage it says *whose desire is to benefit beings*, which means that he is always thinking about benefiting beings. This kind of attitude indicates the practice of compassion. Buddha practiced compassion for all sentient beings of the six realms very seriously for a long time, focusing ceaselessly on their problems as well as on the obstacles of those who have gone beyond samsara. In order to liberate these beings he practiced loving kindness and great compassion. Because he practiced like that for such a long time, of course his compassion improved immensely until he finally reached the highest status of ultimate compassion.

Since Buddha is an infallible person, whatever we need, whatever we wish for, he can satisfy us in accord with our level. This means that from Buddha's side he is completely qualified and ready to help us, but from our side it is we who are lacking in faith, effort, and understanding because we fail to study. Consequently, our road is getting longer and longer and our goal receding farther and farther away. Since Buddha is infallible he can satisfy everybody at their own level. Yet, why would he do this? He does this because he has achieved ultimate compassion, which compels him all the time toward this goal of benefiting all beings in whatever way he can whenever it is necessary. When the time comes his compassion urges him to act. This is what it means to always want to be benefiting beings. What do I mean when I say "when the time comes?" I mean we have to arrange everything from our own side and make a schedule of practice. "When the time comes" for him to act depends upon us, upon our level, upon our aspiration, upon our ability. He will help us to achieve exactly what we wish when we are ready. That is what it means to be infallible. He can do this not only because he achieved ultimate compassion but because he is omniscient.

Buddha's omniscient mind is very clear and expansive and perceives all objects directly. In Tibetan the word for omniscience is *nam kyen* (*rnam mkhyen*). *Nam* refers to all objects; *kyen* means perceiving them directly. How can Buddha's mind do such a thing? Buddha's mind is omniscient because it is not obstructed by obstacles in any way. He can directly see all the problems that sentient beings have.

Compassion and wisdom are different kinds of mind. If he only had compassion without wisdom, he would not be able to accomplish what he wishes. So Buddha achieved wisdom as well. Wisdom is represented by the word *Teacher* (*ston pa*) in the homage. What is the nature of this wisdom and why is it referred to as "Teacher"?

To comprehend this we must first have an understanding of the *status of higher rebirth* (*mngon mtho kyi go 'phang*) and the *status of nirvana and Buddhahood* (*nges legs kyi go 'phang*). The first means an unusually high status, referring to the higher realms of existence. The wheel of samsara is divided into six realms comprising three lower realms and three higher realms. The three lower realms consist of the hell realms, hungry ghost realm, and animal realm. The three higher realms consist of the human realm, demigod realm, and god realm. Because the human realm, demigod realm, and god realm are comparatively high in relation to the three lower realms, they are called "very high" status. In those three higher realms the happiness that the beings experience, their ability, and basic quality are all quite different from that of the beings of the three lower realms. The literal meaning of "definite goodness" (*nges legs*) is something like one hundred percent good and refers to both nirvana and Buddhahood depending on the context.

Although we have achieved the status of a higher rebirth, we are still residing in samsara. Since this privileged status is not secure in the future we will be forced to fall down once again into the three lower realms. The happiness of this higher rebirth is merely temporary. Only when we achieve the happiness of nirvana does that happiness remain without changing, almost like a permanent position. Though we may not believe it this status is achievable; it is certainly possible. But in order to achieve nirvana first we have to know how to achieve it. To learn how to achieve it we need infallible instruction given by an infallible instructor. Where can we find such instruction and where are we to find such a teacher to give us perfect instruction? Who is qualified to do that? Only Buddha is qualified because he is an infallible authority; this is why he is the only true teacher. How can Buddha give us unerring instruction on the way to achieve this goal? Because he teaches everything that he himself experienced, what he perceived, what he himself did to become liberated and achieve Buddhahood. He teaches beings the exact same path that he himself took to achieve it. Through his infallible instruction he shows us the method for becoming liberated from samsara and how to achieve nirvana and Buddhahood.

As a teacher he teaches us about wisdom, about exactly what he himself perceived and experienced.

THE FOUR ARYA TRUTHS

What is it that he perceived and experienced? He perceived the Four Arya Truths (*'phags pa'i bden pa gzhi*) directly and practiced them unerringly until he finally accomplished the ultimate goal. Therefore, what he teaches as a teacher is the Four Arya Truths.

What do we mean by "Arya Truths"? If the Aryas perceive something and believe it to be happiness or the cause of happiness, then it most definitely must be happiness and the cause of happiness. On the other hand, what ordinary people perceive and believe to be happiness and the cause of happiness without a doubt cannot be that, because they perceive things in an erroneous manner. That is why these truths are called "Arya Truths."

The first two truths that the Aryas perceived, the truth of suffering (*sdug bsngal bden pa*) and the truth of origin (*kun 'byung bden pa*), represent objects to be abandoned, while the second two represent objects to be adopted and practiced. What are the objects of the first two truths that are to be abandoned? *Dung ngel* means suffering; *den pa* means true, so true suffering. Are these kinds of suffering really true suffering? Yes, they are true suffering because the Aryas perceived them as such. Who has these kinds of true suffering? We do, we ourselves have them; we are the ones who are experiencing suffering in our mind and body. This is how practitioners should think when they study any subject. They have to immediately apply what they learn to themselves, to their own situation and this is why this method of study is so very different from other ways of studying. We are not just discussing something theoretical and foreign to us but dealing with something we are experiencing insofar as we are the receptacles of this suffering.

Our own suffering, in general, is comprised of four kinds: birth, old age, sickness, and death.[4]

Birth: Once we are conceived in our mother's womb we have to come out. When leaving the womb we are like helpless worms that can do nothing but cry—"Waaaaaaa Waaaaaa Waaaaaa!" If we were happy we wouldn't have to say "Waaaa Waaaa" all the time. "Waaaa Waaaa" shows that we are suffering even though we cannot express our suffering yet in words. This kind of suffering is unbelievably harsh.

Aging: Gradually we grow bigger and bigger, stronger and stronger and continue this way until the process starts to reverse and we start to come down. "To come down" signifies that we grow older and older until the power of our heaps gradually degenerates, getting worse and worse, weaker and weaker. This is the real suffering of old age.

Sickness: Sometimes we are subjected to various kinds of illnesses, some of them curable, some not. These often pose very big problems for us when they occur.

---

[4] The four principal human sufferings: *skye rga na 'chi*

Death: To have to die is the fourth kind of suffering we have to experience. When all our ability is exhausted we are forced to die. Since we cannot stay any longer in this life the body and the consciousness go their separate ways.

These four, being beyond our control, are all definite kinds of suffering of samsara since that is samsara's very nature. Naturally we don't like to suffer and have problems but they come to us automatically without our being able to prevent them. So where does this suffering come from? For example, if we wish to grow a flower first we have to have a seed; then we have to put this seed in some dirt in a flowerpot and add fertilizer and water. We have to tend it regularly to make sure that it has what it needs, enough sunlight, water, protection from insects, and so forth. Eventually the seed will bring forth a sprout, which will slowly grow and begin to produce buds. Later a flower will come, opening up to show all its parts—the stamin, pistil, anthers, and the like. Everything living goes through a similar process. Almost immediately after the fresh, healthy beautiful flower opens, however, that fresh quality begins to degenerate. The flower starts to slump over as the stem becomes more feeble, the petals begin to lose their vivid color and curl and wilt until they eventually fall off the stem. The main power of all of these –the healthy petals, the beautiful color, the sweet scent, the bright green leaves, the firm stem– was in the seed. This seed has a certain potential or completion power, which we call *nü pa* (*nus pa*), to bring about these various qualities that comprise the flower. Of course, that power itself is impermanent so that at some point it too will dissipate, which will result in the flower's eventual death.

Even the happiness of this excellent human being's life, like that beautiful flower with the fresh green leaves, will disappear regardless of our capacity for higher understanding and our exceptional ability to do so many good things. Why? Because those four kinds of suffering, produced as they are by karma and mental afflictions, are always with us and like that seed, which carries those potential qualities within it, must manifest those qualities when it ripens. Karma and the mental afflictions produced both our good human life and the root of our samsaric existence. Additionally, they are responsible for producing the many kinds of suffering that we are compelled to experience throughout our life. Karma and mental afflictions have the power to produce simultaneously a "happy" higher rebirth and the suffering that accompanies it. This is the meaning of samsara's karma. Hence, karma and the mental afflictions are the root causes of samsara's suffering. If we don't have karma and mental afflictions we will no longer have samsara's suffering. It is only due to these that we are forced to experience samsara's suffering. Since Aryas perceive these as the main cause of suffering we can accept their perception as true. If we have no more causes for suffering we have no more suffering. If we have the causes we cannot possibly avoid their result since they possess the power to produce suffering.

In these first two truths we see how Buddha truly perceived and analyzed the nature of suffering as well as the source of that suffering. Not only that, when he realized their true nature he found that there is a hundred percent possibility to become free from them, to put an end to them. That state of freedom from suffering is nirvana or Buddhahood.

How do we achieve this superior status and finally become free? To help followers achieve this Buddha taught the truth of the path (*lam gyi bden pa*). The main path is the wisdom that understands and realizes all the sufferings of samsara and where they come from. So how do we put a stop to this samsaric suffering once and for all? We have to practice true paths. By practicing true paths we can achieve the truth of cessation (*'gog pa'i bden pa*) from the many kinds of suffering. Buddha taught us to try to abandon suffering and the source of suffering. How do we do that? We have to study and practice the paths to achieve the various kinds of wisdom along with compassion. Most of all, we have to acquire the wisdom that understands true sufferings and the true causes of suffering and practice the paths that lead to the cessation of that suffering. We have to use Buddha as our model and study and practice exactly the way he did. Compelled by his compassion over lifetimes to benefit beings, Buddha gained perfection and taught this path in precisely the same way that he achieved it. This is what "*Teacher*" indicates in the homage at the beginning of Dignaga's text.

Buddha gave an example of what he experienced by presenting on his first day of teaching the Four Arya Truths. Just by the very name we can understand that the subject matter of this teaching is true. In fact, all of Buddha's speech can be regarded as true speech just like these Four Arya Truths. What are the four truths and how are we to understand them? As mentioned, the first set of "truths" comprises the objects to be abandoned, while the second set of "truths" comprises the objects to be achieved or adopted. These are true since there is no correct cognition that can find fault with them. What then is the nature of these four truths?

The first two truths are mental afflictions. Altogether there are eighty-four thousand different kinds of mental afflictions. Ignorance is their king while hatred and desire act as its ministers. Motivated by these various mental afflictions people are compelled to do bad things by body, say bad things by speech, and plan bad things by mind. All of these bad deeds, which include both the motivation and the activity itself, that is, the mental afflictions and karma, are the unique causes of suffering and their result encompasses all the suffering of samsara. Whatever suffering there is in the world is the responsibility of the mental afflictions and karma.

Again, we as practitioners of Buddhist philosophy and its tenets, listeners of Dharma, shouldn't be like spectators at a museum. For instance, if I took you to a museum and acted as your guide, and showed you the paintings and said, "This is an extraordinary painting! The painter painted it two hundred years ago. It's really rare. By now it's probably worth around fifteen million dollars!" what would be the fruit of such a visit? You might say, "Oh, today I saw many famous paintings and he told us a lot of stories about the paintings and the painters, etc." Listening to tales about what someone else did and seeing their fruit will not allow us to see the fruit of our own activities. Logic's teaching system should be very different from that kind of spectator's activity whereby subject and object remain separate and things are merely described to us without our participation.

The purpose of every single word of Buddha's teachings is to liberate sentient beings from their suffering. So it is our responsibility to study and learn all his teachings. How, then, do we go about doing this? By first examining our own mind. How? I will tell you. We logicians have an expression: *rang lo rang la gok du ma gyur pa* (*rang blo rang la 'gog du ma gyur pa*), which means "what is in your mind should be clear to you," unless you're crazy. Only you know whether you have ignorance, anger, desire, jealousy or any of the other many kinds of mental afflictions in your mind. These can be counted one by one. Not only do you have mental afflictions in your mind but you are extremely rich in them.

For example, from this morning up to now what have you done physically? What have you said verbally? What have you thought mentally? What kind of thoughts have come into your mind? Of course myriad things have passed through your mind since this morning. Usually thoughts won't stay in the mind longer than two or three seconds because the mind is constantly changing and so it is very difficult to retain them. Were the thoughts you had good thoughts, bad thoughts, or neutral thoughts that are just a waste of time? Perhaps a few of them were very good but more than likely the majority were bad or just neutral thoughts. This reveals that you have mental afflictions and have done many activities by body, speech, and mind that were motivated by them. As you yourself can calculate even in one single day you perform an exorbitant number of bad deeds.

What Buddha taught on his first day of teaching was that all of these mental afflictions are objects to be abandoned. Why should we abandon them? We have to rid ourselves of them because we don't want problems and suffering in the future; we don't want to be unhappy. All the suffering we experience is merely a result of these mental afflictions. If we don't like smoke, for example, we have to extinguish the cause of smoke. Likewise, if we don't like suffering we have to try to abandon its causes—mental afflictions and karma. Therefore, this is a form of truth. We have those qualities so it is true; it is our experience.

At this point you should think, "I see. Now I understand. I don't want to suffer and others don't want to suffer either. Nobody likes suffering. Therefore, I have to try to remove the causes of suffering as Buddha taught us." When thinking this way a qualm may arise in your mind. "Surely I would like to abandon all my suffering as Buddha said, *but* I don't know how to do it." That is why the Buddha taught the second set of truths, which consists of the object to be achieved and the object to be practiced. What are these? The object to be achieved is cessation or freedom from all suffering. Once you achieve that cessation, even if you were to wish to suffer you would not be able to since the status of cessation prevents suffering from ever returning. Cessation really exists. If it did not exist trying to achieve it would be nothing but a foolish waste of time.

"Now that I realize that cessation exists, I have to know what I have to practice to achieve it." This is why the Buddha taught the object to be practiced, which is the wisdom that realizes selflessness (*bdag med rtogs pa'i shes rab*). This is the wisdom that realizes your real nature, the real nature of others, of nations, of the world, of your house, of your body, and the like. While all of these are objects of that realization their unique subject, or mind, that realizes them is the wisdom that realizes selflessness. If you understand your real nature, this is the most powerful wisdom that can put an end to your samsara's suffering.

Now, you might wonder what the most powerful enemies are against which you have to use this powerful wisdom. They are ignorance, hatred, and desire of course. Why are they your most powerful enemies? Because outer enemies can hurt you for perhaps only one lifetime and be forgotten in the next life, but these inner enemies do you harm for lifetime after lifetime for eons and eons. That is why they are your most powerful enemies. This is also a "truth."

Clearly, we are the ones who have those powerful enemies. They are my enemies; they are your enemies. Well then, is it possible to get rid of them? Yes, it is possible. We have to use our logic. When people feel cold they immediately switch on the furnace. Why do they do that? Because the heat from the furnace will eliminate the cold. All cold, no matter how powerful, has its own powerful antidote. That is almost a fact of nature. No matter how dark it gets still, by lighting a match or turning on a light, we can remove that darkness. Every negative thing has its own powerful antidote. Accordingly, our own powerful inner enemy has its own powerful antidote, which is wisdom. Wisdom is that which the Buddha taught us to practice and gain; that is the path.

If we examine the nature of things with logic we will come to discover that this is all true and real, the actual state of affairs and we will come to understand how all of Buddha's speech is infallible and trustworthy, especially these Four Arya Truths. Why is Buddha's speech infallible? Because it has been verified by valid cognition and so we can recognize it as true. By examining these truths with logic our knowledge will become more firm and steady so that we can confidently go about eliminating the object to be abandoned and acquiring the object to be adopted. These four truths –the truth of suffering, the truth of suffering's causes, the truth of cessation, and the truth of the path– are the Four Arya Truths. Since no correct cognition can find fault with them or argue against their validity they are all trustworthy and believable and not just a mere fantasy. This basic knowledge is of principal importance since it obliges us to think all the time about our own nature, about what nature we will have in the future, and so forth.

The knowledge you gain here can be unbelievably useful and not just blind faith as a result of a blind teaching. When you examine what you know with logic, this means that you are searching for a correct understanding of the subject matter through correct cognition, which produces an infallible kind of knowledge. Once you gain infallible knowledge it will stay in your mind very strongly and firmly and will be very difficult for you to lose. Even though you might hear many other different explanations and teachings they won't change your mind very easily as they normally might since you have gained correct cognition that can validate the truth of what you hear. As a result you will naturally inquire further, "Is this true? No, that's not true. I don't believe it." Or, "I believe it because I saw it. I am definitely certain about it since I have gained perfect knowledge about it." Practicing this way, you won't lose your knowledge. Additionally, if you take refuge in the Buddha, Dharma, and Sangha with this kind of certainty through investigation, this mode of taking refuge will bring you measureless, incomparable virtue.

When teaching, it is very important to determine which teaching method is the most appropriate to use. Sometimes we have to teach from the beginning and continue to the end and other times we have to do the reverse, beginning from the end and regressing back to the beginning. We call these two "forward method" (*lugs 'byung*) and "reverse method" (*lugs ldog*). There are also times when it is necessary to pick up at a very crucial point in a teaching and put it all together within the context of the whole. So the method of teaching can be quite different depending upon the context and what is needed at the time, which is determined by both the subject matter and the varying levels of the disciples.

TAKING REFUGE

At the beginning of class we recite the verses for Taking Refuge and Generating Bodhichitta. *Sang gye chö dang tsok kyi chok nam la* means "I take refuge in the Three Precious Jewels." *Chang chub bar du dak nyi kyab su chi* means "I will take refuge in them until I achieve Buddhahood." This implies that we are not only taking refuge in them just once or twice, for a week, a month, or just occasionally, but on the contrary, we are going to take refuge in them continually until we ourselves have achieved Buddhahood. This kind of mind we call *pen pa* (*'phen pa*) or the attitude that makes a powerful decision to do something as in, "I will take refuge in the Buddha, Dharma, and Sangha for however long it takes until I achieve Buddhahood myself."

Why do we have to take refuge for so long? When we take refuge first we have to understand where refuge exists. What is its location? Refuge exists in our mind. If we have a truly strong sense of taking refuge in the Buddha, Dharma, and Sangha we may be considered Buddhist or one of Buddha's followers. If we don't have true refuge in our mind, even though we may be wearing robes and sitting on a high throne we are not Buddhist or one of Buddha's followers. Conversely, though we may be wearing lay clothing and displaying an ordinary aspect so that when people see us they are prone to think, "Oh, he doesn't know anything about Dharma. What can he possibly know?" but in our mind we have strong refuge in the Buddha, Dharma, and Sangha, we are definitely Buddhist and Buddha's follower. In short, whether we are Buddhist or not depends entirely upon whether or not we have truly taken refuge in the Buddha, Dharma, and Sangha. That is the opening, the gateway that grants us entrance into true Buddhist practice. If we lack true refuge we are not Buddhist. No robes or mannerism can make any difference whatsoever.

Once we have refuge in our mind we have got the essential basis of all of Buddha's teaching, practice, and knowledge. Having true refuge we are qualified to take Vinaya vows,

Bodhisattva vows, and Tantric vows. However, if we lack that fundamental basis and proceed to take those vows anyway they will be very strange vows! Therefore, we should have that basis of refuge very nice and firm in our mind. This strong attitude of refuge will certainly bring us great benefit. If we take refuge mentally, recite the verse verbally while making prostrations physically and think deeply about what it is we are doing, such activity is an unbelievably holy and powerful practice. Practicing this way will automatically cause all the bad deeds we collected from beginningless time up to now to diminish or disappear entirely. If we continue to take refuge with strong conviction even the seeds of these bad deeds will eventually disappear. Since bad deeds are the cause of our suffering, if we remove them it is only logical that their result –suffering– will also disappear.

At this point we have to learn the various qualities of taking refuge. There are eight points that signal the effects of taking refuge.[5] The first result determines whether a practitioner is Buddhist. The second result determines whether we have the right to take the various levels of vows. The third result of taking refuge is that all our bad deeds will be diminished and even removed altogether. The fourth result is that by taking refuge we can also collect an enormous amount of virtue incidentally while removing any bad deeds we have previously collected. Fifth, there are many influences originating from external forces that induce suffering, for example, from the

---

[5] The eight excellent results of taking refuge: 1) we become a Buddhist, 2) we got the basis of all of the vows and Buddhist practices, 3) our bad deeds are reduced, 4) our mind becomes richer in virtue and poorer in bad deeds and, as a result, what we wish for will be easily accomplished, 5) humans and non-humans will not be able to harm us, 6) we will not easily fall into the three lower realms, 7) we will be able to accomplish both temporary and ultimate goals effortlessly, and 8) we will achieve Buddhahood very quickly.

elements or disease. What is needed as an antidote is an internal helper to counter these. This can be likened to a corrupt business. Like that business, if our bad deeds are acting as the manager of our mind we will have many bad activities going on so that external bad things will be able to enter our mind very easily due to that connection. Conversely, if our virtue is powerful enough, external good things will be able to enter our mind very easily. This represents the quality of the fifth result of taking refuge. That is, from the outside bad things will not be able to enter our mind and harm us so easily. Sixth, the worst kind of suffering is the suffering that is experienced by the beings of the three lower realms. If we practice taking refuge sincerely with deep conviction we are shutting the door to these three lower realms and securing for ourself protection from those sufferings. The seventh result is that, if we don't have many bad deeds or the traces of bad deeds in our mind but instead have a lot of virtue and good causes, whatever we wish to accomplish, both temporary and ultimate goals, we will be able to achieve with very little effort on our part. The eighth result of taking refuge sincerely and assiduously is that we will achieve Buddhahood very quickly.

Every time we take refuge we can collect an unimaginable amount of virtue, which if it were to take form it would not be able to fit within this great world system. So once we become rich in virtue and poor in bad deeds through taking refuge, all of the Buddhas will be extremely happy with us, because their main purpose is to help all sentient beings and alleviate our suffering. Naturally, it is far easier for them to protect someone who is doing good activities than someone doing otherwise. When beings go in the opposite direction, though they may be very learned, they will encounter big problems and it will be far more difficult for the Buddhas to help them.

When we do what we should do and not do what we shouldn't do, all the Buddhas become very happy with us. Just making the Buddhas happy alone is a source of great virtue. The Sanskrit word for offering is *puja*, which means offering outer things, inner things, secret things, emptiness, and the like. If these offerings actually make the Buddhas happy, we got the true result of making offerings. If the Buddhas are not happy we have not achieved the result. If we practice taking refuge nicely, all the Buddhas will automatically become exceedingly pleased with our activities so we can be sure that we have offered them a very great *puja* indeed.

This is a system of teaching that shows the benefits of an activity from the beginning. If people realize the good benefits of something they will rush to try to achieve it just as ordinary business people do when they hurry to make a profit from some worldly enterprise. Yet profit gained from taking refuge cannot compare with this life's worldly profit; it is many millions of times greater. So, now that we have realized how holy taking refuge is, we have to do it. But how do we do it? We might think, "He is urging me to recite those words because they are so beneficial, so I guess it wouldn't hurt to recite them" or something like that. Even if we don't know anything about taking refuge, but practice it anyway, since we are going in the right direction we can still collect some virtue. But that way of taking refuge is a kind of blind practice. If we have the time and opportunity and wish to achieve the eight good results mentioned above we will have to practice taking refuge sincerely and properly. In order to practice this way with a hope to achieve the eight good results we must gain a clear understanding in our mind of the causes for taking refuge.

What are these good causes? Although gaining this understanding is quite easy unfortunately it is a big obstacle for us that we are not in the least bit curious about what these causes are. As a matter of fact, we rarely even think about them. There are two causes for taking refuge. The first is the fear of suffering and problems of samsara in general and our own individual problems and suffering. We can think about this in various ways. Once we have a vivid sense of the suffering we are forced to experience we will develop fear and dread toward it. When we have realized this very deeply and clearly, we have gained the first of the two causes for taking refuge.

The second cause for taking refuge is strong faith, which can be illustrated in this fashion: "I definitely don't want to experience this kind of suffering. But I am not the only one. No one else wants to suffer either. Everybody should be free from suffering and all these terrible problems. Yet I have no idea how to make others free of suffering let alone myself. Who then does have this knowledge and skill? Who can help us? Who can lead us properly and protect us from suffering?" If we think like this we will want to find an infallible protector, an infallible instructor, an infallible guide. Who has these qualities? The Three Precious Jewels—Buddha, Dharma, and Sangha. Once we realize that only they can help and protect us from our problems and suffering we will develop faith and trust in them as our real protectors.

Even so, as I said, we rarely find ourselves pondering over the general and specific problems of samsara. Usually we spend our time thinking thoughts like these: "I really had a good lunch today. Boy, do I have a terrific job; it allows me to make a whole lot of money so that I won't have any problems in the future. My future's pretty secure so I don't have to worry much about it." These are examples of samsara's temporary happiness. Unfortunately, from beginningless time up until this moment we still find ourselves in samsara and have done absolutely nothing about it. We haven't achieved the slightest independence or power or knowledge. Nothing. How have we spent most of our time up until now? We've spent it suffering as residents of the three lower realms.

And our future lives, do we know anthing about these? Do we ever even think about them? When this life ends will we just disappear? And what about our past lives? What do we know about them? The main purpose of this teaching is to help us come to realize that we have had many former lives and are going to have many future lives as well. From our present condition we can pretty accurately judge that all of our former lives were every one of them samsaric lives in which we experienced nothing but suffering. From this moment on, however, we have the possibilty of making a division in our future lives: they may either belong to samsara or they may transcend samsara. Whichever we achieve, whether a samsaric life or a life that goes beyond samsara, depends entirely upon our practice beginning right now.

It is very easy to tell what our former lives did for us. This excellent human being's life was arranged by our former life due to our having collected a considerable amount of virtue through the practice of morality. As Nagarjuna states: "From giving comes wealth; from morality, a higher rebirth (*sbyin pa'i longs spyod khrims kyi bde*).[6] Every good has its own unique cause. Yet not all causes of our present life are good causes. That is why we don't have a perfect life. Nonetheless, our former life did a very good job in collecting causes to achieve this excellent human being's life. Additionally, our former lives also planted seeds in our mind about Buddhist teachings and practice; otherwise we wouldn't be the slightest bit interested in Buddhism right now. All these propensities were arranged by our former lives, which put good seeds in our mind that are ripening only now. This is why we are striving to learn about Buddhist practice and wish to hear and understand what Buddha taught. In this way we can have some inkling of what it was we did in our previous lives. Those lives did a pretty good job, but still they did many bad things too. Every single problem that arises in this life is a product or result of what was arranged by our previous lives. The primary causes, their main seeds, were collected in our previous lives; the secondary causes, indeed, are our current responsibility and what we are presently arranging in this life.

---

[6] *Precious Garland* (T: *Rin po che'i phreng ba*; S: *Rājaparikathā-ratnāvalī*) v. 438.

Let's pose the question very openly. What are we doing for our future lives? We ourselves know what it is we are doing for them; we know whether or not we are collecting virtue and improving our mind by increasing our knowledge and understanding of samsara's general and specific problems. Everything we don't want to experience comes very easily to us, almost automatically. We often have problems getting the things we want since they are not easily acquired. Such problems are like extra problems added to samsara's general difficulties. As for how we will fare in our future lives, whether we will have a better life or worse one depends solely upon what we do right now in this life. We have the power in our hands at this moment to determine the nature of our future life. If we wish to acquire those eight crucial results of taking refuge and get a better life in the future free from all the various kinds of suffering, this will solely depend upon our mind and activities.

Thus it is critical that we gain conclusive certainty (*nges shes*) about the existence of our past and future lives. We can achieve this type of mind by inquiring where the first moment of this life's mind came from. The very first moment of this life's mind came from the very last moment of our former life's mind. The last moment of that mind was the cause that produced the first moment of this life's mind. While we change our body from an old one to a new one, our mind goes on continually like a stream. The last moment of our former life's mind turned into the first moment of this life's mind. That is one way to understand that we have had a former life.

In general, the continuity of mind is not too difficult to understand. We can see rather clearly how the mind of our present life has had a consistent continuity up to now. For instance, our thinking may go something like this: "When I was a baby I did such and such and used to play like this until I went to school. Then I began working at my job, got married, had kids, and so forth." We can remember all of these things precisely because our mind moves along in a continuum.

Likewise, this life's mind will proceed as a continuum until it reaches the very last moment of mind at the end of this life. When our life reaches the point of death, however, this mind won't just disappear but, as is its nature, will go on continually to become the mind of our next life. Although our old body will be left behind, the mind for its part will continue on to find a new body, which will constitute our new life. This is the kind of understanding we need about former and future lives. Also, all good and bad things that we will experience, both happiness and suffering, are presently in our hands. Both good results and bad results are determined by what we do. We may either be practicing nicely all the time for our own and others' benefit or we may be practicing harming others as well as ourselves.

What do we mean when we say "for our own benefit"? You might think, "In the Buddhist system, especially the Mahayana, shouldn't bodhisattvas be thinking and practicing only for the benefit of others and not for themselves? Isn't it selfish and a big contradiction to say 'for the benefit of others *and ourselves*'"? No. You have to understand what we mean by "our own benefit." If we work for the benefit of other beings they will be able to become happy and enjoy themselves. When beings are happy as a result of our efforts we will collect a great amount of virtue, which of course is a great benefit. That is what it means to bring "benefit to oneself." We don't need any greater benefit than that. Nevertheless, our main purpose, our main job is to work for the benefit of others. To work mainly for our own benefit and only minutely for the benefit of others, as you can imagine, would be absolutely improper.

You can learn everything in class. If it was taught in the class, to ask for a private interview about this is useless. Our teachers and Lamas used to feel very strongly about this. If you were to go to them in private and say, "May I ask you a question?" It would usually disturb them. Since they didn't like it they would say something like, "Were you in that class?" Yes. "Did you hear everything?" Yes. "So what happened?" In answer you were forced to confess that your vessel must have a hole in the bottom since you didn't remember the instructions. That is about the only good answer you can give. So in class you have to listen very carefully and try to catch the meaning of what is being taught. The Lama tries to present a structure for the material, then collects all the crucial points together, and finally shows how to practice what he taught. You have to do it that way. That is why I tell you all the time not to miss class. If you miss, your instruction will be incomplete. Make a special effort to come. Don't miss class thinking, "Well, it's okay if I miss since I can get a copy of the tapes later."[7]

When we were having retreat I made a joke by introducing someone as one of my best students though he rarely attends class. Instead of coming to class he says, "I'm sorry I couldn't come, but I will listen to the tapes." A tape is a tape. If it were so good to just listen to tapes we wouldn't have any need for lineage Lamas since we could get the transmission electronically. A "lineage Lama" signifies that the transmission was passed down from Buddha, to Maitreya, to Manjushri, to Nagarjuna, to Asanga, to Je Tsong Khapa, like that continuing in a direct, unbroken line up to our Lamas, without damage to the instruction, flowing continually from mouth to ear, mouth to ear…and *not* from tape to ear! You have to know this. Listening to tapes is very good especially when listening to songs and so forth. Listening to the radio is even better, though…but you won't get pure instructions with a continuum of blessings. The lineage's blessings come like a current from one Lama to the next in an unbroken succession, so you must receive it like that.

---

[7] Although, of course, these classes are no longer being given the injunction still holds for any student of Dharma who finds him- or herself in a similar situation.

Now that your understanding about former and future lives is a little clearer, you might think, "I want my future lives to be much better than this one!" Why? In order that you don't become too discouraged at this point I have to encourage you a little bit and show you what qualities you do have. On the one hand you have acquired an excellent human being's life this time with a certain degree of wisdom and other fortunate endowments. Be that as it may, do you have renunciation? Do you have Bodhichitta? Correct view? These are the three principal aspects of the path. Do you have a pure attitude of taking refuge in your mind? Do you have good faith in the Buddha, Dharma, and Sangha? Only you yourself can tell whether you have these. Only you can tell what your quality is, your level, your abilities. You may think, "But I don't have any of these qualities. Even so, I don't want my future lives to be like this one." Only you can tell whether your life has been silly or not. If I were to tell you that you are foolish, you would definitely get angry; so only you can say that to yourself. That is what it means to be a Dharma practitioner. You have to think about how to tame your own mind, how to introduce your mind to good things and recognize bad things, find out what you should do and what you shouldn't do. These are the things we as practitioners have to teach our own mind.

ONLY YOU KNOW THE QUALITY OF YOUR OWN MIND

If you wish to have a better life in the future, first you have to study about the qualities of Buddha and his teachings. Initially you can listen to teachings and gain listening wisdom (*thos byung gi shes rab*). This kind of wisdom can be characterized as follows: "He said Buddha is like such and such…and has qualities like this, etc. He told me that there are past lives and future lives, so now I know something about them." Do you know for certain that past and future lives actually exist the way they are described? To gain conviction about their existence you have to begin by examining this life's mind. What's the difference between yesterday's mind and today's mind? What's the difference between today's mind and our mind of tomorrow? The first step in such an examination is to consider those minds closest to your present mind. Do these minds belong to one being or not? Do all these minds –past, present, and future– belong to my own continuum or not? This kind of investigation is a form of checking wisdom, which is the next step after listening wisdom.

At some point in our examination we will find correct reasons in answer to our questions. When we gain these reasons that verify what we discover in our investigations we will have achieved wisdom arisen from contemplation (*bsam byung gi shes rab*). Once we gain wisdom arisen from contemplation we have acquired valid cognition (*tshad ma*), in this case infallible indirect cognition (*rjes dpag tshad ma*), which is a kind of correct knowledge achieved through perfect reasoning. Our infallible indirect cognition realizes that there were former lives and that there will be future lives. Just gaining an incipient understanding like this can be likened to opening the great gate to knowledge. If we lack such knowledge gained through contemplation all other kinds of knowledge will be shut outside and we will be forced to stand inside the door with all knowledge lying beyond it. When we gain that kind of wisdom it is as if a great, wide door has opened up for us and knowledge is allowed to easily enter. This is how we can acquire every kind of knowledge.

Influenced by that inferential cognition we may think, "Since I am going to have future lives they shouldn't be poor like this one but should be much better. Yet I don't know how to accomplish this. Who can help me?" In general, only Buddha, Dharma, and Sangha can help us. Buddha can give us instructions and show us how to obtain a better life in the future. "But who can help me to achieve ultimate happiness?" The Three Ratnas can. Ratna, meaning "precious," signifies their extraordinary qualities. If we achieve these three kinds of preciousness ourselves we will automatically be saved from all our problems. What is it about these three that makes them so precious?

Buddha, the main instructor, can teach us what it is we are to practice, which is Dharma, while the Sangha can assist us in practicing exactly the way the Buddha instructed. Simply put, the only way to achieve the Dharma is to practice according to what Buddha taught. In this way we can realize that all three are there ready for us: the instructor is there, the main object of practice is there, and the helpers are there.

These Three Ratnas we call "causal refuge" (*rgyu'i skyabs 'gro*), or the objects of taking refuge that serve as causes. As we go for refuge to them they serve as causes for us to achieve our own goal. They teach us, help us, and show us the actual paths that we are to practice. We may wonder, "Given that they have such extraordinary qualities, why then don't they just save us outright?" The only way that we can be saved is by listening carefully to teachings and by practicing what is taught. By so doing we too will achieve our own goal, which is Buddharatna, Dharmaratna, and Sangharatna. These are known as "result refuge" (*'bras bu'i skyabs'gro*).

Part of our tantric practice of self-generation[8] includes the recitation of the following line: "I must achieve the status of complete Buddhahood" (*bdag gis rzdogs pa'i sangs rgyas kyi go'phang thob par byas la*). The Buddhahood it is referring to is our own future Buddhahood. We wish to achieve this status so that we might be able to liberate all sentient beings. In order that we may be able to liberate all beings first we ourselves have to become liberated, otherwise we won't have the power to bring things to completion or perform enlightened activities to carry them out. Once we are liberated we will be able to liberate others. Thus, in these lines both causal refuge and result refuge are indicated.

The words "taking refuge" are generally pretty well known. Nevertheless, we have to learn the different classes of taking

---

[8] The tantric practice of *Vajrayoginī.*

refuge. If we are too proud, we won't follow other people very easily, not even the words "taking refuge." As mentioned above there are two sets of refuge: causal refuge,[9] or that which others have already achieved, and result refuge,[10] or that which we ourselves are going to achieve.

To achieve our own three ratnas we have to take refuge in others, that is, Buddha, Dharma, and Sangha, and put our trust in them. The main purpose is to achieve our own three ratnas, however. Although many sage bodhisattvas have achieved that status, even so they cannot help us right away. *They* have achieved that status, but *we* haven't. In order to rescue ourselves from samsara we ourselves have to achieve that status, of course. So going for refuge is not only going for refuge to others who have achieved the status of these ratnas already, but is also going for refuge to our own Buddha, Dharma, and Sangha.

What is refuge? It is the very strong hope that the objects of refuge will help us and give us infallible protection inasmuch as they are perfectly reliable. Since we need helpers to achieve this goal, we believe that they will help us. This kind of unmitigated trust in the Buddha, Dharma, and Sangha is the definition of taking refuge.

Why will Buddha help us? Because he has become perfectly reliable (*tshad mar gyur pa*); he thinks only of benefiting beings (*'gro la phan bshed pa*); he is the perfect

---

[9] The definition of causal refuge is a mind that through its own power puts all hope in the assistance of any of the Three Precious Jewels achieved in another's mind (*gzhan rgyud la grub zin pa'i dkon mchog gsum po gang yang rung ba la rang stobs kyis dpung gnyen du re ba 'cha' ba'i sems pa rgyu'i skyabs 'gro'i mthsan gnyi*).

[10] The definition of result refuge is a mind that through its own power puts all hope in the assistance of any of the Three Precious Jewels that oneself is to become (*rang rgyud la 'byung 'gyur gyi dkon mchog gsum po gang yang rung ba la rang stobs kyis dpung gnyen du re ba 'cha' ba'i sems pa 'bras bu'i skyabs 'gro'i mthsan gnyi*).

teacher (*ston pa*); he is the one who has achieved perfection or Sugata (*bde gshegs*); and he is the perfect protector of other beings (*skyob*). In order to be able to protect other beings a protector needs completion causes. What are these causes? He has achieved ultimate cessations and omniscience so he doesn't have any problems or obstacles and in no way lacks understanding. He sees everything directly. Now, since he has achieved ultimate cessation and ultimate omniscience and has extraordinary power, might he not just want to relax and take a rest for a while after having done such hard work for so long? One might think so but that is not the case. Why? Because Buddha has also achieved ultimate compassion, which urges him all the time to do whatever he can to alleviate the suffering of sentient beings. This is what the words *wishing to benefit beings* in the homage mean and indicates the quality of excellent intention (*bsam pa phun tshogs*).

Buddha also has an excellent practice or method (*sbyor ba phun tshogs*). He completely finished his practice of removing his own problems and knows well how to remove all the problems of other beings. He practiced wisdom for eons and eons, kalpas and kalpas. That is the meaning of *teacher* (*ston pa*) or the wisdom that realizes the real nature of all phenomena (*bdag med rtogs pa'i shes rab*), the main method, tool, and antidote for removing all obstacles.

Why should we have trust in the Three Ratnas? We can trust them because they will help us to bring our ultimate goal to completion. Just giving a little bit of clothing and food and shelter is only temporary help. The Ratnas give us completion help. Since they achieved all knowledge and cessations they possess the ability to help us. That is the special quality of Buddha, Dharma, and Sangha. We have to take refuge both by generating fear, thinking about the general problems of samsara and our own particular problems, and by generating faith, thinking about the special qualities of the Three Ratnas. This is the real way of taking refuge.

Now, since it is very difficult for beginners to have many objects of refuge we have to realize that the Lamas are our main instructors. We cannot see Buddhas. That which Buddha has taught our Lamas will also teach. Our Lamas will satisfy us according to our own level whether it is Hinayana, Mahayana, or that of Tantric practice. Whatever the level, they will give us satisfaction. In general, our object of refuge consists of our Lamas, the four levels of Tantric yidams or tutelary deities, which are like treasuries comprising all our goals, all the Buddhas of the three times –past, present, and future– along with their disciples, dakas and dakinis, and many Dharma protectors. All of them appear in various forms for significantly different reasons. Actually, they are all emanations of the Buddha at the center of our object of refuge. Buddha cannot come presently and show himself in his *nirmanakaya*[11] form. That form already came to India two thousand and five hundred years ago and disappeared from the world. That particular *kaya*, or body, won't come back. Even if it were to come back we would not be able to see it due to our low level. Although his teachings remain adequately intact in the world we still need a teacher to teach them. Because of this the Buddhas emanate in different forms, as a teacher, a sage, a leader, an instructor, a guide, as an assistant, or even as a bridge, an animal, a tree, or water, etc. Emanations are by necessity good forms of which there can be many kinds. It is in this way that we can realize that our Lamas are emanations of the Buddha, like his representatives or messengers.

As beginners, instead of doing a rather complex visualization of so many objects we can take refuge by visualizing a single form, which is Buddha Shakyamuni. It is important to have this knowledge. While the outer form is that of Buddha Shakyamuni his essence is our Lama. The Buddha Shakyamuni that we visualize is a combination of all the levels of Buddhas, from the Lama to the Dharma protectors.

---

[11] Emanation Body (T: *sprul sku*).

Whenever it is necessary he will appear as all these holy beings as a whole set. When there is no longer any necessity, all these beings will dissolve into the Buddha at the center of the object of refuge. The term we have for this is "All-Encompassing Jewel" (*kun 'dus nor bu'i lugs*), which means visualizing a single Buddha's image that comprises all the Buddhas as an object of taking refuge. In general, the purpose of a jewel is to remove a person's poverty. There is outer poverty and inner poverty. In our case our problem is inner poverty, especially a poverty of knowledge. Therefore, this kind of jewel removes our inner poverty. Once our inner poverty is removed, of course our outer poverty will be removed automatically without our having to make a special effort to remove it.

How are we to visualize Buddha Shakyamuni? First we take a look at a good image of the Buddha represented in a thangka. While we are visualizing, however, we shouldn't visualize this image as if it were just a lifeless painting. A painting is what a good painter paints with powder and water and other materials. Powder and water of themselves are not necessarily holy. What is holy is the image of the Buddha. Also, although we may see certain images of the Buddha represented in say clay, bronze, or gold, we shouldn't think that the object of visualization is a solid mass like that. Well then, how should we imagine it?

The essence of all the Buddhas is the Lama. The Lama is a combination of all those objects of taking refuge. The outer form is Buddha's form, a wisdom form unlike our ordinary form. It can appear and disappear easily and dissolve into us without trouble so that we receive his blessings. All of this depends upon the capacity of our knowledge. We have to visualize in this way with strong faith and trust while we think about all of samsara's problems. Then we begin our recitation of taking refuge:

I take refuge in the Lama
I take refuge in the Buddha
I take refuge in the Dharma
I take refuge in the Sangha

lama la kyab su chi'o
sang gye la kyab su chi'o
chö la kyab su chi'o
gen dun la kyab su chi'o

During our actual meditation practice we have to recite each of these lines three times. For the first recitation we go for refuge and make requests. For the second we receive blessings from the object of refuge in the form of nectar and light rays that come and dissolve into us. When doing the third recitation, we visualize that an emanation of the Buddha in the center of the object of refuge comes out and happily dissolves into us. As a result we have the blessing from the *Lama Buddha*. Then we recite three times while we take refuge in the *Buddha* with the order being the same as before, until one emanation comes out and happily dissolves into us. Again we take refuge in the *Dharma* with the same order of repetitions and meditations. Finally, we do the same with respect to the *Sangha*. Once this is completed, we have to recite the following:

I take refuge in the Lama, Yidam, and Three Ratnas
I take refuge in the Lama, Yidam, and Three Ratnas
I take refuge in the Lama, Yidam, and Three Ratnas

lama yidam kön chok sum la kyab su chi'o
lama yidam kön chok sum la kyab su chi'o
lama yidam kön chok sum la kyab su chi'o

Although these lines are not written in "A Necklace for the Fortunate" (*sbyor chos skal bzang mgrin rgyan*), more commonly known as *Jorchö*, when we used to recite this in front of Kyabje Trijang Rinpoche before Lam Rim teachings, this is the way we recited it. While reciting these lines we are to visualize in the same way as we did above. During the first recitation we make requests to them. During the second we receive blessings from them through light rays filled with nectar, which wash away all our problems and bad deeds and clean us of all our stains until our mind is completely lucid and bright. Finally, we visualize that the Buddha also happily comes and dissolves into us so that our body, speech, and mind combine together with the Buddha's body, speech, and mind and we receive the blessings of the Three Ratnas.

Now you have to reflect about what was just taught and do all the visualizations for a minute. It is very important that you think about the instructions and do the visualizations again freshly at least once as soon as you get home after the teaching. Don't forget these teachings but make sure they remain clear in your mind. That is how to make progress. Furthermore, you have to learn logic. If you learn logic, when you take refuge or do any other Dharma activity your practice will become perfect and efficient. Without learning logic, though you may be taking refuge, doing recitations, and visualizations and still be collecting a good deal of virtue, it won't be perfect practice. Only when you do these practices with knowledge will you gain perfection. That is how you have to do it.

Here, in summary, I will mention once again the causes for taking refuge. They are the general problems of samsara, our particular individual varieties of samsaric suffering, and the problems and suffering that we will experience in our future lives. Against these unfortunate experiences we need a protector who can rescue us and in whom we can develop strong faith. Such a protector and refuge is none other than the Three Ratnas. Only they can help us because they have achieved all those unique qualities. These are the two causes of refuge: fear and faith. There are also two kinds of refuge: causal refuge and result refuge.

If we practice refuge in the way described above we can collect a great amount of virtue and will easily gather those eight crucial good results of taking refuge.

PRELIMINARY OBSERVATIONS

The title of this book is LIKE A HEART SO DEARLY NEEDED FOR LIBERATION (*thar 'dod rnams la snying ltar gces pa'i nyer mkho 'ga' zhig bzhugs so*). The Tibetan words *shuk so* at the end of the title mean *herein is contained.* What does this book contain? This book holds very valuable material, which, like a heart, is the most important, most vital organ for us all. Without a heart we could not live. So in order to live we need a good heart. Similarly, those who want very much to become free from the suffering of samsara need very important things that are critical for achieving this. These crucial things are what are contained in this book.

You can perceive many things directly, hear various sounds, see all kinds of visible objects, and so forth. Now, if I were to ask you, "Do you believe in fire?" initially you might think that having a belief in fire doesn't make much sense and isn't so important. Well then, how do you go about gaining a belief in the existence of fire? First you have to learn the definition of fire, which shows how it functions and reveals its characteristics.[12] What are these? If you understand what these are you can gain a belief in the existence of fire. Because you can cook food and burn things you understand that fire has the quality of heat and the function of burning. So, if you need to cook or burn something you know that you will need fire to do so because fire has that quality and serves that function. In the same way, if you want to achieve nirvana and Buddhahood you will have to learn their definition, their function, and their qualities. Once you learn these you will gain faith in them. However, just hearing their names is certainly not enough.

To gain belief in the Buddha you have to learn about the Buddha's qualities and function, not just casually but through correct valid cognition known in Tibetan as *tse ma* (*tshad ma*) and *pramana* in Sanskrit. If you gain correct valid cognition

---

[12] The definition of fire is that which is hot and burns (*tsha zhing sreg pa me'i mtshan nyid*).

about nirvana and Buddha's qualities this will intensify and deepen your faith. What's the benefit of gaining a deep and strong faith in them? Once you gain such a strong faith you will think, "I really want to achieve all those good qualities that I have learned about."

Now, there are instances when one perceives things in a mistaken manner, when one sees incorrectly, hears incorrectly, and so forth. Here, though, we are talking about seeing and hearing not in a mistaken manner but in a real, perfect way. We'll use an example to illustrate these two types of perception. When two people are looking at the same snow mountain, one having a defective eye faculty and the other a healthy eye faculty, the first will see the white snow of the mountain as blue,[13] for example, while the other will see it as white. The one with the perfect, non-defective eye faculty and eye consciousness will see the correct color of that snowy mountain. Perceiving the white color of the snow as white is perfect, infallible perception.

The definition of valid cognition is a new infallible mind (*gsar du mi blu ba'i rig pa*). Dharmakirti in his root text *Commentary to "Valid Cognition"*[14] gives the definition of perfect validity as non-deceptive (*mi blu ba*). When "mind" (*rig pa*) is added to this definition we have infallible, non-deceptive mind or right cognition. This is the kind of mind –an infallible, perfect cognition– that we have to gain about the Buddha. If we don't, just calling ourselves "followers of the Buddha" and saying "Buddha, Buddha" can in no way be considered perfect activities, of course.

How are we to learn about correct cognition? We have to learn the eight logical categories or types[15] pertaining to the

---

[13] This refers to certain "wind" disturbances that are capable of distorting one's perception of colors.

[14] T: *Tshad ma rnam 'grel gyi tshig le'ur byas pa*; S: *Pramāṇa-vārttikakārikā*

[15] *rtog ge'i tshig don brgyad*

subject of "perfect validity" (*tshad ma*). These eight are listed in the following quotation from Dignaga's text *Door of Reasoning*:

THE EIGHT LOGICAL CATEGORIES

།མངོན་སུམ་དང་ནི་རྗེས་སུ་དཔག
།ལྟར་སྣང་བཅས་པ་བདག་རིག་བྱེད།
།བསྒྲུབ་པ་དང་ནི་སུན་འབྱིན་ངག
།ལྟར་སྣང་བཅས་པ་གཞན་རྟོགས་བྱེད།

ngön sum dang ni je su pak
tar nang che pa dak rik che
drup pa dang ni sun jin ngak
tar nang che pa shen tok che

Ngön sum (*mngon sum*) in the first line of the quotation above means direct and refers to infallible, direct perception. An illustration of this type of perception is as follows. What is this? A pitcher. What is this? A flower. What color is this flower? Red. Since you are seeing it directly you can examine it and check each detail yourself, the different colors, shapes, and so forth. You can see these directly with your eye consciousness. This demonstrates the meaning of "direct valid [perception]." Sometimes this is described in terms of its object, as in a "direct object" of valid perception.

Again, the person who sees the color of snow on a snowy mountain as white perceives it with perfect, infallible direct [visual] perception (*mngon sum tshad ma*). Should someone have a visual perception of white snow as blue, that kind of perception is faulty (*ltar snang*) insofar as the object perceived is perceived incorrectly. The opposite of faulty perception is perfect or true perception (*yang dag*). So the quotation above is referring to two kinds of direct perception—perfect direct perception (*mngon sum yang dag*) and erroneous direct perception (*mngon sum ltar snang*).

Je su pak is short for *je pak tse ma* (*rjes dpag tshad ma*) and refers to indirect valid cognition. Although you may be able to see this flower with your direct perception you cannot see its impermanent nature with your eyes; that is something you have to realize through indirect cognition. Gaining an understanding of its impermanent nature through indirect cognition requires the use of a good reason. This good reason has the capacity to produce an indirect valid cognition in your mind, which is the second kind of infallible mind.

Let's examine this more closely by using an example. How long will these flowers stay fresh … maybe two or three days at most? After that what will happen? They will die. Why will they die? They will die because they don't have the causes to make them stay longer. They arise and grow from their causes as perishable. Because flowers grow from their causes, which are seeds, they are impermanent or changing and not unchanging. Needless to say, farmers are very knowledgeable about this. They know which seeds will give good crops and which ones will give bad crops. That is why they are so very careful about buying good seeds for planting in the spring since their goal, of course, is to get good crops in the fall. This kind of understanding is a form of indirect cognition.

Sometimes, though, indirect cognition can be erroneous. Without gathering all the causes a result cannot arise. If all the causes are gathered together they will definitely produce their result. Realizing this is a kind of infallible indirect cognition. However, whenever we think that a result will arise without all the causes being gathered together, the kind of mind that produces such a thought is known as fallible indirect cognition (*rjes dpag star snang*). In short, the first part of this verse – *ngön sum dang ni je su pak*– is referring to four kinds of mind: 1) perfect direct perception, and 2) wrong direct perception, 3) perfect indirect cognition, and 4) wrong indirect cognition.

The next part of the verse reads: *drup pa dang ni sun jin ngak. Drup pa* refers to *drup ngak* (*sgrub ngag*), which means proof statement, and *sun jin* (*sun 'byin*) or *tengyur* (*thal 'gyur*) means refutation. Each of these may be either correct or mistaken, that is, there is a correct proof statement and an incorrect proof statement, a correct refutation and an incorrect refutation, which make up four kinds of cognition, all together giving the eight logical categories.[16]

Here I am just giving you a brief introduction to the root text since you cannot learn everything all at once. The main subject of *Commentary to "Valid Cognition"* by the great scholar Dharmakirti concerns these eight types of logical categories. His commentary consists of four chapters.[17] The main subject matter we are discussing here in this book deals with the material covered in the second chapter of the root text; that is, establishing the means of valid cognition or authority.

---

[16] 1) Perfect direct perception and 2) false direct perception; 3) perfect indirect cognition and 4) false indirect cognition: these are the methods for causing understanding to arise in one's own mind; 5) perfect proof statements and 6) false proof statements; 7) perfect refutations and 8) false refutations: these include the four methods for causing understanding to arise in the mind of others.

[17] Chapter one deals with *inference for oneself* (T: *rang don le'u*; S: *svārthānumāna*); Chapter two deals with establishing the means of valid cognition or authority (T: *tshad ma'i grup pa'i le'u*; S: *pramāṇasiddhi*); Chapter three deals with perception (T: *mngon sum le'u*; S: *pratyakṣa*); and Chapter four treats inference for the sake of others (T: *gzhan don le'u*; S: *parārthānumāna*).

COMMENTARY TO THE TEXT

ལེའུ་གཉིས་པའི་རྒྱ་ཆེར་བཤད་པ་རིགས་པའི་རྒྱ་མཚོ་ལས། ཚད་མ་མདོར།

"The Ocean of Reasoning,"[18] *[which includes] an extensive explanation on the second chapter [of* Commentary to "Valid Cognition"*], quotes the "Sutra of Valid Cognition"*:

The root text upon which this present work is based is the *Compendium of the Means of Valid Cognition,*[19] also known as *Sutra of Valid Cognition,*[20] which was composed by the great Indian Pandit Dignaga. In his homage at the beginning of this text he writes:

ཚད་མར་གྱུར་པ་འགྲོ་ལ་ཕན་བཞེད་པ། །སྟོན་པ་བདེ་གཤེགས་སྐྱོབ་ལ་ཕྱག་འཚལ་ཏེ། །ཞེས་གསུངས།

I prostrate to the One who, wishing to benefit beings became perfectly valid, the Teacher, Sugata, and Protector.

When scholars compose texts they have a system of paying homage to Buddha and his disciples or to Manjushri, among other great beings, at the very outset. Here the author, Dignaga, the great logician, pays homage to Buddha by contemplating Buddha's extraordinary qualities.

---

[18] The complete title of this commentary by *mKhas brub dge legs dpal bzang* is *rGyas pa'i bstan bcos tshad ma rnam 'grel gyi rgya cher bshad pa rigs pa'i rgya mtsho las rang don le'u dang tshad ma grub pa'i le'u.*

[19] T: *Tshad ma kun btus*; S: *Pramāṇasamuccaya*

[20] *Tshad ma mdo*

The homage begins with the words *tse mar gyur pa* (*tshad mar gyur pa*). *Tse ma* (*tshad ma*) generally refers to direct or indirect cognition, signifying a kind of mind. It can also refer to anything infallible or reliable such as a person, speech, or a teaching. Here, when modified by a grammar particle,[21] the text is referring to someone who *has* that quality, someone who *became* that, someone who *is* valid and perfect. Who became an infallible authority, an infallible person? Buddha Shakyamuni. In referring to Buddha as an infallible person this indicates someone we can believe in and whom we can completely trust, someone upon whom we can completely rely. In short, the thesis presented here is how Buddha in fact became that kind of infallible, perfect being.

In order to prove that Buddha turned into an infallible person we have to find good reasons. The first reason given in these lines is that he is always *wishing to benefit sentient beings* (*'gro la phan bzhed pa*). Buddha's main activity is to do beneficial activities for all beings, which indicates that Buddha achieved great compassion.

Without first having accumulated good causes Buddha Shakyamuni would not have been able to turn into a perfectly valid person. It is only by virtue of these causes that he was able to do so. Although there are many Dharma teachers and leaders as well as Dharma inventors, who among them can we actually consider as absolutely infallible, as a reliable authority? Determining this is a follower's main job. If we don't distinguish this well we might follow the wrong leader and end up going in the opposite direction and wind up never reaching Buddhahood. Therefore, learning how Buddha turned into an infallible person is extremely important and necessary for disciples.

How then did Buddha become an infallible person? He did so through having created good causes. The first of these, being the excellent causes in relation to himself (*rang don*

---

[21] *la don*

phun tshogs), consist of the two: excellent mental causes (*bsam pa phun tshogs*) and excellent causes of practice or method (*sbyor ba phun tshogs*). The excellent mental causes comprise ultimate compassion and the excellent causes of practice comprise ultimate wisdom, which caused him to become indisputably reliable and are the qualities indicated by the term *Teacher* (*ston pa*).

What is the main method he used to turn into an infallible person? The main method was ultimate wisdom, i.e. omniscience, which the Buddha in turn taught to his disciples exactly the way he perceived and achieved it. *Teacher* indicates that he taught the principal method for liberating beings from samsara's sufferings and the path to Buddhahood.

Sugata (*bde gshegs*) is a word generally well known among Westerners and refers to a being who has reached the status of ultimate happiness. To attain that status Buddha had to gain some special achievement, which is cessation. For example, when you go to the university you study there until you graduate and get your diploma. Once you get a diploma you have it for the rest of your life, which allows you to maintain your position of knowledge without having to return to the primary classes once again. This means that you have completed your studies and reached a certain status. The same is true of cessation. When Buddhas achieve ultimate cessation they never fall from that status but remain firm in that position. The status of cessation comes from practicing and achieving ultimate wisdom. When you practice and accomplish ultimate wisdom or omniscience, you automatically achieve cessation. Ultimate wisdom and cessation are the excellent causes that benefit oneself (*rang don phun tshogs*), which implies that if you want to become a Buddha you have to achieve two things: ultimate cessation and omniscience. Achieving these you have gained the benefit of your own purpose.

However, the achievement of cessation and omniscience for the benefit of oneself is not enough. Buddha also has to achieve qualities and knowledge that benefit all other beings.

Therefore, Buddha acting as a *Protector* (*skyob*) for all sentient beings is what it means to benefit others. *Protector* here refers to the protection he gives through teaching his followers the exact method, knowledge, and practice he himself engaged in. Having perfected his practice, he proceeded to teach similar activities to his disciples. Of course those disciples who receive his instruction can acquire similar results and achievements. So this is how he protects all sentient beings.

What then do we mean by "protection"? From what is Buddha, as Protector, protecting sentient beings? Generally speaking we have innumerable problems and many kinds of suffering. Needless to say we are very familiar with the words "problems" and "suffering." All problems and suffering are a result of obstacles. There are two categories of obstacles or obstructions: obstructions to liberation or obstructions of the mental afflictions, called *nyön drip* (*nyon sgrib*), and obstructions to omniscience, called *she drip* (*shes sgrib*). The obstructions of the mental afflictions refer not only to the mental afflictions themselves but to their seeds and are the chief obstacles to the achievement of nirvana. What do we mean by "seeds"? Take the mental affliction of anger for instance. Although anger arises in our mind every now and then, it doesn't arise all the time. Our anger lies dormant or inactive most of the time. Nevertheless, anger's seeds remain in our mind as propensities to anger. Sometimes when the right conditions come together those seeds of anger left in our mind immediately flare into anger. We call these seeds *bak chak* (*bag chags*). Generally, *bak chak* means stains. Though our anger may have disappeared for the time being the stains of that anger remain behind in our mind. So *nyön drip* is what mainly obstructs the achievement of nirvana and ultimately the achievement of Buddhahood.

The second kind of obstacle *she drip*, or obstacles to omniscience, can be explained this way. *She*, short for *she ja*, means object of knowledge. *Drip* means obstacle or covering. So *she drip* is a kind of covering that blocks one from seeing all objects of knowledge directly –from "all seeing"– and consequently is the main obstacle to omniscience.

Above we mentioned nirvana and Buddhahood several times. What is the difference between these two? *Nyön drip* and *she drip* are our two main obstacles. *She drip* is the main obstacle to achieving Buddhahood. Since *nyön drip* blocks our achievement of nirvana it also necessarily blocks the achievement of Buddhahood. If I were to say that *nyön drip* blocks the achievement of Buddhahood, this would not be the case for everybody precisely because they do not act as an obstacle for Arhats. Arhats do not have *nyön drip*, obstracles to nirvana; however, since they have not yet achieved Buddhahood they still have *she drip*, or the obstacles to omniscience and the achievement of Buddhahood. The distinction is similar to the following. If you make sweet tea you need tea leaves and sugar. If you lack one of these ingredients you will lack either the tea flavor or sweetness. Whereas the main function of sugar is to make the tea sweet and not to give the flavor of tea, the main function of tea is to give the smell and the flavor of tea and not the sweetness. It is the combination of both of these that gives you good, sweet tea. Likewise, as explained, *nyön drip* and *she drip* each have their own main function. The meaning of each comes in their definitions.[22]

[22] The definition of a mental affliction obstacle is, of the two kinds of obstacles –obstacles to liberation and obstacles to omniscience– that which functions principally to hinder the attainment of liberation (*thar pa dang thams cad mkhyen pa gnyis kyi nang nas gtso bo thar pa thob pa la gegs byed kyi sgrib pa'i rigs su gnas pa nyon sgrib kyi mtshan nyid*).

The definition of an obstacle to omniscience is, of the two kinds of obstacles –obstacles to liberation and obstacles to omniscience– that which functions principally to hinder the attainment of omniscience (*thar pa dang thams cad mkhyen pa gnyis kyi nang nas gtso bo thams*

ཕྱག་འཚལ་ཞེས་བྱ་བ་བཤད་པའི་གཞིའོ།

The basis of this explanation is the phrase "I prostrate [to the Teacher, Sugata, and Protector]."

Quoted from Pandit Dignaga's homage to the Buddha at the beginning of his book, these words form the basis of the explanation of the present text. One way of showing homage is *to make prostrations* (*phyag 'tshal*).

།གང་ལ་ན་ཚད་མ་ལའོ།

To whom does he make prostrations? To the Infallible One.

Dignaga is paying homage to an infallible object, to the one who became perfectly valid.

།ཚད་མ་ཇི་ལྟ་བུ་ལ་ཞེ་ན།

What kind of infallible object is this?

He explains by way of a description:

།རྒྱུ་མེད་རང་བྱུང་གི་ཚད་མ་མ་ཡིན་གྱི།

This Infallible One neither arose without a cause nor was he self-produced, but...

---

cad mkhyen pa thob pa la gegs byed kyi sgrib pa'i rigs su gnas pa shes sgrib kyi mtshan nyid).

Here he is distiguishing between Buddha and other teachers together with their respective philosophies. What does it mean "to arise without a cause and be self-produced"? Do you know who Brahma is and where he resides? Brahma is a god who resides in the form realm. The form realm itself may be divided into seventeen different levels. The first three levels are Brahma's domain. For Buddhists, the philosophy and tenets that maintain belief in Brahma are quite peculiar. His followers say that Brahma's physical body will never change but remains the same forever. When each of his lifespans finishes a new Brahma will arise, yet his outer form always remains the same. According to this philosophy Brahma (*tshangs pa*), is permanent, non-momentary, or unchanging. His followers for their part, however, are functioning entities (*dngos po*) and therefore are changing, momentary, or impermanent. Brahma is their god, their leader, and the creator of the philosophy to which they ascribe. According to these tenets permanent objects do not have causes. Brahma, as a permanent entity, exists without having been produced by any causes and will never change or disappear because he does not possess the causes to bring about such a change or dissolution. This is the kind of view being refuted here by saying *without* having any *causes* producing its existence (*rgyu med*).

Another quality mentioned is to be *self-produced* (*rang byung*) or existing by itself without causes. According to their philosophy Brahma is a reliable authority (*tshad ma*) and an infallible god. However, no infallible object can arise and exist by itself without having been produced by causes. *It is not like that* (*ma yin gyi*). The author is saying that the object to which he is paying homage cannot be described as having characteristics such as these.

།རྒྱུ་ཕུན་སུམ་ཚོགས་པ་ལས་ཚད་མར་འབྱུངས་པར་གྱུར་པ་ཞིག་ལའོ།

[I prostrate] to the Infallible One who was born from excellent causes.

The author is making prostrations *to* the one who turned into an infallible object *through having gathered excellent causes* (*rgyu phun sum tshogs pa las*).

།རྒྱུ་ཇི་ལྟ་བུ་ལས་ཚེད་མ་ཇི་ལྟ་བུའི་ངོ་བོར་འབྱུངས་པ་ལ་ཞེ་ན།

You may wonder from what causes he arose as that kind of infallible nature.

Two thousand and five hundred years ago Buddha Shakyamuni was born as Prince Siddhartha of the Shakya clan. Later, due to his having gathered excellent causes he turned into an infallible person i.e., he became a Buddha.

།རྒྱུ་བསམ་སྦྱོར་ཕུན་སུམ་ཚོགས་པ་ལས།

From excellent causes of intention and practice,

Intention (*bsam*), one of the excellent causes, is a kind of mind and refers here to compassion. *Practice* (*sbyor*) or method refers to the excellent cause of wisdom. From the accumulation of excellent causes one gets excellent results, which are mentioned in the next line.

འབྲས་བུ་དོན་གཉིས་ཕུན་སུམ་ཚོགས་པའི་ཚད་མར་འཁྲུངས་པ་ལའོ།

[I prostrate] to the one who was born as an infallible person, the result with the two excellent purposes.

The *two purposes* (*don gnyis*) are the goals for the benefit of oneself and for the benefit of others. "Benefiting oneself" refers to achieving ultimate cessation and omniscience. "Benefiting others" refers to protecting all sentient beings. How does he protect beings? Buddha protects beings by teaching them a perfect method for proceeding along the path to Buddhahood.

།དེ་ཡང་རྒྱུ་བསམ་པ་ཕུན་སུམ་ཚོགས་པ་ནི། འགྲོ་ལ་ཕན་བཞེད་པ།
ཞེས་པས་བསྟན་ཏེ།

Moreover, excellent intention is indicated by the phrase: "Wishing to benefit beings."

What does excellent intention (or excellent mental causes) refer to? This wish and willingness *to benefit beings* reveals an excellent kind of mind and superior intention. What is the nature of these excellent mental causes?

འགྲོ་བ་མཐའ་དག་སྡུག་བསྔལ་ལས་སྒྲོལ་བར་བཞེད་པའི་ཐུགས་རྗེ་
ཆེན་པོའོ།

He has great compassion that wishes to liberate all sentient beings from their suffering.

Buddha has a strong wishing mind characterized by *great compassion* (*thugs rje chen po*), which is the essence of these excellent mental causes. What then is the nature of the excellent causes of practice?

༄ སྦྱོར་བ་ཕུན་སུམ་ཚོགས་པ་ནི། སྟོན་པ། ཞེས་པས་བསྟན་ཏེ།

The excellent causes of practice are indicated by the word "Teacher."

Teacher implies one who gives instructions. What is it that the Teacher (in this case, the Buddha) teaches?

བདག་མེད་མངོན་སུམ་དུ་རྟོགས་པའི་ཤེས་རབ་འཁོར་དང་བཅས་པའོ།

[He teaches the] wisdom that directly perceives selflessness together with its attendant minds.

Selflessness (*bdag med*) according to the Madhyamika-Prasangika School means shunyata, *emptiness*. What kind of emptiness? Emptiness (*bdag med*) can be classified into two kinds: emptiness of inherently existent person (*gang zag gi bdag med*) and emptiness of phenomena (*chos kyi bdag med*). These may be described as follows.

You are a person. Your body, nonetheless, is not a person but a person's body. "Your body" implies a person's body. "You" implies a person. Just as a person and a person's body are different likewise your shunyata and your body's shunyata are different. Your shunyata is your characteristic (*khyad chos*) while you are the basis (*khyad gzhi*). Shunyata is your real nature and that real nature is your characteristic. Your body's shunyata is your body's real nature while your body is the basis whose shunyata is a characteristic. Since there are five heaps that exist in relation to your body, there are five different kinds of shunyata in relation to those heaps. In fact, there are many, many different kinds of shunyata.

Why are we still living in samsara and experiencing suffering? We have not escaped from suffering because we have not been able to perceive our own real nature, our own selflessness (*bdag med*) directly. Not only have we not perceived our real nature directly, we have not even come to perceive our real nature indirectly through inferential valid cognition. Consequently, we are forced to remain in samsara and experience all kinds of suffering. So, if we don't like to experience suffering we have to find a way to become liberated from it. The main method for doing so is to gain the wisdom that perceives our real nature and the real nature of our five heaps. If we gain this wisdom it will lead us to nirvana and Buddhahood. This is the excellent cause, the main practice of wisdom (*rgyu sbyor ba phun sum tshogs pa*) that the Buddha taught us and the perfect way for us to achieve the ultimate status.

Wisdom is only one kind of knowledge. Above it mentions wisdom *along with its attendant minds* or retinue. We can achieve this wisdom that perceives our own real nature if we practice properly. To achieve this wisdom it must be accompanied by a kind of recognition of "who we are," which is one kind of knowledge. This identification of "who we are" is not our real nature but merely a relative object. The kind of mind that thinks "I am such and such" is a type of distinguishing mind known as discriminating conception (*'du she*). "I am that; he is that; she is that" and so forth, all represent types of discriminating minds. In addition, we have sensory feelings that induce us to think such things as "I'm feeling well," or "I'm not feeling so well," etc. These feelings we call *tsor wa* (*tshor ba*), which accompany every mind. In short, *retinue* refers to the many mental factors (*sems byung*) that accompany wisdom even during our meditation.[23]

།འབྲས་བུ་རང་དོན་ཕུན་སུམ་ཚོགས་པ་ནི།

The excellent results for one's own benefit...

BUDDHA, THE *SUGATA*, OR EXCELLENT RESULTS FOR ONE'S OWN BENEFIT

Compassion and the wisdom that perceives our own real nature are the two excellent causes of intention and practice respectively. From these two excellent causes come *the excellent results for one's own benefit.*

བདེ་གཤེགས། ཞེས་པས་བསྟན་ཏེ།

...are indicated by the word "Sugata."

Sugata (*bde gzhegs*), the "One Gone to Bliss," indicates the cessations that Buddha achieved. Since we have many, many obstacles there are many, many cessations. Although our obstacles will disappear in some manner as a result of our practice, at some point the same obstacles, the same problems will return. Cessations, however, by nature do not have that quality of disappearing and then returning again. Cessations are achieved through practicing wisdom. By practicing wisdom we abandon our obstacles one by one. Once we have thoroughly abandoned our obstacles they can never return because we have destroyed them by applying their antidotes

[23] These are known as the five ever-present mental factors (*kun 'gro lnga*).

and thereby achieved cessation, which maintains its status. Buddha's cessation is what is being described here.

དེ་ཡང་། ལེགས་པར་སྤངས་པ་དང་། སླར་མི་ལྡོག་པར་སྤངས་པ་དང་། མ་ལུས་པར་སྤངས་པ་སྟེ། ཁྱད་པར་གསུམ་ལྡན་གྱི་སྤངས་པ་ངོ་བོ་ཉིད་ཀྱི་སྐུ་དང་།

> *Furthermore, the Nature Truth Body is a [Buddha's] cessation comprised of three qualities: good cessation, non-returning cessation, and all-abandoning cessation.*

THE THREE QUALITIES OF BUDDHA'S CESSATION

These lines are describing Buddha's cessation, which has three characteristics.[24] The first is *good cessation* (*legs par spangs pa*), meaning that Buddha's cessation has the quality of having perfectly abandoned the two kinds of obstacles –obstacles of the mental afflictions (*nyon sgrib*) and obstacles to omniscience (*shes sgrib*)– through the practice of wisdom. The second is *non-returning cessation* (*slar mi ldog par spangs pa*), meaning that all the obstacles have been abandoned without ever returning. Although we, for our part, may have practiced the antidotes and abandoned some of the obstacles on the lower paths, we may not be able to sustain this kind of practice continually with fortitude and, as a result, the power of the antidotes that we apply diminishes so that the obstacles eventually return. A Buddha's cessation, however, lacks that quality since it is a non-returning cessation. The third kind of cessation is *all-*

---

[24] "The Sugata has three qualities [representing] the abandonment of the cause [of suffering]" (*rgyu spangs yon tan gsum bde gshegs*). *Pramāṇavārttika*, v. 139.

abandoning cessation (*ma lus par spangs pa*), signifying the abandonment of all obstacles without exception. We have already mentioned the rough categories of the two principal obstacles *–nyön drip* and *she drip–* yet there are many other kinds of mental afflictions. Each of these will plant seeds in our mind and act as obstacles. Although there are numerous objects and levels of knowledge, we cannot perceive them due to our having countless obstacles. To achieve Buddhahood we have to get rid of each and every one of these obstacles without allowing a single one to remain.

A Buddha's cessation is comprised of these three qualities and is known in the Dharma field as the Nature Truth Body,[25] which is one of the four bodies of a Buddha. A Buddha's wisdom is also comprised of three qualities, which are described below.

དེ་ཁོ་ན་ཉིད་མཁྱེན་པ་དང་། མཁྱེན་པ་བརྟན་པ་དང་། མ་ལུས་པ་མཁྱེན་པ་སྟེ། ཁྱད་པར་གསུམ་ལྡན་གྱི་རྟོགས་པ་ཟག་པ་མེད་པའི་ཡེ་ཤེས་གཉིས་ལ་བདེ་བར་གཤེགས་པ་ཞེས་བརྗོད་དོ།

> *The epithet "Sugata" [The One Gone to Bliss] refers to the two—[ultimate cessation and] the uncontaminated wisdom of omniscience comprised of the following three qualities: that which perceives suchness [the real nature of all phenomena], whose knowledge is firm, and that which knows all things without exception.*

The first quality of Buddha's omniscient wisdom is the exceptional ability to perceive *suchness* (*de kho na nyid*) directly, referring here to the real nature of all phenomena. The

[25] T: *ngo bo nyi kyi sku*; S: *svabhāvikakāya.*

second quality is that *the knowledge* he possesses is *very firm* and stable (*mkhyen pa brtan pa*) insofar as its quality does not degenerate. The third quality is the ability *to perceive* the real nature of all phenomena *without exception* (*ma lus pa mkhyen pa*) since it grants the ability to perceive directly the problems of each and every being. *Uncontaminated* refers to the fact that this wisdom *completely lacks* the stains of the mental afflictions. *These two* refers to ultimate cessation and ultimate omniscience. The one with these qualities is what is being referred to as *Sugata*, the One Gone to Bliss, in the homage.

I have only given you a brief introduction to this subject. If we go much further into detail you will get completely confused like Alice in Wonderland. In any case it's very important that you get the ideas we have already covered as clear in your mind as possible. Next time we will discuss the main points that are critical for all Buddha's followers. You have to hear these things. If you miss this kind of discussion it's like trying to eat an apple without dentures—you won't be able to bite into it nicely and will leave a lot of gaps. To help you remember I will summarize here what was taught up to this point.

Because we are Buddha's followers or practitioners of the system that Buddha taught it is critical that we know what the Buddha is and why it is we are following him. This is what is being discussed in this text. To help you to keep the main points of the discussion clear in your mind and to serve as a resumé of the Buddha's qualities it is useful to memorize these lines of homage of the root text explained above:

tse mar gyur pa dro la pen she pa /
tön pa de shek kyob la chak tsel lo /

Tse ma (*tshad ma*) means valid or infallible, which can refer to an infallible person, an infallible mind, or any infallible thing. Buddha Shakyamuni is being used here as an example of an infallible person. Within the field of logic, however, when we use the term "Buddha," it may refer to various things; for instance, it can refer to his omniscience, which is not a person but a kind of mind. In like manner "Buddha" may refer to his cessations, which are not changing but unchanging. Buddha Shakyamuni himself is an Emanation Body or *nirmanakaya* (*sprul sku*). Before achieving the *nirmanakaya* he has to achieve the Complete Enjoyment Body or *sambhogakaya* (*longs spyod rdzogs pa'i sku*). Since the *sambhogakaya* is a Buddha deity's form he is not able to teach human beings while in that form but has to change his physical form into that of a human being. That is why he took birth as a *nirmanakaya*, that is, as a prince in India twenty-five hundred years ago. So, given that "Buddha" can be classified in many different ways, in this text, when the author refers to Buddha as an infallible person he is principally referring to Buddha Shakyamuni in his *nirmanakaya* form.

To whom is the author paying homage? To infallibility. What kind of infallibility? To someone who embodies that quality of infallibility once he has turned into that quality. Who did that? Buddha Shakyamuni, he is the one who turned into an infallible person.

Validity (*tshad ma*) is a major subject in Buddhist thought. What do we mean by "validity"? Let's take an example. Here on the table we can see this small plant with its many leaves and various colors. Because we are observing it correctly we have experienced an infallible eye consciousness. Since our eye consciousness perceives this plant here in front of us unmistakenly, our eye consciousness is considered valid. In this case our infallible eye consciousness is taking this plant as its principal object. We call this kind of validity "direct valid perception" (*mngon sum tshad ma*).

In the Madhyamika-Prasangika school system we refer to this plant, which is the principal object of our eye consciousness, as the "principal object of apprehension" (*rtso bo 'dzin stangs kyi yul*). Because the consciousness perceives the object the way it is [conventionally without looking for its ultimate nature], this consciousness is unmistaken or non-deceptive (*mi blu ba*) and is what is meant by "validity." So, just as Buddha Shakyamuni was born as a prince in India due to various good causes, he was also born as or became a perfect, infallible person through being produced from two very excellent causes (*rgyu phun sum tshogs pa gnyis*).

What are these two excellent causes? The first excellent cause is Buddha's compassion, which he practiced for eons and eons until he eventually achieved ultimate compassion. Due to his attainment of ultimate compassion and under its powerful influence he gained many other good qualities as well. This attainment is indicated in the homage by the words *wishing to help sentient beings* (*'gro la phen gzhes pa*). Buddha is thinking all the time about how he can be of benefit to beings. This also implies that he is lacking even the slightest obstacle. The second excellent cause is indicated by the word *Teacher* (*ston pa*) in the verse. In general, when using the term "teacher" this refers to someone who shows or teaches something. In this case, *Teacher* refers to the wisdom that perceives the real nature of all phenomena. These then are the two excellent causes of Buddha, the Infallible One.

Further, these two excellent causes brought about the two excellent results that are special qualities of the infallible Buddha. The first is the excellent result that is for the benefit of oneself (*'bras bu rang don phun tshogs*); the second is the excellent result for the benefit of others (*'bras bu gzhan don phun tshogs*). The first result may also be classified into two: Buddha's cessation and Buddha's knowledge or omniscience. Buddha's cessation is ultimate cessation and implies the abandonment of all obstacles through the application of their individual antidotes. This is a true kind of abandonment. Buddha's cessation has three characteristics. The first characteristic is good cessation (*legs par spangs pa*). The second is non-returning cessation (*lar mi ldog par spangs pa*), which means abandoning obstacles in such a way that they never return. The third characteristic of Buddha's cessation is all-abandoning cessation (*ma lus par spangs pa*).

There are many levels of obstacles and many levels of knowledge. It may be the case that we have abandoned only some obstacles but not all of them. When we achieve the path of insight (*mthong lam*), for instance, at that point we have abandoned all obstacles pertaining to the path of insight but have yet to abandon those obstacles pertaining to the path of meditation (*sgom lam*). The obstacles of this path are known as *gom pang* (*sgom spangs*), obstacles abandoned on the path of meditation. Even at this level still we have not gotten rid of all our obstacles. Buddha's cessation is such that *all* obstacles have been abandoned. This is the meaning of excellent cessations (*spang pa phun sum tshogs pa*).

As mentioned, the first excellent result comprises the qualities of cessation and omniscience, which we call the *"cessation of a Sugata"* (*spang pa bde dshegs*) and the "*omniscience of a Sugata*" (*rtogs pa bde dshegs*) respectively. Sugata (*bde bar gshegs pa*) refers to the status of ultimate happiness that a Buddha achieves.

།འབྲས་བུ་གཞན་དོན་ཕུན་སུམ་ཚོགས་པ་ནི། སྐྱོབ་ཅེས་པས་བསྟན་
ཏེ། རང་གིས་གཟིགས་པའི་མངོན་པར་མཐོ་བ་དང་། ངེས་པར་
ལེགས་པའི་ལམ་མཐའ་དག

The word "Protector" indicates the excellent results for the benefit of others since [Buddha] perceived all paths to higher rebirth and to Buddhahood…

The word *kyob* (*skyob*) here in this verse means *Protector*. Who is being protected? All sentient beings. How does Buddha protect them? He protects them by teaching. How does his teaching protect them? Since Buddha himself has already become an infallible authority through having achieved those two excellent results from those two excellent causes, Buddha can teach his followers exactly how he achieved his status, how he obtained perfect results so that his disciples can learn to do exactly what he himself did. Many of Buddha's followers have achieved enlightenment by practicing in the same exact way as Buddha Shakyamuni. That is how he protects beings and why the author makes prostrations to the *Protector* (*skyob*), which shows the qualities of the result for the benefit of others (*'bras bu gzhan don phun tshogs*).

BUDDHA, THE PROTECTOR, OR EXCELLENT RESULTS FOR THE BENEFIT OF OTHERS

Samsara is divided into six realms—three higher realms and three lower realms. *Higher rebirth* (*mngon par mtho ba*) refers to the three higher realms, more specifically, taking rebirth in the gods' realm, demigods' realm, or human beings' realm. Of course there is an immense difference between the kind of life in terms of ability and enjoyments experienced by beings of the higher realms and those experienced by beings of the lower realms. The life of a being of the three higher realms has more so-called "happiness" in samsara due to being a result strictly related to its unique causes. The life of a being in the lower realms, which is a result of having accumulated bad deeds, is also strictly related to its own unique causes. Buddha perceived directly the kind of good causes that are necessary to achieve the status of all the higher realms' happiness as well as all the causes of suffering of the lower realms.

Nirvana or *Buddhahood* (*nges par legs pa*) means something like "one hundred percent good," or very, very good, implying that not a speck of anything bad has been mixed with it. *All the paths* (*lam mtha' dag*) refers to all the causes or paths to achieve the higher realms' happiness and all those necessary to achieve nirvana and Buddhahood. As I mentioned before, Buddha protects all sentient beings by teaching them these paths to Buddhahood.

།རང་ཉིད་ཀྱིས་ཇི་ལྟར་གཟིགས་པ་ལྟར་གཞན་ལ་བསྟན་པའི་སྒོ་ནས།
འགྲོ་བ་སྡུག་བསྔལ་ལས་སྒྲོལ་བའི་ཕྱིར་སྐྱོབ་པ་ཞེས་བྱའོ། ཞེས་དང་།

He is called the "Protector" because he liberates beings from suffering through teaching them exactly what he himself perceived.

To be concise, Buddha is called the *Protector* of all beings because he is able to liberate them from suffering by means of this teaching system, that is, by teaching them the paths exactly as he experienced and perceived them, as well as how to gather excellent causes for achieving these paths.

ཡང་དཀོན་མཆོག་གསུམ་ལ། ཚད་མས་དྲངས་པའི་ངེས་པ་རྙེད་པ་
དེ་ཉིད་ནས་བཟུང་སྟེ། སྐྱབས་སུ་འགྲོ་བ་ལན་ཅིག་ཙམ་བསྒོམ་པ་ཡན་
ཆད་ཀྱང་།

Also, from the very moment you have gained absolute certainty induced by valid cognition about the Three Precious Jewels, just meditating once on taking refuge…

POWER OF TAKING REFUGE AFTER GAINING CERTAINTY

To *have gained absolute certainty induced by valid cognition* is similar to the American expression "I know, I know, I know" in response to something we feel we are absolutely sure of. If we really "know" something, what we know is brought to our mind through some form of valid cognition. The text in this case is referring to indirect valid cognition rather than direct valid perception. If we practice taking refuge in the Three Precious Jewels just once while having a definitive understanding about them in our mind our practice will become far more powerful.

While studying this subject we have to gain valid cognition. As previously mentioned, there are two types of valid cognition: direct (*mngon sum tshad ma*) and indirect (*rjes dpag tshad ma*). An example of the first is like seeing something directly with our eye consciousness. The second, *je pak tse ma*, can be explained this way. *Je* means "after," implying an understanding achieved "after" a certain mental process. *Pak*, in general, means "to guess" or surmise. In this case, however, it does not imply being unsure about the object under investigation but, on the contrary, signifies having perceived or inferred something correctly through the use of good reasoning and thereby having gained infallible cognition. At present, even though as rookies you may not be able to perceive Buddha's qualities and his achievements in the same way as you are able to see this plant that is directly in front of you, if you are sharp enough you can, nevertheless, gain indirect valid cognition about such things.

For example, we can gain indirect valid cognition by considering the following. How did Buddha become an infallible person? He became infallible through having first accumulated the two excellent causes, which brought him the two excellent results of benefiting himself and benefiting others. We can use this as a perfect reason to prove why he became an infallible person. Once we gain an indirect valid cognition realizing how Buddha became a reliable authority, we will have a deeper understanding of Buddha's qualities. Just having the words "Buddha, Dharma, and Sangha" in our mind alone makes us very lucky even if we practice without understanding. But when we take refuge in Buddha influenced by that kind of understanding our taking refuge will become incomparably more powerful and beneficial.

What is Buddha? What is Dharma? What is Sangha? We should be able to say, "Buddha means such and such...; Dharma means such and such...; Sangha means such and such... ". Through having gained good reasons explaining why these objects of taking refuge are the way they are, we will find them worthy as objects of refuge. If we take refuge in them with this understanding our practice will become very extraordinary and extremely virtuous. Why? By taking refuge with this understanding we can collect an enormous amount of virtue, which, were it to take form, all the worlds would be far too small to contain it. So, this is why I have said this is very important. Taking refuge with an understanding gained through infallible cognition is an extraordinary activity. Conversely, though we might still collect a little virtue, without having that kind of understanding as we take refuge we are just taking refuge blindly.

When we say "*namo Buddhaya* / I take refuge in the Buddha," does this mean we are taking refuge only in Buddha Shakyamuni? As I mentioned before "Buddha" can be classified into four *kayas* or bodies: *nirmanakaya*, *sambhogakaya*, *svabhavakaya*, and *jñanadharmakaya*. The *sambhogakaya* refers to the Buddha's deity form while the *nirmanakaya* is a manifestion form like Buddha Shakyamuni. Had we been living twenty-five hundred years ago in India we would have been able to see the *nirmanakaya* of Buddha Shakyamuni. The *nirmanakaya* and *sambhogakaya* are known as the Form Bodies of a Buddha (*gzugs kyi sku*). The Buddha Jewel, or *Buddharatna*, consists of these four *kayas*. The Dharma Jewel, or *Dharmaratna*, consists of Buddha's cessations and omniscience. The Sangha Jewel, or *Sangharatna*, consists of Aryas.

What is it that qualifies one as Sangha? When a practitioner meditates with the objective of perceiving the real nature of all phenomena, he must have first gained listening wisdom (*thos byung gi she rab*). In that way he can gain a realization of the real nature through indirect valid cognition (*rjes dpag tshad ma*). By practicing continually, eventually he will perceive the real nature of all phenomena directly, that is, he will gain a direct valid perception (*mngon sum tshad ma*) of the real nature of all phenomena. Once he achieves that, at that point he has reached the status of an Arya. Of course, Buddha Shakyamuni perceived the true nature of all phenomena eons and eons ago and, because of that, is *Sangharatna*. Therefore, Buddha comprises all three ratnas: he is *Buddharatna*, *Dharmaratna*, and *Sangharatna* together. Once we understand this we will gain a strong belief in Buddha as a real infallible protector and valid teacher.

སྲིད་པའི་རི་བོ་ཕྱིར་བསྙིལ་བ་ལ་མཐུ་དང་ལྡན་པ་འགྱུར་གྱི་གཞན་དུ་ན།

> *...you will have great power to destroy the huge mountain of your samsara, when otherwise not.*

Here poetic language is being used to describe samsara as *the mountain of samsara* (*srid pa'i ri bo*). The image represents our not having been able to purify or even reduce our own samsara from beginningless time until now so it still remains with us like some gigantic mountain. Be that as it may, by practicing taking refuge while having this definitive understanding about the qualities of the Three Precious Jewels in our mind, we will gain the power to destroy (*bsnyil ba*) our own samsara. Sometimes in the city we see demolition crews destroying very tall buildings with dynamite and reducing them to dust. Similarly, even though samsara may be as huge as a mountain we can still demolish it as they do those tall buildings.

What does *otherwise not* imply? The text is saying that if we are lacking a good understanding about the qualities of the Three Precious Jewels or about how Buddha achieved Buddhahood, we will be powerless in the face of our samsara.

ཇི་སྲིད་དཀོན་མཆོག་གསུམ་གྱི་ཡོན་ཏན་ལ་གཞན་གྱི་ཚིག་ཙམ་གྱིས་རྗེས་སུ་འབྲངས་ནས་དད་པ་བསྒོམ་པ་དང་། དཀོན་མཆོག་གསུམ་ལ་ཡོན་ཏན་དེ་ལྟ་བུ་ཡོད་པའི་རྒྱུ་མཚན་རྟེད་པ་ལྟ་ཞོག །དཀོན་མཆོག་གསུམ་པོ་དེ་ཉིད་སྤྱིར་ཤེས་བྱ་ལ་ཡོད་པ་ཙམ་གྱི་རྒྱུ་མཚན་གང་ཡང་མ་མཐོང་བཞིན་དུ། ནན་གྱིས་སྐྱབས་སུ་འགྲོ་བའི་ཚིགས་སུ་བཅད་པ་དགྲངས་ཀྱི་ང་རོ་དྲག་པོས་དུས་ཚིགས་མང་པོའི་བར་དུ་བསྒྲགས་ཤིང་།

Should you proudly proclaim that you are assiduously taking refuge by repeating an exorbitant number of recitations of the Refuge Verse, as long as you just practice by faithfully following another's words regarding the excellent qualities of the Three Jewels and needless to say have not yet gained certainty through reasoning about their qualities or even know whether these extraordinary Three Jewels really exist, and...

In short, though you may not know anything about the Three Jewels, you may still be taking refuge in them just because someone told you about them saying something like, "The qualities of the Three Jewels are unbelievably great! I cannot even begin to describe them to you since their power is so magnificent. If you take refuge in them they will gradually remove all of your problems and you will be able to achieve whatever you wish." If someone were to describe the Three Jewels in this way, even though you may not know a single thing about their real qualities, most likely you will think, "Oh, I really want to take refuge in these three precious ones—Buddha, Dharma, and Sangha."

These are very good instructions. In the past I have come across people who have made pronouncements to me that they are spending all of their time practicing. When I ask them what it is they are practicing they often say, "Oh, I have just finished practicing *kyamdro*, taking refuge practice." Then I might ask them how many they have completed. "Oh, about a million." So I tell them, "That's very good; you did a very good job. But, let's see, can you tell me a little bit about the qualities of the Buddha, Dharma, and Sangha?" In answer to this they have no choice but to reply like Ronald Reagan used to: "Well…actually…I don't know very much about that." So, just counting millions and millions of recitations without having any knowledge about what it is you're doing doesn't have much meaning.

རྒྱུ་མཚན་གང་ཡང་བཤད་དུ་མེད་པའི་མིག་གི་ཆུ་རྒྱུན་ནམ་མཁའི་ཆར་
ལྟར་བབ་ཀྱང་། མཚན་བརྗོད་པ་ཙམ་ཞིག་གི་ཕན་ཡོན་འབྱུང་བ་
ཟད་ཀྱི། སྐྱབས་འགྲོའི་དོན་གང་ཡང་ཚང་བ་མ་ཡིན་ནོ། །ཞེས་དང་།

...though you may not know anything about the Three Jewels or have any good reason [why you are taking refuge in them], and may shed tears [of devotion] like rain falling from the sky, you will only receive the virtue of reciting their holy names. Still you have not acquired the real meaning of Taking Refuge.

Since we haven't gained true understanding about the Three Jewels we truly don't know what it means to take refuge. This is very important. I want very much to tell you about this so you understand it well. Therefore, try to make a special effort to come here to class. We have to realize what this means and always keep it in our mind when taking refuge. When we begin to take refuge, at first, for just a short time we should think about the qualities of the Buddha, how he is a reliable, infallible person and how Buddha, the Teacher, has completed his practice and achieved the two purposes (*don gnyis mthar phyin ston pa rdzogs sangs rgyas*)—for the benefit of himself and for the benefit of others. We don't need a third kind of benefit; two are enough.

Earlier I mentioned Brahma. There are many tenets that hold various views about creation. Having some knowledge of these will help in understanding the main subject of *Sutra of Valid Cognition* (*tshad ma mdo*) by the great pandit Dignaga and the greatest commentary on this text, *Commentary to "Valid Cognition"* by the holy Dharmakirti.

PROVING BUDDHA AROSE FROM CAUSES

Buddha didn't just turn into an infallible person without any causes. That status of infallibility is related to many causes. Among these are two main ones comprised of the two collections: the collection of virtue (*bsod nams kyi tshogs*) and the collection of wisdom (*ye shes kyi tshogs*). The first refers to compassion, which the Buddha practiced for eons and eons to benefit beings. The latter refers to wisdom, which he also practiced for eons and eons until he accomplished its perfection. These are the two major causes that brought about his achievement of Buddhahood and allowed him to become a valid authority.

ཡང་སྐྱེ་བ་སྔ་ཕྱི་མེད་དོ་ཞེས་གྲུབ་པའི་མཐའ་བཅས་ནས་སྨྲ་བའི་སྒྲོ་འདོགས་ཀུན་བརྟགས་མངོན་གྱུར་རྒྱང་ཕན་སོགས་ཕྱི་རོལ་པ་ཁ་ཅིག་མིན་པ་ལ་མེད་ཀྱང་།

Also there is no lack of non-Buddhists such as the followers of the Charvaka School, who have the actual acquired wrong view that asserts: "Past and future lives do not exist."

If you are a practitioner listening to these teachings, when you hear the words "former lives" and "future lives," you should automatically apply what you hear to yourself, to your own situation, and think: "*My* future lives" and "*my* former lives." In India, there were quite a few non-Buddhist schools at the time this logic text was written, among them one was the *Charvakas*, known in Tibetan as Gyang-penpa,[26] whose followers did not believe in former and future lives.[27] The term

---

[26] (T: *rgyang phan pa*; S: *Charvakas*) *rJe btsun dkon mchog 'jigs med dbang po* writes in his *Grub mtha' rin chen phreng ba'i tshig 'grel thor bu*: "With regard to the 'Gyang-penpa,' they assert that we do not come here from a previous life because no one has ever seen a previous life. They also hold that an adventitious mind comes from an adventitious body just as a temporary flame arises from a temporary lamp. Additionally, they believe that we do not go on to a future life from our present life. This is due to the fact that, since body and mind are of one substance, when the body disintegrates the mind likewise will disintegrate. For example, when a stone is destroyed the drawing rendered on that stone is likewise destroyed."

[27] Dharmakirti responds to this belief in his work, *Pramāṇavārttika*, with the argument: "Just because you don't perceive something (past and future lives in this case), it doesn't mean they don't exist" (*ma mthong phyir na med pa min*). This accords with perfect reason of

exaggeration (*sgro 'dogs*) is used here synonymously with wrong view (*log lta*), in this case referring to the lack of belief in former and future lives. This particular wrong view comes from having cultivated bad tenets. If we hear and study a lot of bad tenets, every single word puts seeds in our mind that will eventually grow into mistaken ideas or wrong views. These we call "acquired wrong view" (*kun btags*) as opposed to "innate wrong view" (*lhan skyes*). The belief that we have one single life without former and future lives mentioned here is a good example of an acquired wrong view, which usually originates through the cultivation of bad tenets. As for innate wrong view every ordinary person has it.

Actual acquired wrong views (*kun btags mngon gyur*) may be explained this way. When we get angry, for instance, we have actual anger present in our mind and when we stop being angry that manifest anger vanishes from our mind temporarily. However the potential, that is to say, the seeds of anger still remain dormant until anger arises once again when prompted by the appropriate conditions.

The *outsiders* (*phyi rol pa*) referred to above are any proponents of tenets other than the system of Dharma propounded by Buddha.

སྒྲོ་འདོགས་དེ་ཉིད་ཀྱི་ས་བོན་སོ་སོ་སྐྱེ་བོ་ཕལ་ཆེ་བ་ལ་ཡོད་དེ།

---

non-observation in logic whose classic example is the following: Consider this place in front of us, in the mind of a person who does not have the spiritual capacity to perceive a ghost there does not exist a factually concordant analytical consciousness that ascertains a ghost, because the mind of that person has no validating perception of a ghost (*mdun gyi gzhi 'dir chos can, sha za bskal don du song ba'i gang zag gi rgyud la sha za nges pa'i dpyad shes don mthun med de, gang zag de'i rgyud la sha za dmigs byed kyi tshad ma med pa'i phyir*).

Most ordinary people have the seeds of such acquired wrong views.

The fact that most ordinary people have seeds of acquired wrong views in their mind can be proven with logic. We might think about it this way: "How can I possibly have such seeds in my mind? I've never studied wrong tenets in my life so I shouldn't have any such seeds. How is that possible?" Even though we may have not studied wrong tenets in this life, since we have had countless lives in the past we cannot be absolutely sure that we have never studied and cultivated wrong tenets in the past. In fact, it is more than likely that we have acquired them and not only once but many, many times! Each time we studied wrong views we collected seeds that remain in our mindstream. This is the reason why any ordinary person can have seeds of acquired wrong views in their mind.

SEEDS OF ACQUIRED WRONG VIEWS

སྔོན་སྐྱེ་བ་གཞན་དག་ཏུ་རྒྱང་ཕན་སོགས་ཀྱི་གྲུབ་པའི་མཐའ་དང་། གཞུང་ལུགས་ཐོས་པའི་སྟོབས་ཀྱིས་བག་ཆགས་བཞག་པར་གྱུར་པའོ།

On the strength of studying the tenets and scriptural systems of such schools as the "Gyang-penpa" in our previous lives we have planted seeds [of wrong views in our mindstream].

Therefore, we have accumulated a great collection of harmful seeds from listening to and studying wrong tenets in numerous previous lives.

།དེ་ལྟ་མ་ཡིན་ན། གྲུབ་མཐས་བློ་མ་བསྒྱུར་བའི་སོ་སོ་སྐྱེ་བོ་དག་གི་རྒྱུད་ལ་མཐོང་སྤངས་གཏན་ནས་མེད་པ་ཐལ་བར་འགྱུར་རོ།

If that were not the case, it would absurdly follow that, since his mind has not been transformed by tenets, an ordinary person would have no obstacles to be abandoned on the Path of Insight.

To better understand this we have to discuss the cessations, which were only briefly touched on earlier. Cessation can be classified into two kinds: the cessation of obstacles abandoned on the Path of Insight (*mthong spangs*) and the cessation of those obstacles abandoned on the Path of Meditation (*sgom spangs*). What is the nature of this "Insight"? If we have *insight* about the real nature of all phenomena –our real nature, our heaps' real nature, the real nature of other beings– and perceive them directly with our cognition during meditation, the wrong views along with their seeds that we gained through hearing and studying wrong tenets in this and previous lives will most definitely disappear. When we perceive the real nature of these things, the view that holds their nature in an erroneous way will certainly be destroyed. Those obstacles that hinder the perception of this real nature are what we call "obstacles to be abandoned on the Path of Insight" (*mthong spangs*). Upon achieving the Path of Insight, subsequent to the Path of Accumulation (*tshogs lam*) and the Path of Preparation (*sbyor lam*), through gaining a direct perception of emptiness we achieve the real *Dharmaratna* as well as become an Arya (*'phags pa*) or real *Sangharatna*. So, the abandonment of acquired wrong views along with their seeds through the application of special wisdom is what is known as the "first cessation" and that which is achieved on the Path of Insight.

།གཞན་ཡང་སོ་སོ་སྐྱེ་བོ་ཕ་མལ་པ་ཕལ་ཆེ་བ་དག་གི་རྒྱུད་ལ་སྐྱེ་བ་སྔ་ཕྱི་འཇལ་བའི་མངོན་སུམ་ཚད་མ་མི་སྲིད་ཅིང་།

Furthermore, it is not possible for most ordinary people to have a direct valid perception in their mind that comprehends [the existence] of former and future lives and...

This is a very important quotation. "Ordinary person" here is one who pertains to the first two of the five paths. When the practitioner achieves the third path, the Path of Insight (*mthong lam*), he becomes an Arya (*'phags pa*), or superior being, and is therefore no longer considered *ordinary* (*so so skye bo*). Two ways of perceiving our former and future lives is either through some form of direct valid perception or through indirect valid cognition. Most ordinary people do not have direct valid perception of either their own or other people's former and future lives. If someone were to ask you, "Are you able to perceive your former and future lives directly?" Of course you will say "no." Although you may not have a direct perception of those lives, nevertheless, you may have an indirect cognition about them. Even having an indirect cognition about former and future lives is still quite difficult to accomplish.

དེ་སྲིད་སྐྱེ་བ་སྔ་ཕྱི་ཡོད་པར་སྒྲུབ་པའི་རྟགས་ཡང་དག་མ་མཐོང་བ་དེ་སྲིད་དུ་རྗེས་དཔག་ཀྱང་མི་སྲིད་ལ།

As long as you are lacking perfect reasons to prove the existence of former and future lives it will be impossible for you to have an indirect valid cognition about them.

Not only do ordinary people lack direct perception of these lives, they don't even have an inferential cognition of them either. In other words, we need infallible reasons in order to gain an indirect cognition of the existence of former and future lives. For example, what do you see me holding in my hand? A stick of incense. You can see it through your direct visual perception. Now what do you see here? Smoke. Since you can see this smoke directly, you have an infallible direct perception of this smoke as well. Why is smoke rising from this incense holder? When you ask the question "why," this indicates that you are looking for good reasons to validate what you are experiencing. You think, "If there is smoke, there must also be fire. Smoke is coming out of that box because fire is burning up the incense. Because there is smoke, there is fire." This realization –that there must be fire because there is smoke– is an infallible inferential cognition. When you realize that there is fire in the incense holder, you do so not directly but indirectly through the use of a good reason. The reason used in this case is the very smoke that you see. It is based on a factual object. The knowledge concluding that fire must be present in the incense holder by virtue of the presence of smoke is a kind of infallible knowledge or indirect valid cognition (*rjes dpag tshad ma*), whereas the eye consciousness that perceives the smoke directly is a kind of direct valid perception (*mngon sum tshad ma*), the other kind of infallible knowledge. Therefore, to have an indirect valid cognition you need good reasons to substantiate your thesis. Through these good reasons you will come to realize that what you are investigating is real.

VALID INFERENTIAL COGNITION REQUIRES CORRECT REASONS

Now, you may not have a direct perception of former and future lives at present, but do you have an indirect cognition that perceives them? Only you can tell whether you do or not. Until you have studied sufficiently and formulated an understanding through the use of good reasons concerning their existence, it will not be possible for you to have an indirect cognition about your former and future lives or about the former and future lives of others.

དེ་ཉིད་འཇལ་བའི་ཚད་མ་རྣམ་པ་གཉིས་གང་ཡང་རྒྱུད་ལ་མ་སྐྱེས་
པར།   །དེ་ཉིད་ངེས་པའི་ངེས་ཤེས་སྐྱེ་མི་སྲིད་པའི་ཕྱིར།

Without there arising in the mind either of these two kinds of valid cognition perceiving their [existence], an ascertaining consciousness cannot arise to validate them.

Above we have already mentioned *two kinds of valid cognition*—direct and indirect. *Ascertaining consciousness* (*nges shes*) is a kind of unequivocal conviction about something, which can be described in the following way. What did I show you only a moment ago? I showed you a stick of incense and then I showed you some rising smoke. Since you did not see the source of the smoke, namely the fire, you had to realize the source of the smoke by using good reasons. An ascertaining consciousness is a kind of mind that remembers that which it has already experienced directly. "Because I saw smoke directly I can still remember it. Since there cannot be smoke without fire this correct reason makes me realize that there must be fire in the incense holder." So, the first *ascertaining consciousness* was induced through your having had a direct perception, and the second was induced through the application of a correct reason. In a similar way, without perceiving former and future lives directly or indirectly you cannot possibly have an *ascertaining consciousness* to verify them.

སྐྱེ་བ་སྔ་ཕྱི་མེད་པར་འཛིན་པའི་སྒྲོ་འདོགས་མངོན་གྱུར་ཡང་སྐྱེ་བ་ལ་
འགལ་བ་མེད་པ་ཡིན་ནོ།

Though you may not actively hold the wrong view denying the existence of past and future lives, there is nothing to prevent its arising.

Many people have acquired the wrong belief that holds the opposite view about the existence of former and future lives, yet their view may not necessarily always be active. For example, it's possible that you got very angry this morning, at which time you had *actual*, manifest anger. Though your anger has subsided since this morning and you are presently a little calmer after the fire has died down, this does not mean that you don't have anger in your mind necessarily. Just because you do not manifest your anger now doesn't mean that you were not angry before or might not get angry sometime in the future. This shows that it is possible for anger to arise in your mind given the proper conditions since there is nothing to oppose it. What does this mean? As we said earlier, there are two major kinds of valid minds: direct and indirect. If you have not acquired either of these with regard to former and future lives, it is certainly possible that you are holding the wrong belief that there are no former or future lives, even though that wrong view may not be manifest at present. It's always possible that at some moment it may arise in your mind. There is absolutely no reason why this cannot happen since you have neither gained a direct perception nor an inferential cognition supported by good reasons to substantiate the correct belief that former and future lives do in fact exist. What else could deter you from having such a wrong belief?

།དེ་ལྟར། སྐྱེ་བ་སྔ་མ་དང་ཕྱི་མ་ཡོད་པའི་ངེས་ཤེས་རྒྱུད་ལ་མ་སྐྱེས་པ་དེ་སྲིད་དུ། བདག་ཉིད་ཀྱི་སྐྱེ་བ་དུ་མར་སྙིང་རྗེ་ལ་སོགས་པའི་ལམ་བསྒོམས་པ་ལ་ངེས་པ་རྒྱུད་ལ་སྐྱེ་མི་སྲིད་ཅིང་།

Accordingly, as long as an ascertaining consciousness has not arisen in your mindstream regarding former and future lives, you cannot have absolute conviction about your having meditated on a path such as compassion throughout many rebirths...

Compassion is mentioned here as one of the many kinds of knowledge or paths we may have meditated on in our former lives. Other kinds of knowledge include charity, morality, patience, virtuous effort, concentration, wisdom, and so forth. *Path* in this context refers to the way one travels to reach nirvana and Buddhahood. What is the definition of *path*? The definition of *path* is a realization that is influenced by the thought of renunciation.[28] Two synonyms for path (*lam*) are the "Mother" (*yum*) and "knowledge" (*mkhyen pa*). All forms of path knowledge are gained through meditation. If we cannot recognize our former lives with direct or indirect cognition, it will be impossible for us to remember that we had practiced compassion, patience, wisdom, or any of the other paths in our previous lives. The reason we cannot remember what happened in our former lives is because we have no *ascertaining consciousness* (*nges shes*) about them.

[28] *nges 'byung gi bsam pas zin pa'i mngon rtogs lam gyi mtshan nyid*

དེ་དག་སྐྱེ་བ་དུ་མར་བསྒོམས་པ་མི་སྲིད་པའི་སྒྲོ་འདོགས་གཅོད་མི་ནུས་ལ།

Nor are you able to dispel the exaggerated view that it's impossible to have meditated on those paths in many of those former lives.

If I were to ask you, "Do you remember having practiced those kinds of knowledge in your former lives?" You might answer, "I'm not really sure whether I did or not." This reveals a kind of doubt or hesitation in your mind. If you don't wish to have such doubt and want to be absolutely sure that you did indeed practice those paths in former lives you will have to gain a recollection of these. If you have recollection you will be able to readily say, "Yes, I definitely practiced these paths in the past because I remember when I was born as such and such and I studied with a very good teacher in that life and learned and practiced, and so forth. I did this not only once but in several of my previous lives." There are many people who can remember their past lives like that. So, in order to remove your doubt, you need a good memory that can recall what happened in your former lives.

དེའི་ཕྱིར། ཇི་སྲིད་སྐྱེ་བ་སྔ་ཕྱི་ཡོད་པར་སྒྲུབ་པའི་རྟགས་ཡང་དག་ལ་བརྟེན་ནས་ངེས་པ་མ་རྙེད་པ་དེ་སྲིད་དུ། བདག་གིས་སེམས་ཅན་ཐམས་ཅད་ཀྱི་དོན་དུ་སངས་རྒྱས་ཐོབ་པར་བྱའོ་སྙམ་པའི་སེམས་བསྐྱེད་ཀྱང་རྣལ་མ་སྐྱེ་མི་སྲིད་ཅིང་།

Therefore, until you gain certainty based on perfect reasons proving the existence of former and future lives, it is impossible for true bodhichitta to arise that reflects, "I must achieve Buddhahood for the benefit of all beings."

In order to establish the existence of former and future lives you need to prove their existence through the use of *perfect reasons* (*rtags yang dag*). A perfect reason may be like the one I gave you earlier. For example, what perfect reason proved that there was fire in the incense holder? "I realized there was fire in the incense holder because I saw smoke coming from it." Since you saw smoke coming directly from the incense holder this caused you to realize that fire must be inside. *Until you gain certainty based on perfect reasons* that you have perceived or realized something you will not be able to have perfect knowledge.

WITHOUT CERTAINTY GAINED THROUGH PERFECT REASONS TRUE BODHICHITTA CANNOT ARISE

Bodhichitta is the mind that wishes to achieve complete Buddhahood for the benefit of all beings[29] and is one of the three principal aspects of the path. For us to gain *true bodhichitta* we must have good recollection of having practiced bodhichitta previously, of having practiced compassion and perfect love over many lifetimes. The perfection of these kinds of practices in this life is contingent upon our having practiced them in our past lives. For example, without meat we cannot make delicious momos. Though we may have meat, if we have no flour we cannot make momos. Also, if we don't have the proper skill we cannot make momos. Therefore, each one of these "ingredients" relies upon the other. We have to apply our logic this way. To have the result of delicious momos we must first gather the necessary

---

[29] The definition of bodhichitta as given in the *Abhisamayālaṃkāra* (T: *mNgon rtogs rgyan*) is *sems bskyed pa ni gzhan don phyir / yang dag rdzogs pa'i byang chub 'dod/* Ch. 1, v. 19.

causes. The first ones are causes, the latter ones are results. Subsequent results are related to former causes. If we want something we have to create the causes for it; without causes we will never be able to experience the results. This is what *impossible* refers to above.

དེར་མ་ཟད། ཚེ་ཕྱི་མ་ངན་སོང་དུ་ལྟུང་གིས་དོགས་པ་དང་ལྷ་མིའི་
གོ་འཕང་ཐོབ་པར་བྱ་བའི་ཕྱིར་དུ། དགེ་སྡིག་ལ་བླང་དོར་བྱེད་པའི་
ཚུལ་ལ་ཡང་། ངེས་པ་རྣལ་མ་སྐྱེ་མི་སྲིད་པས།

> *Not only that, it will be impossible for you to have perfect certainty about the need to adopt the practice of virtue and abandon the practice of non-virtue in order to achieve the status of a human and to hestiate from doing bad actions out of fear of falling into the lower realms in your future life.*

Fear here refers to having intense anxiety about something, in this case, about the possibility of falling into the three lower realms in a future life. This kind of dread or apprehension indicates a very crucial point, which is that if we are a real Dharma practitioner and really want to practice Dharma, we have to realize that it is definitely possible that we fall into one of the three lower realms in our future life. There are various levels of certainty about this. We may be *absolutely sure* that we will fall, we may think that there is *a pretty good chance* that we will fall, or we may think it is *only vaguely possible* that we will fall. Being *absolutely sure* implies that we know we are doing nothing but bad things all the time and collecting bad deeds so that there is absolutely no way to avoid falling into the lower realms. Thinking that we have *a pretty good chance* of falling implies that our activities are about fifty fifty, or equally divided between doing good things and doing bad things. Thinking that it is *only vaguely possible* means that we are doing bad deeds about one third of the time and practicing virtue for the other two thirds. *The status of a god or human* is referring to the three higher realms—human beings' realm, demigods' realm, and gods' realm (*mngon mtho*).

The sense of this passage is as follows. We may think, "I may fall into one of the three lower realms in my future life. If that should happen, I will have made a tremendous mistake since I didn't do anything to avert it. Therefore, I must look after my future life and achieve a higher realm's rebirth!" If we are perfect practitioners, especially perfect Tantric practitioners, we have received instructions and specific methods for achieving Buddhahood. From the Dharma's side everything is ready; it is only we who are lacking from our side. We are the ones who are poor, not the Dharma. If we cannot achieve the ultimate state of Buddhahood in this lifetime we will need an excellent life that is conducive to practicing the paths of Dharma in the future to achieve Buddhahood. The kind of excellent life we will need is a higher realm's life, most especially a human being's life, which is what we have right now. It is extremely important that we realize that we have acquired a very useful life this time and that we should not fail to make good use of it. So, whether we achieve a higher realm or fall into a lower realm in the future depends entirely upon our own practice from this very moment until the time we die. It is entirely up to us. That being so what then must we do?

If we wish to achieve a higher realm's rebirth for the ultimate purpose of achieving Buddhahood and not fall into the lower realms, we have to follow this system of collecting virtue and giving up doing bad deeds as much as we can. *Perfect certainty* refers to having acquired direct perception or indirect cognition about our former and future lives.

ཇི་སྲིད་སྐྱེ་བ་སྔ་ཕྱི་ཡོད་པར་རིགས་སྟོབས་ཀྱིས་མ་ངེས་པ་དེ་སྲིད་དུ། མངོན་པར་མཐོ་བ་དང་ངེས་པར་ལེགས་པའི་ལམ་ཐམས་ཅད་ཀྱི་སྒོ་འགགས་ཏེ་འདུག་པ་ཡིན་ནོ།

Until you have realized on the strength of logic that former and future lives exist, the door to all paths that lead to higher rebirth and definite goodness will be closed.

Higher rebirth (*mngon par mtho ba*) refers to a life in one of the three higher realms, which is of course a "nice" life compared with life in the three lower realms. *Definite goodness* (*nges par legs pa*) refers to nirvana and Buddhahood. These are called "good" because they are definitely a good objective to strive for. To achieve these we have to enter the paths (*lam*) that lead there. Again, we have to understand that we need all the proper "ingredients" and causes to practice the paths. If we lack any of them we will not be able to reap the fruits since *all the paths* to higher rebirth, nirvana, and Buddhahood *will be closed* (*lam thams cad kyi sgo 'gags*) to us. In any case, we cannot sit around idle for eons and eons just waiting for the paths to open up for us; we ourselves have to try to open them with our practice.

།དེས་ན། འདི་ཉིད་ལ་ངེས་པ་རྙེད་པ་དང་། སྐྱེ་བ་སྔ་ཕྱི་མེད་པའི་སྒྲོ་འདོགས་ཆོད་པ་ནི། ལམ་སྒོམ་པ་ལ་ཐོག་མ་ཉིད་དུ་ཆེས་ཆེར་གལ་ཆེ་ཞིང་། ཞེས་དང་།

Therefore, gaining certainty and dispelling any doubts you may have regarding the existence of former and future lives is of the utmost importance at the beginning of practicing the paths.

GAINING CERTAINTY AND REMOVAL OF ALL DOUBT ABOUT PAST AND FUTURE LIVES THROUGH REASONING

It is vital that we gain strong conviction and remove all our doubts and skepticism about the existence of former and future lives. If we want to practice something and achieve it we have to know the chief thing we are to do at the outset. Here, at the very beginning of our practice it is critical that we have these two, namely, good certainty and removal of all doubt.

ཡང་སྐྱེ་བ་སྔ་ཕྱི་ཡོད་པའི་སྒྲུབ་བྱེད་དགོད་པ་ནི། ཐ་མལ་པ་སྐྱེས་མ་ཐག་གི་རིག་པ་དང་པོ་ཆོས་ཅན། རང་རྒྱུ་རིག་པ་སྔ་མ་སྔོན་དུ་སོང་སྟེ། རིག་པ་ཡིན་པའི་ཕྱིར།

One way of establishing the proof of the existence of former and future lives is as follows: Consider the very first moment of mind of an ordinary newborn baby, the unique cause of that mind was a preceding moment of mind because its nature is mental.

ESTABLISHING PROOF OF PAST AND FUTURE LIVES FROM PRECEDING MIND

At this point we should decide to gain certainty about our former and future lives first through inferential cognition, like the example given earlier proving the presence of fire by the perception of smoke, then later through direct valid perception. We have to have perfect reasons to convince ourselves that former and future lives exist. As proof of their existence the text gives the example of an ordinary person (*tha mal pa*) who has just been born. As we know there are many babies born in hospitals everyday. As soon as they're born they make a loud noise –"Waaaa waaaa!"– which comes from their trying to express their feelings. What they are feeling at the time of their birth is great discomfort and very unpleasant sensations. If we wonder what this feels like, it is as if someone were to catch us in the winter, take off all our clothes and throw us into the snow. If that happened of course we would suddenly feel terribly uncomfortable! In a similar way, to the tender skin of a newborn baby who has just arrived in this strange new place everything feels very harsh and irritating so it automatically begins to cry out in pain. These cries arise from feeling (*tshor ba*), a mental factor that accompanies the main mind. Since the mind of a newborn baby is one thing while its body is another it is evident that the mind and the physical body each has its own unique causes.

For example, every crop of vegetables must first be planted. These vegetables likewise have their own unique causes and secondary conditions. The unique, principal cause of a vegetable is a seed. The secondary conditions are heat, fertilizer, dirt, water, sunlight, and so forth, which in combination help the seed to mature. When the seed matures it gives forth a sprout. Without the assistance of the four elements a seed will remain as dry as a bone and fail to bring forth a sprout. For a seed to grow it needs the help of these elements. Therefore, the principal cause producing a sprout is a seed while the secondary conditions are the four elements [earth, water, fire, and air]. Similarly, the mind of a newborn baby has its own unique principal cause as does its physical body.

Just from looking at this newborn baby we can see that it has found a new body, which has come from the combination of the parents' substances. But what about the newborn baby's mind –the mental part– where did this come from? Did it come from the parents as well? What is the main seed, the unique principal cause of this mind? Is it something that originated from the parents' mind or did it come from something else?

In general –and I imagine Western scientists believe likewise– form cannot turn into mind just as mind cannot turn into form. Rocks cannot turn into something mental nor can mental things turn into rocks. Hence, what is mental must come from what is mental and what is physical must come from what is physical. Accordingly, the very first moment of mind of this life must have had its own unique principal cause, which can only be mental. We call this unique principal cause the substantial cause (*nyer len gyi rgyu*). The substantial cause of mind has to be mind, just as it is described in the *Commentary to "Valid Cognition"*: "Thus, it is proven that what is not mental cannot be the substantial cause of what is mental."[30] Where did that mind come from then? To whom did that mind belong before the mental continuum of this life began? Surely mind must have had its own unique causes.

THE SUBSTANTIAL CAUSE OF MIND IS MIND

Above, the text states that *the unique cause of that mind was a preceding moment of mind.* What is the definition of mind? The definition of mind is that which is clear and knowing.[31] *Lo* (*blo*), *rik pa* (*rig pa*), and *she pa* (*shes pa*) are synonyms. The first moment of this life's mind must have had its own unique mental cause preceding it, which existed at the very final moment of our previous life's mind. This life's mind arose immediately after the last moment of the mind of our former life and so these two are very closely related.

Let's take a sprout as an example. Before the first moment of the arisal of a sprout its main nature is evident as a seed.

---

30 *rnam shes min pa rnam shes kyi / nyer len min pa'i phyir yang 'grub* / v. 164.

31 *gsal zhing rig pa blo'i mtshan nyid*

The very first moment it becomes a sprout it is no longer a seed. We can see the succession of cause and effect in this succession of seed to sprout. Likewise, the first moment of this life's mind comes from the last moment of mind of our previous life in a succession of cause and effect. Why is this? As the text states, *because its nature is mental.* This should be very clear. Because mind has a mental nature the unique cause of mind should be mental as well. Mental comes from mental; physical from physical.

དཔེར་ན། ད་ལྟའི་རིག་པ་འདི་བཞིན་ཞེས་པའི་རྟགས་ལས། ཐ་མལ་པ་སྐྱེས་མ་ཐག་གི་རིག་པ་དང་པོ་ལ། རང་རྒྱུ་རིག་པ་སྔ་མ་སྔོན་དུ་སོང་བ་འགྲུབ་པས་སྐྱེ་བ་སྔ་ལ་ཡོད་པར་འགྲུབ་ཅིང་།

For example, the logical reason that states "[because] it is similar to this present mind" proves that [the newborn baby's] mental continuum existed in a previous life preceding it since the unique cause of the first moment of mind of that ordinary newborn baby is a previous moment of mind.

If I were to ask you, "Do you know where you live? Can you recognize your house?" Everybody will easily answer, "Why, yes, of course I do." "Did you just realize it at this moment for the first time?" "No, I have known this since the time I started living there." This particular knowledge evolved from that time and has continued up to the present moment and will stay firmly in our mental continuum over time. In this way we can understand how knowledge comes from unique mental causes passing from one moment to the next in a succession reaching up to the present moment. This is what is implied by *similar to this present mind* (*da lta'i rig pa bzhin*), which we are experiencing right now. It is in this exact same way that the mind of a former life, the mind prior to that former life, and the one prior to that one, and so on, continue up to the present moment in a continual mental stream from one life to the next.

We can understand from the reason given above how the mental continuum continues from beginningless time up to this very moment and how this life's mind has originated from our previous life's mind. Once we logically realize that we must have had a life prior to this life we can no longer be fooled. This realization, produced by an indirect inferential cognition, should prove definitively to our mind the existence of former lives.

What does it mean above by *until you gain certainty based on perfect reasons definitively proving the existence of former and future lives*? How can we definitively prove this? When a baby is born it has a mind, which is made up of a continuum of instants of mind. Here, the subject under discussion is that very first instant of a newborn baby's mind. Because that mind is an entity it most certainly had its own cause. Since every entity must arise from its own unique cause the first moment of that infant's mind likewise must arise from its own unique cause. What then is its unique cause? The unique cause of that ordinary baby's first moment of mind is a previous moment of mind. The general rule is that a cause comes before its effect. Accordingly, the very first moment of that newborn baby's mind is the result of a previous mind existing before it, which serves as that later moment of mind's unique cause. Why is the cause of that newborn baby's mind a previous mind? Because it is mind; or as given above *[because] it is similar to this present mind.* The mind that we have presently at seven o'clock came from the mind that existed previously at the very last moment of six fifty-nine.

If the unique cause of that baby's mind had to have come from a previous mind, to whom did that previous mind belong? It belonged to the very last moment of mind of that baby's previous life. So there must have been a previous life. We have to logically prove the existence of a previous life through the relationship of cause and effect and use *present mind*, which we see is similar, as an example to substantiate it. That is how we can prove that the mind at the very beginning of this life comes from the previous mind, namely, the very last moment of mind of our former life.

Once you have proven to your own mind that you have had previous lives, you will easily come to realize that you will have future lives as well. You shouldn't think about this just in a general, abstract way, but rather you have to apply it to yourself, thinking, "*I* have a present life. *I* have had previous lives. *I* will have future lives." Understanding the existence of all of these as they pertain to *you* will contribute to making your understanding firm and help you to generate a strong conviction about them, not to mention it will compel you to act more decisively. You should reflect on this: What did your previous life do for you? What are you doing now in order to help your future lives? Now that you have gained the tools to understand your situation with unerring logic, you won't need to go to Mickey the Psychic to get a prediction about your future. Do you know who Mickey is? She is someone who can tell you the winning lottery numbers. Or at least that's what it says on TV. At night they often show her advertisement that says: "Go ask Mickey. She will give you a prediction for winning the lottery. Mickey knows everything." But, in your case, you don't have to go to Mickey to get a prediction about your future lives! If you use logic you will be able to recognize them very clearly yourself.

IF PAST LIVES EXIST, THEN SO TOO MUST FUTURE LIVES

What did your previous lives do for you, both in terms of good things and bad things? Samsara, as you know, has two divisions: higher realms and lower realms. Rebirth in one of the higher realms is a result of virtuous deeds; rebirth in one of the lower realms is the result of non-virtuous deeds. This excellent human life of the higher realm that you have achieved this time is the result of having done good deeds in the past. Who was it that collected those good deeds? Of course it was your previous life that worked very hard for you and did a very good job insofar as the virtue that your previous life collected gave you this excellent human being's life. Nevertheless, this life is still accompanied by many kinds of problems and suffering all of which can be counted as the results of bad deeds. Who was it that collected these bad deeds? Most of them were collected in your previous lives, although some of them you may have collected last year or when you were a child even. In this way you can see how your previous lives did both good and bad things for you.

Now, most important, what are you doing for your next life? You can tell that clearly. If you are collecting good deeds, mainly through practicing morality, these deeds will bear the fruit of your having a good life in the future. By practicing morality you will achieve an excellent human being's life. By practicing giving you will become rich in your future life. By practicing patience in the future you will be a noble person. By studying a lot and collecting a good deal of knowledge in the future you will be a good scholar endowed with the ability to study, think, write, teach, and other such activities. Similarly, the practice of concentration and the practice of wisdom will render their individual fruits. There is absolutely no doubt that if you gather such causes you will experience the corresponding results.

We have to realize that when we die the connection that ties the body and the mind will be broken, which will result in the two being separated. The mind will continue, however, and acquire a new life by changing the body. The main key is to understand that the very last moment of this life's mind is not just going to disappear, to vanish into nothingness like a candle flame, but will act as the unique cause of the first moment of mind of our next life. So, once we fully understand this, once we are truly convinced that

THE UNIQUE CAUSE OF FUTURE MIND IS PRESENT MIND

there are future and past lives, whenever we study or make a concerted effort to do anything, our activities will become very meaningful and precious for us and not just be useless. This is the essential point of the teaching being given here; it is not merely an idle description or imaginative story.

We have to see how logic texts have a unique quality to help us undertand everything by using reason. If we understand through using logic, the knowledge we acquire will become correct, infallible knowledge (*tshad ma*). Whatever an infallible mind perceives, learns, or understands, the object of that mind, lacking all error, too becomes infallible. Everything that an infallible mind perceives must necessarily exist precisely because it is an object of valid mind. Because the mind is unerring the object of that mind is likewise unmistaken. This is a rule of logic. So the study of logic texts gives us a very good opportunity. However, in the same way as medical books can only teach doctors or others interested in medicine, logic texts can only teach logicians, of course. That is why we here are very lucky to engage in learning these important crucial points through using logical reasoning.

དེ་ལྟར་གྲུབ་པ་ན་སྐྱེ་བ་སྔ་མ་ནས་འདི་ཉིད་དུ་མཚམས་སྦྱོར་བའི་ནུས་
པ་དང་ལྡན་པ་མཐོང་བ་གང་ཡིན་པ་དེ་ལ། རྒྱུ་ལྷག་པོ་ཅི་ཞིག་ཡོད་
པར་གྱུར་ཅིང་རྒྱུ་གང་ཞིག་མེད་པའི་རྒྱུ་མཚན་གང་གིས།

Once you prove that, you will realize that the mind has the power to join the previous life to this very life. So why should extra causes be required for that connection since it can be understood from this reason alone?

Once we realize the necessity of the existence of previous lives we will realize that our mind at the present moment, the previous moment of mind, and the former life's mind all belong to the same mental continuum. This allows us to confidently say, "My former life's mind; my mind of this morning, my mind at the present moment; my mind of this evening; and –in a logical progression– my mind of the next life." This is how mind proceeds, which can be easily verified through logic.

When the passage states *that the mind has the power to join* (*mtshams sbyor ba'i nus pa dang ldan pa*), this means that when changing lives from our previous life to this life, our mind in our previous life was endowed with the power to connect to this life's mind. What is the agent that joins our lives? The agent is the power of mind. It is like this. If we wish to produce rice, we must plant rice seeds. If we wish to produce wheat, we must plant wheat seeds. Each seed has the power to produce its own kind of grain. If such is the case with material phenomena, of course the cause-and-effect relationship between inner mental phenomena is far more powerful. Every seed has the power to produce an effect of the same class. Consequently, we can realize that every mind originates from a previous life's mind and it only makes sense that the very first moment of this life's mind comes from the very last moment of our previous life's mind since that last moment of our previous life's mind had the unique ability to produce this present mind. Due to that the last moment of our previous life's mind joined the very first moment of our present life's mind. In short, our previous life's mind had the unique ability to produce its result, which is our present life's mind going continually from life to life. Additionally, once we recognize this power of the mind to produce a mental result we can see both how a previous life's mind produced this life's mind and how this life's mind will continue on to produce the mind of our next life.

MIND'S POWER TO CONNECT LIVES

If mind itself has that power, why should extra causes (*rgyu lhag po ci zhig*) be required to connect one life to the next?

How do we know we will have a future life? Because our previous life's mind is the unique cause of this life's mind and this life's mind is the unique cause of our next life's mind. If we check we won't be able to find any extra causes that connect our previous life's mind to our present life's mind. The reason given here to prove the mutual correspondence and connection between our past life and our future life should be adequate without requiring any additional causes to make this occur.

ཐ་མལ་པའི་འཆི་སེམས་ཐ་མས་ཕྱི་ནས་རིགས་འདྲ་ཕྱི་མ་མཚམས་སྦྱོར་བ་མེད་པར་འདོད་པ་ཡིན་ཏེ། དེས་ན་རྒྱུ་ཚོགས་ཁྱད་པར་མེད་པའི་ཕྱིར་ཐ་མལ་པའི་འཆི་སེམས་ཐ་མས་ཀྱང་། རང་འབྲས་རིག་པ་ཕྱི་མ་མཚམས་སྦྱོར་བ་ཡོད་པར་གྲུབ་པ་ཡིན་ནོ། །ཞེས་དང་།

We accept that the very last moment of mind of an ordinary dying person does not join to mind of like nature much later on in a future life. So, without need of other extra causes we can prove that future lives exist because the last moment of mind of an ordinary dying person joins that mind to the [first moment of] mind of a future life through producing its own unique result, which is mind.

Join (*mtshams sbyor*) here refers to putting two things together that are of the same nature. Our previous life's mind, insofar as it is mental, can only join to that which is mental, namely, our future life's mind, and cannot transform, say, into the physical body of our next life. It does not work like that. Why does this previous mind not join to a mind much later on in the future? This cannot happen because the last moment of our previous life's mind connects directly without break to the very first moment of mind of our present life. We can think about it this way. When will our mental continuum at the end of this life produce its result? We don't have to ponder hard over this and have all manner of doubt thinking, "Maybe it will produce its result in a month or so, or in a year, or sometime much, much later in the future." The very last moment of an ordinary dying person's mind immediately produces the next life's mind in the very next moment.

The very last mind of an ordinary person who is just at the point of death retains its mental nature since it is a continuum of mind and therewith connects to a future mind in the next moment. When an ordinary person dies the mind, leaving the old body behind, seeks a new body in which to take birth. Thus, the mind goes on continually while the physical body is discarded.

The very last moment of mind of an ordinary dying person is endowed with the power to produce the next life's mind immediately in the subsequent moment. When ordinary mind produces a resultant mind it cannot occur much later on, say, after one or two years, but necessarily joins to the mind of a new life immediately after the passing of the previous mind of the old life.

You have to think a lot about this in as many ways as you can. Did you go to grade school? Did you eventually finish high school? If you say "yes," it implies that you acquired high-school level knowledge. Did you finish college? Again, if you answer "yes," it means that you acquired college-level knowledge. The mind that you developed in high school must be connected to the mind that you developed later in college. After finishing college it connects with the mind that continues after college. In such a way the mind goes on continually. "I remember when I was in college; I remember when I was in high school; I remember when I was in grade school." The very fact that you are able to say this reveals how your present mind passed through those various stages in a continuous manner. Your mind continued its existence through college, through high school, through the time when you were a very small child, from the time when you were just born, and so on in a continuum from your previous life as well. Why? Because all of these moments of consciousness are mind (*rig pa*), and only mental can come from mental.

Have you heard of the Brahmaputra River? This is the principal river in Tibet. Once it crosses the border out of Tibet and enters the plains of Assam in northern India it is no longer called by that name but is known as the Dihang River. From there it continues on through Bangladesh, moving through India where its name changes from the Jamuna River to the Padma River, then to the Meghna River before it finally loses itself entirely as it empties into the Bay of Bengal. Just as the names of this same river change as it crosses the border from one country to the next so too do our names change as we change lives due to the power of the same mental continuum that joins each of our lives together. In the same way this single river has no need of special causes to join together the rivers of different names as it wends its way through the various countries. The power of the continuum of the river itself will carry these nominally different rivers eventually to the ocean.

So, did you have former lives? "I think so." Why? "Because my present mind came from yesterday's mental continuum and so on from the time I was born and will continue on similarly in the future. Additionally, since there can be no unique cause of mind other than mind this mind had to come from the mind of a previous life. Since a mental cause can only produce a mental result, my present life's mind is the result of my former life's mind." You have to think about it in this way.

If it is true that the mind goes on in a continuous manner, how is it that our mind is sometimes very good and at other times very bad? Here we are talking about mental consciousness. Generally speaking, mental consciousness is neutral. However, occasionally this neutral mental consciousness associates with mental factors such as anger. Anger influences the neutral mind thereby making it bad by association. At some point, though, we may come to realize that this anger is destructive insofar as it creates all sorts of negative results for ourselves and everyone else. Realizing this through applying good reasons induces us to practice compassion. As a result of this practice the mind gradually gets better and better. Even though the mind moves in a continuum, the improvement or damage of the mind depends upon the person. Every person can control in which direction the mind is to go.

The argument given above concerning an ordinary person's mind who is about to die is used to convince us that there are former lives. Accordingly, the example of an ordinary newborn baby's mind is given. That baby's mind had its own unique causes, which are a previous mind. If mind has a mental nature it should have had its own unique mental causes to produce that very first moment of mind. Why? Because that brand new mind is a kind of mind. Logicians express this argument for past lives with the following logical statement:

Consider the mind of a newborn baby, that mind had its own prior mental causes because it is the nature of mind, just like our present mind.

chi pa te ma tak pe lo chö chen, rang gyu rik pa nga ma ngön du song te, rik pa yin pe chir, ta te rik pa de shin

If mind has a mental nature its own unique substantial cause must also be of a mental nature. Assuming by necessity that causes appear before their results, since our present mind is the result of a mental cause, that cause must have occurred before this present mind. This is the idea being presented in logical language above. If our present mind had its own unique cause we can easily realize how our mind at the present moment of two o'clock should have had its own preceding cause of mind at one fifty-nine. First comes the cause, next the result. The mind at the first moment is a cause that produces the second or subsequent moment of mind, its result. If the cause is mental, the result likewise must also be mental since mind must have its own unique substantial mental cause. In this way we can come to appreciate how the first moment of mind of an ordinary newborn baby had its own unique mental causes prior to its birth.

Well now, what is this argument trying to prove? It is trying to prove that our present mind originated from a prior mind belonging to a previous life. *We accept* (*'dod pa yin*) implies that there might be someone who objects because he believes that a previous life cannot join to this present life without there being additional causes to bring this about. That person might think that in order for two lives to join special causes other than the one given here are required. Some non-Buddhist scholars who have no comprehension of the mind's unique power to join lives together in this way fail to believe in former and future lives.

We have to have a special skill in reading logic texts to decipher the exact meaning of the subject here under discussion.

ཡང་ཤེས་པ་སྔ་མ་ལ་ལྟོས་མི་དགོས་པར་འབྱུང་བ་ཁོ་ན་ལས་ཤེས་པ་སྐྱེ་བ་ཡིན་ན། གང་དུ་དྲོད་གཤེར་ལ་སོགས་པ་སྐྱེ་བོ་སྐྱེ་བར་མི་འགྱུར་བའི་ས་སོགས་ཆ་དེ་འགའ་ཡང་མེད་པར་འབྱུང་བ་ཡོད་ཙམ་གྱིས་ཤེས་པ་སྐྱེ་དགོས་པ་དེའི་ཕྱིར། ས་སོགས་ཐམས་ཅད་སེམས་ཀྱི་བདག་ཉིད་ཀྱི་ས་བོན་དུ་ཐལ་བར་འགྱུར་རོ། ཞེས་དང་།

If it were the case that consciousness arose only from the elements without having to rely upon a previous consciousness [for its substantial cause], consciousness would arise from the mere presence of the elements without there being any part of the elements, earth element for instance, that would not become a conscious being wherever there were [the conditions of] heat and moisture and so forth. From this it would logically follow that all the elements such as earth contain the natural seeds that germinate into mind.

Some say that the elements alone can produce mind without having to depend upon a previous consciousness as its substantial cause. If that were the case then consciousness would have to arise just from the mere presence of the elements –earth, water fire, or air– without need of any other factors to produce a being.

REFUTING BELIEF IN THE ELEMENTS AS THE EXCLUSIVE CAUSE OF MIND

Formerly in India, some of the major non-Buddhist schools held the belief that mind has no need of unique mental causes for its production since the elements are a sufficient cause to produce the next life's mind. They believed that when one is born the mind is merely a result of the gathering of the elements. Now, let's say, for instance, that mind does not need the unique mental cause belonging to a previous mind to bring it about. If that were so, then how exactly does a new mind come into being? There is a logical way to pursue this.

Does the arising of a new mind require the gathering of the elements or not? This question implies that there are two views with one side asserting that the gathering of the elements alone can produce mind and the other asserting that a mind cannot be produced by these alone. Let's see what the nature and function of the four elements are. The air element functions to make things move and progress. The fire element has the function of ripening and maturing. The earth element has the quality of hardness and serves to obstruct. Finally, the water element is moist and has the function of holding things together. The elements can gather anywhere, be it inside a house, outside in the garden, or even in a mother's womb. However, it is not a given that just from the gathering of these elements a new person is going to arise. Logicians would say "*ma kyab*" (*ma khyab*) meaning "this is not necessarily so." A being may or may not be produced depending upon many other conditions. In the Vinaya Sutra it says, "If three conditions are gathered in a mother's womb a new creature will be generated." Therefore, in accord with this scriptural view the gathering of the four elements is not enough for the production of a new person since, for this to happen, at least three conditions are necessary. These three are the following: 1) in order to be a mother two qualities should be present. The first is that there should be a mutual relationship or former connection between the mother and new child so that the mother is the mother of that child and the child the offspring of that mother. The second is that she must also possess the unique substance that has the power to produce a new baby's body, which implies that she has to be fertile. If she doesn't have these two qualities, she won't be able to produce a new baby; 2) the parents must come together to combine their unique substances; and 3) the bardo being must be looking for a new life.

If these three qualities are present then a new life will be produced. From this you can understand that the mere gathering of the elements will not produce a new mind since several other special conditions are required. The wood of the trees outside, for example, cannot turn into a person's mind. Turning into a person's mind requires the unique quality of a previous mind to produce it and not just the gathering together of the four elements. Can water turn into mind? Can fire turn into mind? Can earth turn into mind? Can air turn into mind? Can the combination of all of these turn into mind? Certainly not. As was just mentioned, even the gathering of the inner four elements cannot produce a new person or new mind. If indeed they could turn into mind then we would have no way of distinguishing between sentient beings and the elements for they would all possess the same quality; that is, sometimes they might be elements and sometimes they might be living beings. Not only that, anywhere where there are elements consciousness would automatically arise and there would be no need for unique causes and secondary conditions to produce anything.

To understand this we have to be familiar with the dual classification of causes into primary causes and secondary causes. The primary or unique cause of mind is only mind. The secondary causes can be the gathering together of the elements. What would happen if you were to put your finger in fire? You would say "ouch!" naturally due to the feeling of intense heat. But what would happen if you were to put a spoon in the fire? Would the spoon say "ouch!" or not? Is a spoon capable of feeling intense heat? No, it is not. But doesn't a spoon possess elements? Yes, it does. Does your finger possess elements or not? Your finger, hand, body, and so forth are all a combination of the elements. For that matter, spoons, tables, even the stove itself that holds the fire are all a combination of elements. Why then do we feel pain when our finger touches fire? Our finger feels pain because, as it says above, it *has the nature of mind* (*sems kyi bdag nyid*), which means that it is associated with mind. Our body in general is associated with mind. If we hurt it in any way we immediately feel pain; if we alleviate it the pain subsides and we feel better.

Seeds (*sa bon*) refer to unique causes. For example, grain, rice, barley, wheat, each has a seed that is the principal cause of each of their respective crops, whereas the elements are secondary causes. Similarly, mind is the principal cause of mind and is associated with its secondary minds through which the feelings of happiness and suffering and so forth arise. Now, when scholars propose that the elements are the sole producers of consciousness, all the elements, both inner and outer, should have the nature of mind. If that were the case it would logically follow that were we to smash one of those elements it too would feel some kind of suffering, but obviously it does not.

Only a human being's body, which is a combination of mind and the elements, can produce a human being's life, whereas a spoon cannot possibly produce a human being's life. So, if I were to say to the scholar who believes that, "According to your view, since the mind does not have to rely on mind for its production but just a combination of elements can produce consciousness, why then wouldn't it be possible for a human being to arise from a spoon? Doesn't that follow from what you say about the gathering of elements, since a spoon likewise possesses a combination of those elements?" That scholar cannot accept his own ridiculous assertion; he cannot accept that the mere association of elements can produce a human being's life. If that were so, then why wouldn't trees and steel and rocks and so forth all give rise arbitrarily to a human being since they too are made up of a combination of elements? Of course they cannot produce a human being precisely because they are lacking the primary, unique cause of mind, which is mind. This is the basis of the argument presented above.

ཕྱི་མ་ཡོད་པའི་སྒྲུབ་བྱེད་ནི། ཐ་མལ་པ་འཆི་ཁའི་བློ་རྟོག་པ་ཆོས་ཅན། རིག་པ་ཕྱི་མ་མཚམས་སྦྱོར་ཏེ། སྲེད་པ་དང་བཅས་པའི་རིག་པ་ཡིན་པའི་ཕྱིར།

A correct reason proving that there are future lives is the following: Consider the mind of an ordinary person just on the verge of death, his mind will turn into the next life's mind, because that mind is accompanied by craving [for a future life].

What does this mean that *mind is accompanied by craving* (*sred pa dang bcas pa*)? This means that the mind of an ordinary person on the verge of death is associated with desire. Desirous craving (*sred pa*) is one limb of the "twelve limbs of dependent origination" (*rten 'brel bcu gnyis*). Buddhas, bodhisattvas, Aryas, and Arhats won't take rebirth in samsara as a samsaric being, because their birth and an ordinary person's birth in samsara are completely different. Why? When seeing the suffering of ordinary beings, through their great compassion, prayers, and wishes they take rebirth in samsara voluntarily strictly for the purpose of helping those beings as did Buddha Shakyamuni and many other sages. However, an ordinary person's rebirth is not like that, since it occurs strictly involuntarily through their falling under the control of karma and the mental afflictions.

TWELVE LIMBS OF DEPENDENT ORIGINATION

To explain this we have to understand the workings of the twelve limbs of dependent origination. Arya Nagarjuna states in this regard:

།དང་པོ་བརྒྱད་པ་དགུ་ཉོན་མོངས།
།གཉིས་པ་བཅུ་པ་ལས་ཡིན་ཏེ།
།ལྷག་མ་བདུན་ནི་སྡུག་བསྔལ་ཡིན།

The first, eighth, and ninth are mental afflictions;
The second and tenth are karma;
The remaining seven are suffering.[32]

[32] *Verses on the Essence of Dependent Origination* (T: *rTen cing 'brel bar 'byung ba'i snying po'i tshig le'ur byas pa*), v. 2.

The "first" refers to *ignorance* (*ma rig pa*) or the view of the transitory collection (*'jig lta*), the main root of the mental afflictions, the"eighth" refers to *craving* (*sred pa*), and the "ninth" refers to *grasping* (*len pa*), all three being mental afflictions. The "second" refers to *compositional factors* (*'du byed*), while the "tenth" refers to *existence* (*srid pa*), both comprising karma. The "remaining seven," which include *consciousness* (*rnam shes*), *name and form* (*ming dang gzugs*), the *sense doors* (*skye mched*), *contact* (*reg pa*), *feeling* (*tshor ba*), *conception* (*skye ba*), and *old age* and *death* (*rga dang shi*) are results that make up the suffering of samsara. The second, *compositional factors*, is a form of "propelling karma" (*'phen byed kyi las*), while the tenth, *existence*, is a form of "completing karma" (*'grub byed kyi las*). The eighth, *craving*, and ninth, *grasping*, are types of desire.

Ignorance, the first, produces karma insofar as it motivates the second and tenth limbs, *compositional factors* and *existence*. This motivating ignorance requires a powerful secondary agent, in this case, karma, represented by *craving* and *grasping*, the eighth and ninth limbs. Although this subject can be rather involved, a brief sketch of the twelve limbs of dependent origination will help you to understand this present text.[33]

---

[33] To summarize these twelve links, Kaydrup Je in his *Ocean of Reasoning* (*Rigs pa'i rgya mtsho*) quotes the *Sutra Discriminating Differences* as follows: "Because this exists, this arises; because of that having arisen, that arises. How is this? Due to ignorance we have compositional factors. Due to compositional factors we have consciousness. By virtue of consciousness name and form come into being. Due to the existence of name and form the six sense doors arise. By the very existence of the six sense doors contact occurs. Through contact we have feeling. Due to feeling craving comes into being. Due to craving we have grasping. From grasping arises existence. Due to existence there is birth. From birth come old age and death. This process yields only misery and lamentation,

The critical time just before death is when an ordinary person "chooses" the karma that will be influential in forming his next life. His choice may have either a good karmic result or a bad karmic result. A typical scenario of someone's thoughts at the time of death might go like this: "My life is coming to an end. Now I am going to die. This is terrible! I'm losing my eyesight, all my faculties, my body, my family, my relatives, friends, everything!" This type of desire that contemplates all that one is losing and proceeds to crave after it illustrates how one "chooses" bad karma, which will subsequently mature. The tenth limb, *existence*, is the matured karma that is chosen by the strong desire of the eighth, *craving*, and ninth, *grasping*, limbs.

Conversely, another scenario might go this way: "Now my life is almost finished and I will soon die. So far I have done a very good job. I spent my time meditating and reciting prayers, and I did as many virtuous activities as I was able. Now I don't have any regrets. Even though I didn't achieve nirvana or Buddhahood in this life, in the future I really do hope that I can finish all the practices and achieve the supreme goal as soon as possible." These aspirations and wishes are a type of desire that "chooses" a good future life and is the result of good deeds. We, as Dharma practitioners, at the very least should have this kind of attitude.

When we are just about to die we may have a strong desire for a next life. This is an extremely important time since it is at this time that we "choose" the karma that will become our next life. If at that time some good knowledge such as faith in the Buddha or our regular practice of taking refuge should come to mind for even a brief moment, it will help us to "choose" good karma and might give us a good next life. However, if such virtuous thoughts don't come at that time, we will "choose" a bad karma and have an unfortunate rebirth. Since that is how it

---

suffering, unpleasantness, and myriad disturbances; its only result—a great heap of suffering." (p. 398)

functions this is why our regular practice is so important and why I told you it is crucial to clearly remember your object of taking refuge. Practitioners should think about the Three Ratnas –the object of taking refuge– all the time, just like a baby who thinks about its mother incessantly, "mom, mom, mom."

IMPORTANCE OF REFUGE AT THE TIME OF DEATH

The time of death is one of the most important times for us to recall our daily practice. If our mind has grown used to our practice the habitual behavior we developed previously will arise at the time of death. If it has become a habit with us of course we will remember it. That habitual knowledge and the Three Ratnas' power will come together in our mind at that time and we will then be able to "choose" a good next life. Although the moment of death is very brief it is unbelievably important and can give rise to a very good result. Nevertheless, that next life will still be a samsaric life because the main karma that produced it is motivated by ignorance, which is a mental affliction. The mental afflictions produce *compositional factors*, the second limb, which is karma, in this case "propelling karma,"[34] while the tenth limb, *existence*, represents "completing karma," or the power to complete what the karma of craving and grasping has chosen. The remaining seven limbs are their result, which is our suffering samsaric nature.

Since *the mind of an ordinary person just on the verge of death* is associated with desire –the main factor in the twelve limbs– it will definitely join to a next life's mind. We have many debates about this subject in the monastery. Let's examine the logical statement that was presented earlier:

---

[34] This limb as described by Pabongka Rinpoche in *Liberation in Our Hands* (*Lam rim rnam grol lag bcangs*): "Compositional factors are like doing work. Motivated by ignorance, we perform the karma that creates the heaps of a future life." (p. 74, Vol. 3)

Consider the mind of an ordinary newborn baby, it came from its prior mental continuum, because it is mental, like our present mind.

chi pa te ma tak pe lo chö chen, rang gyu rik pa nga ma ngön du song te, rik pa yin pe chir, ta te rik pa de shin

When giving "because it is mental" as the reason to prove the thesis, namely, that a newborn baby's mind came from its own prior mental continuum, we are implying "mind" in general. In light of this, using the reason "because it is mental" is not a sufficient reason. This is why when debating, since everything is done carefully and in such great detail, we are forced to add the further qualification "because it is a mind *accompanied by desire*." Why do we need to add this?

Since the various vehicles arise in accord with the level of the disciple's mind, there are different levels of tenets. For example, there are three types of renunciation (*nges 'byung*): that pertaining to persons of small capacity (*skye bu chung*), that pertaining to persons of intermediate capacity (*skye bu 'bring*), and that pertaining to persons of greatest capacity (*skye bu chen*). These can be classified into a Listener's renunciation (*nyan thos kyi nges 'byung*), a Solitary Realizer's renunciation (*rang rgyal gyi nges 'byung*), and a Mahayanist's renunciation (*theg chen gyi nges 'byung*), a classification referred to in the Tantric texts as "renunciation pertaining to the three types of vehicles" (*theg pa gsum gyi nges 'byung*).

When Buddha taught Dharma he taught it in such a way so as to fit the minds of all his disciples. Consequently, those disciples for whom certain advanced teachings were not appropriate simply did not hear them and so they came to the conclusion, "If there were a highest vehicle, Mahayana, Buddha would have taught it to us, but he didn't. Therefore, the Mahayana doesn't exist." Such arguments would often arise. Again, when Buddha taught, the main language he used was Sanskrit. But how many different languages did his disciples speak? The Buddha didn't have an interpreter; he didn't need one. When he taught in Sanskrit the Pali speakers would hear it in Pali; the gods would hear it in the god's language; the nagas would hear it in the naga's language; and other ordinary common people would hear it perfectly in their own languages. Nevertheless, many people argue that Buddha taught only in Pali and not in Sanskrit. Others, on the contrary, maintain that his principal language was Sanskrit and not Pali. These apparent discrepancies arose for the same reason given above, that is, that when Buddha taught each individual would hear the teaching in his own language. This is just one example of the inconceivable qualities of the Buddha's speech (*gsung ba bsam gyi mi khyab pa*).

The main belief upheld by Dharmakirti in his *Commentary to "Valid Cognition"* is in accord with the Sautantrika School (*mdo sde pa*), sometimes in combination with the Yogachara or Mind Only School (*sems tsam pa*). According to the Sautrantika and Yogachara Schools there are two types of nirvana: nirvana with remainder (*lhag bcas nyang 'das*) and nirvana without remainder (*lhag med nyang 'das*). When a practitioner achieves nirvana without remainder and becomes an Arhat, according to them, he no longer needs to study since he has achieved everything upon reaching his main goal. At this stage, known as "the cutting of the physical and mental continuum" (*bem rig rgyun bcad*), there is nothing left of form, of person, of knowledge, of mind, and so forth. Believing that they have achieved their ultimate goal they don't think it necessary to enter the Mahayana path. As a consequence for them the Mahayana School system doesn't exist. But of course that is not the case. Arhats, after waking up from their nirvana meditation have to enter the Mahayana path in order to achieve Buddhahood since they have what is called "the seeds for a Buddha's mind" (*rang bzhin gnas rigs*).[35]

[35] "The definition of the seeds for a Buddha's mind is that which belongs to the sphere of Dharma and is suitable to become a

Now, as for "the cutting of the physical and mental continuum," if upon reaching the state of nirvana their mind were to completely disappear so that nothing remained of their mental continuum, obviously their mind would not be able to continue to join to the next life's mind. The higher school systems, for their part, don't accept this. They believe that even though those beings in nirvana don't have suffering, they still have to take on a next life, and the best kind of life they can adopt for practicing to achieve Buddhahood is a human being's life. In debate we describe this with the reason "because theirs is a mental continuum endowed with desire" (*chags bcas rgyun ldan gyi rig pa yin pa'i phyir*).

Now we can clearly understand how we have had many past lives and not just this single life that we have at present. Buddha himself never said to anyone, "Your very first life was like this and this!" Since life is beginningless we all have had many former lives. Likewise, we are going to have many future lives as well. We have to think about this logically. "When I die and my body is buried or cremated, my mind won't just disappear but will continue on to the next life. That is why I need a good life in the future and what I am praying for now. I need good knowledge, good health, excellent wisdom, superior ability, all such qualities." Whatever our previous life did for us in the past we can easily recognize by the results right here and now through judging who we are and what we are experiencing. Every goodness, every happiness, including our collection of virtue, were all arranged by our previous lives. Of course, even the suffering we feel is also a result of our former lives, which collected suffering's causes. This reveals the absolute strictness and infallibility of karma and why, even though we may not be able to achieve a certain level in this life with our practice, if we do good things and

---

Buddha's Essence Body (*svābhāvakāya*) (*chos dbyings gang zhig ngo bo nyid skur 'gyur rung rang bzhin gnas rigs kyi mtshan nyid*)." From *Phar phyin mtha' spyod spyi don.*

continue to practice Dharma, our life is still very meaningful and has great purpose since this will result in our future life being much better than our present one. Conversely, if we do bad things these actions will hurt our future life so that it will be much, much worse. This is why it is a very important practice to think about our previous lives, about our happiness and suffering and what we are doing in this life, and about what will come in the future as a result.

We logicians have an expression: “You don’t have to go to a fortuneteller to get a prediction about your future.” If you need a prediction, ask yourself what it is you are thinking and doing right now and what you have done in the past, and realize that results in exact accordance with these will come in the future. Since everything we do is meaningful and a way of collecting seeds that will accompany us in the future, we have to practice virtue as much as we can and restrain ourselves from doing bad things and collecting non-virtue.

ཐ་མལ་པ་འཆི་ཁའི་དབང་པོ་ཐ་མ་ཆོས་ཅན། དབང་པོ་ཕྱི་མ་གཞན་མཚམས་སྦྱོར་ཏེ། ལུས་ལ་སྲེད་པ་དང་བཅས་པའི་དབང་པོ་ཡིན་པའི་ཕྱིར།

Consider the last moment of the [mental] sense power of an ordinary person just about to die, it will join to the [mental] sense power of the next life because that last moment’s [mental] sense power is associated with craving for the body.

Sense power here refers to the mental sense power, which is one of the six sense powers. The six sense powers are: the eye sense power, ear sense power, nose sense power, tongue sense power, body sense power, and mental sense power. The first five are physical form, while the sixth is mental and, though possessing a different nature, it performs a similar function as the others. These six sense powers are the unique causes of the six consciousnesses: eye consciousness, ear consciousness, nose consciousness, etc. Just as each of the five sense consciousnesses relies upon a unique sense power in order to function so too does mental consciousness. It is by virtue of the sense consciousnesses that we are able to see, hear, smell, taste, touch, and feel. These sense consciousnesses are a combination of consciousness and mental sense power insofar as a mental consciousness is produced immediately after any of these consciousnesses via the mental sense power. When we use such expressions as "I saw such and such; I heard such and such," and so forth, this signals the presence of mental consciousness, which is produced by any of the six consciousnesses just before they have passed.

An example of the mental sense power is as follows. What is this? This is a letter opener. To perceive this letter opener as an object you had to use your eye sense power and eye sense consciousness; that is, that eye sense consciousness was produced by the combination of the object and your eye sense power. What did I show you just a moment ago? A letter opener, right? Do you still remember it? Of course you do. That memory is a type of mental consciousness produced immediately after the eye sense consciousness through the mental sense power. Although mental consciousness itself is not capable of seeing this letter opener directly, it does have the power to clearly remember and comprehend the object that was directly apprehended by the eye sense consciousness. The very moment a sense consciousness terminates it produces a mental consciousness. So, any consciousness that occurs prior to the mental consciousness is described as a mental sense power since it is the unique cause of that mental consciousness.

The last refers to the last moment of the mental sense power. This sense power is the unique cause of the very first moment of the next life's mental sense power. This sense power at the time of death will continue on and *join to the next life as its mental sense power* preceding the next life's mental consciousness. More specifically, the very last moment of consciousness of the previous life turns into the very first moment of consciousness of the next life. How can this happen? *Because that last moment's [mental] sense power is associated with desire* for a next life.[36]

When we wish to put two material things together we join them with glue. Desire is like the glue that joins the previous life to the next life. Since desire strives to take to the next life what we wish for in this one, consciousness accompanied by craving desire is that which joins the consciousness of the previous life to the consciousness of the next life.

འཁོར་བ་ཐོག་མ་མེད་པ་སྒྲུབ་པ་ནི། འདོད་ཆགས་དང་ཞེ་སྡང་ལ་སོགས་པ་ཆོས་ཅན། རིགས་འདྲ་སྔ་མ་སྔོན་དུ་སོང་སྟེ། རང་ཉིད་གོམས་པ་ལས་གོང་ནས་གོང་དུ་རང་གི་ངང་གིས་ཆེས་གསལ་བར་སྐྱེ་བ་མཐོང་བའི་ཕྱིར། ཞེས་དང་།

To prove that samsara is beginningless [we can use the following proof]: Consider desirous-attachment, hatred, and so forth, the same kind of mind preceded them as their own unique causes, because we clearly see how they

---

36 Kaydrup Je, in *Ocean of Reasoning*, lists three types of craving (*sred pa gsum*): "1) desirous craving that wishes to achieve happiness; 2) fearful craving that wishes to be rid of suffering; and 3) craving for existence, which is a craving attachment for the contaminated heaps." (p. 400)

automatically grow stronger and stronger [in our mind] through [the process of] habituation.

PROVING SAMSARA HAS NO BEGINNING

Once we realize the truth of the existence of former and future lives, we will also come to realize that samsara is beginningless, both general samsara and our own specific samsara. Understanding that our mind came from a previous mental continuum of a former life, and that that life's mind came from a mental continuum of a life prior to it, we will realize that we can never say something like "This is my first samsaric life," since samsara has no beginning. But how do we go about proving this?

What does *samsara* mean exactly? Samsara is the perpetual cycle of suffering existence. If that's the case, do we have samsara? What does our samsara look like? [37] We always have to think about these things by applying them to our own individual situation so that we can gain deeper awareness. Samsara is a kind of condition that is quite easy to understand. Most every amusement park, "Great Adventure" in New Jersey, for instance, has a ferris wheel. A ferris wheel is a large wheel with many spokes covered with bright colored lights and filled with people yelling and screaming as it turns and turns. As that big wheel turns on its axis one side goes up while the other side goes down as does our samsara, circling incessantly in the six realms. What is the power that drives this ferris wheel? Electricity. In order to stop the machine there must be a person at the controls who is able to turn it off with a switch

[37] Kaydrup Je describes a samsaric person as follows: "That person is never separate from clinging to a 'self' and always craves for 'mine,' and all his endeavors of taking on and abandoning things is done solely for the sake of making this 'self' happy. To accomplish this he is never free of mental afflictions and karma. This is what a samsaric person is like." (Ibid, p. 557)

otherwise the wheel would continue to spin endlessly. Similarly, our samsara's wheel turns incessantly under the power of karma and mental afflictions and, if we wish to stop it from spinning once and for all, we have to turn off the switch of karma and the mental afflictions.

The definition of samsara is "the condition of taking birth involuntarily by the power of karma and mental afflictions."[38] In other words, due to the power of karma and the mental afflictions we are "helpless" insofar as we have no choice in the matter of our conception or rebirth since that is imposed upon us by our karma and mental afflictions. This is a vital point regarding our turning in samsara and represents this same *joining* of one life to the next as mentioned in the lines above. Our lives, which are joined together by the power of karma and mental afflictions, follow eachother one after one after one, sometimes going to the higher realms and sometimes going to the lower realms, but mostly to the latter, which is like our "permanent" address.

Do we have that condition of samsara? Certainly we have it. We are still turning on that wheel. When did samsara's wheel start turning? If we ponder this we'll soon discover that we have been turning perpetually in samsara life after life, life after life, and this has always been our condition, in our previous life, in the life prior to that previous life, and so on, turning and turning helplessly. Therefore, since our samsaric lives are beginningless, samsara too is beginningless. In our future lives we will also turn in the same way until we finally achieve nirvana and stop our samsara for good. This is how we can gain inferential cognition of the beginninglessness of our own samsaric lives.

Desire (*'dod chags*) mentioned above, is a secondary motivation or mental factor that accompanies the other mental afflictions from one life to the next. In fact, desire is what

---

[38] *las dang nyon mongs pas dbang gyis rang dbang med par nying mtshams sbyar ba'i cha 'khor ba'i mthan nyid*

essentially joins these lives together. For example, when political candidates give speeches they say things like, "I want to become the next president of the United States, so vote for me. I will do this and that for the country, and so forth." Everything they say, of course, is incited by desire, which most often is their main motivation. *Hatred* (*zhe sdang*) or animosity can be described this way. Again, using the example of political candidates, when they say such things as, "My opponent has done a terrible job. His plans for the future of this country aren't as good as mine but will only help to ruin the economy. He failed in all his promises in the last term and almost destroyed the country. But I am definitely not going to do that. I am going to do much, much better!" It isn't difficult to see how such statements are motivated by a mind of animosity.

And so forth refers to the many other mental afflictions apart from these two just mentioned. Nevertheless, desire and hatred are the most powerful ministers of the king of the mental afflictions. Who is the king? Ignorance. Ignorance is an afflicted mind that grasps at the "I" as if it were inherently existent. Ignorance believes this "I" to be an independent person who doesn't rely on anything else. We call this king "self-grasping ignorance" (*bdag 'dzin*). This ignorance grasps at you, your mind, your life, others, at all things as if they existed from their own side independently without having to depend on anything else for their existence. This self-grasping mind constantly produces the other two principal mental afflictions –desire and hatred– very easily. That is why these three are samsara's main root, which are often depicted in the drawing of the Wheel of Life as three distinct creatures—a pig, a cock, and a serpent. The pig represents ignorance, the cock represents desire, and the serpent represents hatred. These three are the main causes of our specific and general samsara that overwhelms us.

Which of these two do you think is worse, hatred or desire? I say desire is worse. Generally, hatred is very bad but not as bad as desire. Hatred only comes intermittently and can be alleviated through steady practice. Desire, however, bothers us constantly from morning to night, from the time we get up to the time we go to bed. So, in terms of time, we can see how hatred is less of a danger than desire since desire influences our mind all the time without respite.

The *basis* of the argument above refers to the mental afflictions, which is the subject under discussion. *Desirous attachment, hatred, and so forth*, i.e., the other mental afflictions, all had their own unique prior causes, which were desire, hatred, and so forth. *The same kind of mind preceded them* means that hatred belongs to the same class of mind as the previous hatred that was its direct cause, for instance; or, desire belongs to the same class as the desirous mind prior to that. *They grow stronger and stronger in our mind through habituation* means that, without trying to reduce or get rid of them, we generate these mental afflictions *automatically* such that they stay nice and secure in our mind. If we spend our time mostly practicing desire and hatred, our mind will certainly become accustomed to them. Not only that, our desire and hatred will grow greater and greater, *stronger and stronger*, gathering strength through our habituation.

We can see very clearly how they naturally grow greater and greater in our mind. How does this happen? To use a familiar situation by way of illustration: "He hurt me last year. Not only did he hurt me last year, he hurt me many, many times. This has been going on for a good long time now. That is why I am going to do such and such…" and so it goes. This is an example of how our hatred increases and gathers strength, becoming more powerful the more we meditate on an object of hatred. This is precisely how we develop and nurture it. Sometimes it gets so severe that we feel as if we cannot even stay put in our chair but have to jump up at once and fight or even kill our enemy. If we practice this way the situation will turn out just like that. On the other hand, if we practice compassion, which is the opposite of hatred, our desire will gradually decrease and we will gain more satisfaction. As our hatred diminishes our mind will gradually get softer and softer, more subdued, until eventually it will lead us to the peace of nirvana. From this we can see how the way of growing accustomed to different minds, be they positive or negative, is very similar.

Practitioners need this kind of instruction. Whenever our practice is failing, the fault is not due to our lacking something outside but rather to our lacking something inside, inside our own mind. Even though we may be listening well in class and studying a lot, yet afterwards our mind doesn't seem to change in the very least, something most definitely is wrong. Either there is something wrong with our practice, something faulty with the method we are using, with our effort, or lack of faith, or simply because we lack understanding about the subject. If our practice goes this way, of course our mind will have no chance to improve.

So, due to our natural habituation to these mental afflictions and their automatic increase in strength, we have found one way of proving the beginninglessness of our samsara. In short, our samsara is beginningless because the causes of samsara are beginningless. If the causes are beginningless then so too are the results.

ཡང་འཁོར་བ་ཐོག་མ་མེད་པར་གྲུབ་སྟེ། སེམས་ཅན་མིན་པ་སེམས་ཅན་དུ་གསར་དུ་སྐྱེས་པའི་རིག་པ་མེད་པའི་ཕྱིར། དེར་ཐལ། རྣམ་ཤེས་ཀྱི་རྫས་མིན་པ་རྣམ་ཤེས་ཀྱི་ཉེར་ལེན་དུ་རུང་བ་མིན་པའི་ཕྱིར། ཞེས་དང་།

Samsara is also beginningless because there never was a mind that arose newly as a sentient being which was not a sentient being previously. That logically follows because what does not have the quality of consciousness cannot become the substantial cause of consciousness.

There is another way to prove that samsara has no beginning. For instance, we would never be able to say, "Last year that wasn't a sentient being, but now it is." It would be impossible for something that is not a sentient being suddenly to become a sentient being. We cannot find a single good reason to prove that this has ever happened nor can we legitimately say that eons and eons ago there were just physical things until at some point these things just suddenly turned into sentient beings.

SENTIENCE CANNOT ARISE FROM NON-SENTIENCE

Sometimes we hear about people clearing away a forest to make a field for planting. After clearing the trees away they begin to plant seeds in the field, tend the crops, harvest them, cook the food they have harvested, and then finally eat it. However, trees themselves obviously will not do all of that of their own accord nor will we ever find the Rocky Mountains, for instance, suddenly turning into sentient beings. It doesn't happen like that. If something is not a mental "substance" (*rnam shes kyi rdzas*) in the first place, it cannot turn into something that is mental later. If it is not a sentient being then it is not something that has consciousness. If it does not have consciousness it cannot suddenly turn into something that has consciousness.

Another way of revealing the beginninglessness of samsara is by exposing the natural tendency of things. *It is not an appropriate way* (*rung ba min pa'i phyir*) for things to function when *what* is not *the substantial cause of consciousness* (*rnam shes kyi nyer len*) suddenly becomes its substantial cause. When stating above that non-consciousness such as physical form cannot turn into consciousness, it is indicating indirectly that samsara is beginningless. How? Since what was not consciousness previously cannot turn into consciousness later, consciousness has necessarily always been the main cause of consciousness in a beginningless regression.

Also, if we generate desire and hatred without trying to reduce these mental afflictions or get rid of them altogether, their power will never diminish but only increase and continue endlessly. Since ignorance, hatred, and desire are the main causes of our perpetual uncontrolled rebirth in samsara, if we never work to eliminate them from our mind, they will grow stronger and stronger and compel us to remain perpetually trapped in this endless cycle of existence. On the other hand, if we make an effort to weaken their power and diminish them considerably our mind will become habituated to that and will gradually improve.

ཡང་དངོས་པོ་སྟོབས་ཞུགས་ཀྱི་རྟགས་ཀྱིས་ཐར་པ་སྒྲུབ་པའི་རིགས་
པ་གཞུང་གི་ཆ་གོང་འོག་དག་ལས་གསུངས་པ་དག་གི་དོན་བསྡུས་པ་
ནི་འདི་ཡིན་ཏེ།

"Reasoning by the power of things" is a reason used to prove the existence of liberation [and Buddhahood] critical to arguments found throughout [Buddhist] scriptures, and in fact condenses the entire meaning of the Buddha's teachings.

It is extremely important that you understand this passage. If you understand it well your every effort and activity will become meaningful.

REASONING BY THE POWER OF THINGS

"*Reasoning by the power of things*" (*dngos po stobs zhugs kyi rtags*) is a logical term referring to one of three types of inferential reasoning. These include: reasoning by the power of things (*dngos po'i stobs zhugs kyi rtags*), inferential reasoning through convention (*grags pa'i rtags*), and inferential reasoning based on trust (*yid ches kyi rtags*). One way to understand this first type of inferential reasoning is through the following syllogism:

Consider sound, it is impermanent, because it is produced.

sgra chos can / mi rtag ste / byas pa yin pa'i phyir

To illustrate let's take the clock on this desk. Is this clock permanent or impermanent? It is impermanent because someone produced it with various materials. If someone produced it it must necessarily be impermanent due to its being created by various causes and conditions. There is no such thing as a permanent cause or a permanent result arising from an impermanent cause. This clock is something that came into being through causes and conditions and will eventually fall apart and disappear since perishing is also a quality of its transitory nature. The reason used here, "because it is produced," is an example of a "reason by the power of things," and can be used to prove that this clock is impermanent.[39]

---

[39] This type of reason is explained in some detail in *Extensive Signs and Reasoning* (*rTag rigs rgyas pa*): "There is a reason by the power of things because that is just what 'a product' is. This is so because 'a product' is the correct reason by the power of things used to prove that sound is impermanent. Let's consider 'a product,' it is a correct reason of the power of things that is used to prove that sound is impermanent because, first of all, 'a product' is a correct reason in that proof; second, impermanence being of a slightly hidden nature is the explicit object held as the quality to be proved in that proof and, third, a spiritually shortsighted person can ascertain 'a product' by valid cognition through the mere power of things. The third part of this reason holds true because sound itself is a manifest phenomenon and, although sound's impermanent nature is slightly hidden, based on that [manifest object] an ordinary person is able to ascertain its

There is another way to characterize this type of reason. Do you see this bright light above us? We use this light to help us see; without it we would be left in the dark. Therefore, this light has a very useful function. Since it is something that functions it must have had a cause to bring it about. Anything that functions is a "functioning thing" (*ngos po*), which comes about through causes and conditions. Now, because of our being able to see in this otherwise dark room we realize that the light switch has been turned on; we don't have to go over to the light switch to determine whether it has been switched on or not. Just by the power of seeing the light burning up there on the ceiling we can judge correctly that the switch is on. The understanding that the light switch is on due to the power of seeing the light burning is an example of "an inferential cognition that arises through the power of things." This is the type of reason that is being used above to prove the existence of *liberation* (*thar pa*).

We have already discussed the definition of samsara. Samsara is that which causes migrators to take birth as one of the beings of the six realms without respite. So, does general samsara exist? Does our own particular samsara exist? We can safely say that general samsara and our own particular samsara exist. Now, is there something beyond general samsara and our own specific samsara? Does liberation exist? Since we can abandon both general samsara and specific samsara of course liberation exists. Once we have abandoned samsara we have achieved the condition of nirvana. So we can confidently say that there is such a condition as liberation. Here, what is being referred to as liberation is "supreme liberation" or omniscience (*thams cad mkhyen pa*), which is another term for Buddhahood. It is extremely important for us to realize that these –liberation and Buddhahood– exist. Should we be unsure or doubtful about their existence, in one sense, our resolve will

---

impermanence by means of valid cognition through the force of things." (pp. 49–50)

weaken and we may become discouraged and begin to feel that any effort we expend toward achieving these goals will be futile.

How then can we prove that they exist? We can prove their existence by using good reasons. Where will we find such good reasons? There are many places in the Sutras, Tantras, and logic texts as well as their commentaries where such good reasons are mentioned. The essence of all of these reasons may be condensed into one main crucial type of reasoning (*gsungs pa dag gi don bsdus pa*), which is inferential reasoning by the power of things. Since this type of reasoning is so important, so critical in proving the existence of nirvana and Buddhahood, it is like a logical key for opening our understanding to all the Buddhist texts.

This being a logic text we are reading here, we have to learn and investigate everything by using logic, by using our own inferential cognition through applying correct reasons and not just follow other's words and hope for the best.

གང་རང་གི་རྒྱུའི་རིགས་ལ་གནོད་བྱེད་སྟོབས་ལྡན་དང་བཅས་པ་ཡིན་ན། རང་གི་རྒྱུན་གཉེན་པོའི་སྟོབས་ཀྱིས་ཟད་པ་ཡོད་པས་ཁྱབ་སྟེ།

Whatever has sufficient power to harm something's cause is necessarily a sufficient antidote to damage its continuum.

This phrase can be explained with an example. Sometimes due to cold induced by wind, snow, ice, rain, and so forth goosebumps arise on the skin. Cold is the unique cause of goosebumps. Now, can goosebumps, which are a result of the cold, be removed? Of course they can. How? They can be removed by the application of heat. Heat has the power to hurt the cold and finally destroy it. In destroying the cold heat thereby also destroys the cause of goosebumps and indirectly eliminates those goosebumps. From this we can see how goosebumps have a unique enemy that can destroy them, which is heat.

Our samsara's suffering can be likened to those goosebumps; if left alone without being countered by a powerful antidote it will stay interminably. So what do we do? How can we remove our suffering? Just as we can apply heat to destroy the cold we have to apply the main antidote that will destroy the very cause of our many kinds of suffering and troubles. Just as there is a unique, powerful antidote against that which causes our goosebumps, namely heat, there is likewise a unique, powerful antidote for countering the causes of samsara's suffering. If there is such a powerful antidote to the causes of samsara's suffering, why would it not be possible to completely eliminate suffering at some point once and for all?

A POWERFUL ANTIDOTE THAT DESTROYS THE CAUSE DESTROYS THE CONTINUUM AS WELL

When we apply a powerful heater to eliminate the cold, the goosebumps that arise as a result of the cold will automatically disappear as well. Likewise, when a powerful antidote puts an end to the causes of samsara's suffering, that resultant condition is liberation (*thar pa*). Since there is general samsara and *my* samsara, similarly there is general liberation and *my* liberation. Therefore, we do have some hope of becoming free and have no need to get discouraged.

Our situation can be described by the following thesis:

Consider the appropriated heaps, their continuum can definitely be terminated by a powerful antidote…

nyer len gyi phung po chos can / rang gi rgyun gnyen po'i stobs kyi zad pa yod pe khyab te

The basis of this thesis or the subject under discussion is the *appropriated heaps*.[40] Where do we find these appropriated heaps? The appropriated heaps that we are talking about here are our own mental and physical heaps. These heaps, both mental and physical, were produced by karma and mental afflictions. We acquired them from very close causes (*nye bar len pa*) or causes that are very closely associated with us, namely, karma and the mental afflictions. Owing to these, our life is a samsaric life. Why? Because these appropriated heaps are our life's basis. We shouldn't be thinking about this in the abstract but rather should think about how these heaps pertain to us directly, as in: "This is *my* samsaric body! This is *my* samsaric mind! These are *my* contaminated appropriated heaps!" and so forth. We are not discussing things that exist far, far away, but on the contrary, they are intimately close to us.

What does it mean to say that "we can definitely put an end to their continuum by a powerful antidote"? Will this continuum of the appropriated heaps that are a result of karma and mental afflictions remain for kalpas and kalpas? If we are logical we will answer "no." Why? To give a logical answer means to supply good reasons. That continuum can be cut because its causes –the mental afflictions and karma– have a powerful antidote. What is that antidote? Though not explicitly stated here in the text the antidote is the wisdom that perceives the selflessness (*bdag med rtogs pa'i shes rab*) or the real nature of our body, of our body's continuum, of our mind, of our mind's continuum, and so forth. We can combine these elements and make a logical statement this way:

Consider our contaminated physical and mental heaps, they as results, will be exhausted at some point because their causes –

[40] The contaminated appropriated heaps are a substantial result arisen from prior karma and mental afflictions that will become the substantial cause of future karma and mental afflictions.

karma and mental afflictions– have a powerful antidote, which is the wisdom that realizes selflessness.

དཔེར་ན། གྲང་རེག་ལ་གནོད་བྱེད་སྟོབས་ལྡན་མཐོང་བས་ཀྱང་འབྲས་སྤུ་ལོང་བྱེད་ཀྱི་རྒྱུན་ཟད་པ་མཐོང་བ་བཞིན།

For example, when we see something that has great power to damage the cold we realize that it can destroy the continuum causing goosebumps, an effect of the cold.

What is it *that has great power to damage the cold*? Heat. Given that goosebumps are *the result of the cold*, if we destroy the cause of that cold, we also eliminate the effect that cold causes, which are those goosebumps. Since goosebumps arise, abide, and disappear this shows that they exist as a *continuum* (*rgyun*). So, we can see (*mthongs bas*) how the continuum of goosebumps, which are the result of cold, won't be able to stay indefinitely if we counter the cold with heat, its specific powerful antidote.

ཟག་བཅས་ཀྱི་ཕུང་པོ་འདིའི་རྒྱུའི་རིགས་ལ་ཡང་གནོད་བྱེད་སྟོབས་ལྡན་མཐོང་བ་ཡིན་ནོ།

[Likewise] we see that there is also something that has great power to damage the causes [karma and mental afflictions] of [our] contaminated heaps.

Similarly, we can apply this same reasoning to our own contaminated heaps (*zag bcas kyi phung po*). *Contaminated* refers to the mental afflictions. Our five heaps are under the power of karma and the mental afflictions since these are what produced them. As mentioned before, the first, *ignorance*, eighth, *craving*, and ninth, *grasping*, limbs of the Twelve Limbs of Dependent Origination represent the mental afflictions, while the second, *compositional factors*, and the tenth, *existence*, represent karma. These are the causes of our samsara. Therefore, we can realize that just as the cold, which is the cause of our goosebumps, has its own powerful antidote, so too do the causes of our mental and physical heaps. Once we practitioners truly realize the treacherous nature of general samsara and of our own specific samsara, we will not want to remain even a second longer in this samsaric condition with its perpetual suffering and problems. Is there something we can do about it? Yes. We can apply the main powerful antidote against samsara's causes, which is the wisdom realizing selflessness (*bdag med rtogs pa'i shes rab*). We have to strive hard to gain this kind of wisdom.

If everyone has only understood just this one single point, they have gained enormous benefit from coming here and listening to these teachings.

།ཞེས་བྱ་བ་ནི། འགལ་ཟླ་དམིགས་པའི་དངོས་པོ་སྟོབས་ཞུགས་ཀྱི་རྟགས་ཡང་དག་གོ

This [reason] is called "a perfect reason of the power of things through observation of its opposite."[41]

We have to discuss this in more detail using the logical statement given above.

---

41 In *bLo rtags 'dres ma*, Cone Lama gives the definition of this kind of reason as follows: "The definition of a reason through observation of the opposite is a perfect reason of non-observation suitable to appear that is used in that proof and is either an affirming negation or a positive entity." (p. 73)

Consider my contaminated appropriated heaps, they have a powerful antidote that can definitely cut their continuum, because their causes have a powerful antidote.

A PERFECT REASON OF THE POWER OF THINGS THROUGH OBSERVATION OF THE OPPOSITE AS APPLIED TO OUR SAMSARA

The subject (*chos can*) of debate is “my contaminated appropriated heaps” (*zag bcas nyer len gyi phung po*). The object to be proved (*bsgrub bya’i chos*) is “*they have a powerful antidote that can definitely cut their continuum*” (*rang gi rgyun nyen po’i stobs kyi zad pa yod te*). The thesis (*bsgrub bya*) combines these two: “*Consider my contaminated appropriated heaps, they have a powerful antidote that can definitely cut their continuum.*” Now, what is a perfect reason we can use to prove that this thesis is correct? A perfect reason we can use is “*because their causes have a powerful antidote.*” This kind of reason is called “a perfect reason by the power of things through observation of its opposite.” “Opposite” in this case refers to things that have an opposing or mutually contradictory nature such as “that which is permanent” and “that which is impermanent,” for instance. In order to qualify as “opposite” it is not necessary that both contradictory entities exist. For example, although self-existence does not exist, self-existence and self-existentlessness are still considered opposites. In addition, it is not possible for one thing to possess both opposing qualities. For instance, one thing cannot be both permanent and impermanent.

If you want to learn what this means you’ll have to go to India to study debate and eat chapati and dhal. If you can’t go there you can come here to debate class and study seriously and say, “Oh, that’s interesting, that’s really interesting. I want to hear a debate about that.” “To be interesting” is definitely not the main goal of debate. The main goal of debate is to learn. “Interesting” won’t last very long but vanishes only too quickly. Therefore, you have to learn by training your mind deeply with logic.

We can make a similar logical statement: *Consider a huge fire raging in the east* (*me stobs chen pos khyab par non pa'i shar gyi phyogs na chos can*). This is our subject of debate (*chos can*). *The cold and goosebumps cannot stay there continually* (*grang reg sbu long bcas rgyun chags su gnas pa med te*). This is what we are trying to prove (*bsgrub bya'i chos*). How can we prove it? By supplying a perfect reason to prove our thesis, namely, "*because there is a powerful antidote [a raging fire] that damages its continuum* (*rang gi rgyun rigs la gnod byed stobs ldan yod pa'i phyir*). This means that the powerful heat of that raging fire in the east will destroy any cold in that eastern place. If the cold cannot remain there, needless to say, nor can the result of the cold, namely those goosebumps, remain there indefinitely either. If we apply this logic to our own condition we might present the following statement:

This samsaric continuum of mine cannot remain for a very long time, because its causes –karma and the mental afflictions– have a powerful antidote, which is the wisdom realizing selflessness (*bdag med rtogs pa'i shes rab*).

In short, by using a reason of the power of things through observation of its opposite, we can prove that the end of our samsara is possible. What is it that we are "observing"? We are observing with our wisdom the true nature of reality, which is the opposite of, and powerful direct antidote to, the causes of our samsara, namely karma and the mental afflictions, and indirectly to our suffering, which is the effect of those causes.

IT IS POSSIBLE TO PUT AN END TO OUR SAMSARA

འདིའི་ཁྱབ་པ་མངོན་སུམ་ཚད་མས་གྲུབ་ལ།

Its entailment is established by direct valid perception ...

The cause of something and a powerful antidote applied against that cause are mutually contradictory opposites. Just so, the continuum of something that is caused, in this case these contaminated samsaric heaps of ours, and a powerful antidote, namely the wisdom realizing selflessness, applied to the cause of that continuum, specifically karma and the mental afflictions, are opposites. We can realize this by direct valid perception. For example, anger and compassion are opposites; the one is the antidote to the other. *Entailment* (*khyab pa*) can be described this way. If someone is drunk, it “entails” that that person has had a good deal of alcohol. Similarly, if a powerful antidote is applied to a cause it entails that it will also destroy the continuous effect brought about by that cause.

Now, what is the meaning of *direct valid perception* (*mngon sum tshad ma*) in this case? Let’s take this flower, for example. What kind of flower is it? A hyacinth. You recognize it as a hyacinth since you see its shape and color and so forth directly with your direct visual perception; that is, you perceive it without having to use a form of reasoning to get at it. In like manner you can realize the samsaric nature of your five heaps, specifically through the use of direct valid mental perception (*yid kyi mngon sum tshad ma*). You know that by applying a powerful antidote to their cause, the effects, which would ordinarily arise from that cause, cannot arise because their cause has been eliminated.

ཕྱོགས་ཆོས་སྒྲུབ་པ་ནི།

The property of [the reason present in] the subject is proven ...

The subject or basis of debate (*chos can*) in this case is our five contaminated appropriated heaps (*zag bcas nyer len gyi phung po*). The property (*chos*) of the subject (*phyogs*) refers to the characteristic of the reason being present in the subject. So, our statement, "*This samsaric (mental and physical) continuum of mine cannot remain for a very long time, because its cause, karma and the mental afflictions, has a powerful antidote*" reveals that an important characteristic of these five heaps is that their cause has a powerful antidote. In short, the subject, or first part of the statement, possesses the characteristic described in the third part of the statement. How do we know that the causes of our five contaminated appropriated heaps have a powerful antidote? Because the cause of our heaps, especially ignorance –the king of the mental afflictions, which views these heaps in an erroneous manner– can be destroyed by correct view or the direct perception of the true nature of our heaps.

གང་དངོས་པོའི་གནས་ལུགས་ལ་ལོག་པར་ཞུགས་པ་དེ་ལ།
དེའི་རིགས་ལ་གནོད་བྱེད་སྟོབས་ལྡན་ཡོད་པས་ཁྱབ་སྟེ།

Any mind that engages the true nature of things erroneously necessarily has a powerful destroyer...

Ignorance, the main cause of our appropriated five heaps, holds the true nature (*gnas lugs*) of our five heaps in the wrong way or erroneously (*log par zhugs pa*), that is, as if they were self-existent.

དཔེར་ན་དུ་བ་དང་ལྡན་པའི་ལ་ལ་མེ་མེད་པར་འཛིན་པའི་བློ་འདོགས་བཞིན། གང་ཟག་གི་བདག་ཏུ་འཛིན་པ་འདི་ཡང་དངོས་པོའི་གནས་ལུགས་ལ་ལོག་པར་ཞུགས་པའི་བློ་ཡིན་ནོ། ཞེས་བྱ་བའོ། །གང་ཟག་གི་བདག་འཛིན་ལ་གནོད་བྱེད་མཐོང་བས་སྡུག་བསྔལ་གྱི་རྒྱུ་ལ་གནོད་པར་གང་གིས་འགྲུབ་ཅེ་ན། དེ་གཉིས་རྒྱུ་འབྲས་སུ་ངེས་པར་བྱེད་པའི་ཚད་མ་ལས་འགྲུབ་སྟེ། གོང་དུ་བཤད་པ་ལྟར། གང་ཟག་གི་བདག་ཏུ་འཛིན་པ་ལས་བདག་དང་མི་འབྲལ་བར་འདོད་པའི་སྲེད་པ་རང་སྟོབས་ཀྱིས་འདྲེན་པ་མངོན་སུམ་གྱིས་འགྲུབ་ལ། དེ་ལས་བདག་གི་བདེ་བ་ལ་སྲེད་པ་དང་། དེ་ལས་བདག་གི་བདེ་བ་སྒྲུབ་བྱེད་དུ་ལྟར་གྱི་དབང་སོགས་དང་། ཕྱི་རོལ་གྱི་ཟས་གོས་ལ་སྲེད་པ་དང་། དེ་ལས་བདག་གི་བདེ་བ་སྒྲུབ་པའི་ཆེད་དུ་སྒོ་གསུམ་གྱི་ལས་མངོན་པར་འདུ་བྱེད་པ་དང་། དེ་ལས་འདོད་པའི་དོན་མ་ཐོབ་པ་དང་། མི་འདོད་པའི་དོན་ཐོབ་པའི་ཚོར་བ་སྡུག་བསྔལ་སྐྱེ་བ་མངོན་སུམ་ཚད་

མས་གྲུབ་པའི་ཕྱིར། ཚེ་འདིའི་སྡུག་བསྔལ་དང་བདག་འཛིན་རྒྱུ་
འབྲས་སུ་མངོན་སུམ་ཚད་མས་གྲུབ་ལ།

For example, this grasping at a self of person is a mind that holds the true nature of things erroneously and is similar to the wrong belief that holds that there is no fire on a mountain pass that has smoke, as it says. We may wonder how it is proven that perceiving the destroyer of the self-grasping of person does harm to the cause of our suffering. This is proven by valid cognition that ascertains the two – grasping at an inherent self of person and suffering– as cause and effect, respectively. As explained above, it is proven that grasping at an inherent self of person directly elicits by its own power the desirous craving not to be separated from that self. From that arises craving for the happiness of the self, from which arises our acting to accomplish the happiness of that self and to crave external things like food and clothing. So, in order to accomplish the happiness of that self we perform karma by way of the three doors [body, speech, and mind]. Hence, it is proven by direct valid perception that a feeling of suffering arises whenever we do not get what we wish and whenever we get what we do not wish. The fact that this life's suffering [is related to] self-grasping in a cause-and-effect [relationship] is established by direct valid perception.

As mentioned previously, the way of teaching varies. Sometimes we have to teach by starting from the bottom and going up to the top; other times we have to start at the top and go to the bottom. Here it is easier for you to understand if we begin from the bottom and work our way back.

Bad feelings come to us very often. This is what we call "painful feeling" (*tshor ba sdug bsngal*). Why do these feelings come to us? They come to us whenever we cannot achieve what we want and when we achieve the opposite instead. What is the origin of these bad feelings? Bad feeling originates from having done some bad action in the past through the activities of the three doors –body, speech, or mind. We do these actions very often in relation to external things such as food and clothing or whenever we go to the store and want to buy things that don't match the amount of money we have in our pocket. This is how these bad actions happen.

Of course we think, "I want to be happy and don't want to suffer." To achieve this goal it is necessary to behave in such a way that the effects correspond to what we wish; however, we allow all our activities of body, speech, and mind to behave in the opposite way so that we get results that are opposite to what we wish. Our bad actions of the three doors come primarily from this desire to have happiness and to be free of suffering. Desire's object can be either good or bad. Thinking, "I don't want suffering" means that we have the desire not to suffer. We can also have a desire to achieve the so-called "good things" of samsara, which in fact is a deluded mind that is produced exclusively by ignorance (*bdag 'dzin*) or profound self-grasping. So, desire comes from ignorance; ignorance being perishable has a powerful antidote that can eliminate it if we are diligent enough about applying it.

Why is ignorance perishable and consequently able to be abandoned? Ignorance can be abandoned because ignorance itself is a wrong view, a mistaken way of holding its object. The object in this case is our five contaminated heaps. Since ignorance is a wrong view its antidote, correct view, is definitely able to defeat it. By using these steps we can understand how the causes of these heaps have a powerful antidote. For clarity this can be stated as follows:

Consider ignorance, it is perishable, because it has a powerful antidote that can eliminate it.

This is the meaning of *the property of the subject is proven* (*phyogs chos sgrub pa*), that is, that the quality stated in the reason can be validly applied to the subject under investigation. Or more explicitly, a quality of *ignorance* is that *it has a powerful antidote that can eliminate it*, which validates the fact that ignorance is perishable.

Is it okay or is this making you dizzy? Now, before going to sleep tonight try to remember all the points I mentioned. Whenever problems or feelings of happiness come we usually have to experience them whatever they may be whether good or bad. Where do these experiences come from? What is their origin? This is what we have to examine and how we have to practice. Whenever we achieve the opposite of what we desire and feel badly, we have to realize that that bad feeling is deeply rooted in our self-grasping mind (*bdag 'dzin*) whose nature is also suffering. Since there is a very close relationship between a cause and its effect, if the cause is bad we will definitely experience a bad effect. Due to this very close relationship we are forced to experience suffering almost all the time because our mind is imbued with this ignorance.

After learning logic you will be able to examine things with a logical mind and understand that something happens because it has the causes for it to happen. You will realize that, "Because of this cause, that result has come; this problem arises from that cause," and so forth. If you learn that way you will spend your energy trying to fight with the causes rather than with the effects. Once the effects have come out it's already too late! Therefore, you have to fight causes with powerful antidotes. By practicing in such a manner you will be able to defeat the causes of suffering. This is what "practice" means.

འཆི་ཁའི་སྲེད་པ་ལས་རིགས་འདྲ་ཕྱི་མ་མཚམས་སྦྱོར་བ་དངོས་སྟོབས་རྗེས་དཔག་གིས་གྲུབ་པ་ན། མཚམས་སྦྱོར་བའི་རིགས་འདྲ་ཕྱི་མ་དེ་ཉིད་ཀྱང་སྡུག་བསྔལ་ཞེས་ཐ་སྙད་དུ་བྱ་བ་ཡིན་པས་ཕྱི་མའི་སྡུག་བསྔལ་དང་རྒྱུ་འབྲས་སུ་དངོས་སྟོབས་རྗེས་དཔག་གིས་ངེས་སོ།

If it is established by inference through the power of things that a future life of like kind arises from craving at the moment of death, that future rebirth of like kind to which the previous life is joined may also be termed "suffering." Therefore, it is ascertained by inference through the power of things that the suffering of our future life is an effect [brought about by a prior] cause.

If we think deeply about this we will soon come to realize that all our suffering and problems, every sickness, every difficulty, each and every one of our troubles is strictly a result of self-grasping mind (*bdag 'dzin*), specifically from the mental afflictions and karma it occasions. These are the causes of our suffering and the answer to our question of where our suffering comes from.

When an ordinary person is *just about to die* (*'chi kha'i*) *craving* (*sred pa*) functions like this. We think, "Now that I am going to die I am going to lose my body. What kind of future life am I going to have? I want a good body in my future life." That desire goes on continually to join to our next life in such a way as to become our next life's desire so that the two lives are connected through this craving. This is how one life joins to the next and explains the meaning of *craving* at the time of death. *We can realize this by inference through the power of things* (*dngos stobs rjes dpag gyis nges*). To use our previous argument:

Consider the mind of an ordinary person who is just about to die, that mind joins to a similar mind in the future precisely because it is mind.

tha mal pa 'chi kha'i blo rtog chos can / rigs 'dra phyi ma mthsam sbyor te/ rig pa yin pa'i phyir

We generally give the reason "because it is mind," but as mentioned before this response can foster a big debate. We might argue saying, whatever is mind (*rig pa*) will definitely join to the next life's mind since that is mind's nature. Well then, if this is what we maintain, there is a problem. What about the mind of a Buddha? Doesn't Buddha have a mind (*rig pa* and *blo*)? Of course Buddha has a mind but Buddha's mind won't join to a samsaric life! This is why we have to qualify our reason as done above by saying "because it is a mind accompanied by craving-desire" (*sred pa dang bcas pa rig pa yin pa'i phyir*).

There are lots of debates like this. You, though, are very, very lucky since you don't have to go to debate! Once you become used to wrestling with logic, soon even the specialized words of logic will come to your mind automatically and you will be more and more compelled to question "why" whenever you hear something new. That way you will eventually acquire a logician's mind and, since you'll be used to asking "why" about everything you hear, you will begin to look for good reasons to substantiate your beliefs. If you can't find a good reason to resolve something, you won't be obliged to believe just anything you hear. That way you won't jump into a deep abyss with your eyes wide open. If you do jump with your eyes wide open, this clearly shows that you don't have a logician's eyes. Just opening your ordinary eyes is not enough.

རིགས་འདྲ་ཕྱི་མ་དེ་དོན་ལ་སྡུག་བསྔལ་ཡིན་ཡང་། ཚེ་འདིའི་ལས་ཉོན་དང་ དེ་གཉིས་རྒྱུ་འབྲས་སུ་ངེས་པ་ཙམ་གྱིས་དེའི་སྟེང་དུ་སྡུག་བསྔལ་གྱི་ལྡོག་པ་དངོས་སྟོབས་ཀྱིས་ཇི་ལྟར་ངེས་ནུས་ཞེ་ན།

The continuum of the next life will be the same in kind [as that of the present life] insofar as it will also be [of a] suffering nature. However, if we understand that the two – karma and the mental afflictions of this life and [our future life]– have a cause-and-effect relationship, on that basis how can we ascertain the defining characteristic of suffering through the power of things?

The continuum of the next life will be the same in kind [as that of the present life] means, for example, that my body today is the same continuum of body as I had yesterday and my mind today is the same continuum of mind as I had yesterday. Similarly, tomorrow I am going to have the same continuum as I do today. Hence, the continuum of my next life will be *the same in kind* as the continuum of this life; my present samsaric life and my future samsaric life will have the same continuum inasmuch as they are of the same nature or of like kind (*rigs 'dra*). Given that they are of like kind, they *will also be [of a] suffering nature* (*sdug bsngal yin yang*). Since truly there is no real happiness in samsara because all samsara's nature is nothing but suffering, my future life, which is the same in kind as the continuum of this present life will also be a samsaric life with its corresponding suffering.

If we understaind that the two –karma and the mental afflictions of this life and [our future life]– have a cause-and-effect relationship means the following. As logicians you should understand by now that this life's mental afflictions and karma, which of themselves have a suffering nature, are the causes of the next life. In brief, this life's karma and mental afflictions are in a relationship of cause-and-effect with regard to our next life such that everything in our next life will be a result of this life's mental afflictions and karma. Just by understanding how the one is the effect of the other allows us to realize the infallibility of their relationship. Why is it so that just because they have a cause-and-effect relationship our next life is going to have a suffering nature? The reason follows.

ལས་ཉོན་གྱིས་འདུས་བྱས་པ་སྡུག་བསྔལ་གྱི་དོན་ལྡོག་ཏུ་དངོས་
སྟོབས་ཀྱི་ཚད་མས་ངེས་ནུས་ལ།

We can realize by valid [inferential] cognition through the power of things the meaning distinguisher of suffering, since that which is produced by karma and mental afflictions [is the definition of suffering].

By using this reason of the power of things we can understand that our next life will also have the nature of suffering.

Meaning distinguisher (*don ldog*) is a logical term. Here I will introduce you to two kinds of distinguishers: *meaning distinguisher* (*don ldog pa*) and *designated distinguisher* (*tha snyad ldog pa*). *Meaning* (*don*) in this case refers to something's definition; what is *designated* (*tha snyad*) refers to the actual thing that is being defined. For example, thing (*ngos po*), is a *designated distinguisher*. The *meaning distinguisher* (*don ldog*) of "thing" is "that which is able to perform a function" (*don byed nus pa*). This refers to its usage, that is, a thing is something that can be

WE CAN REALIZE BY INFERENCE THROUGH THE POWER OF THINGS THAT OUR FUTURE LIFE WILL HAVE THE NATURE OF SUFFERING

used. All impermanent entities are "things." So any impermanent "thing" can be a *designated distinguisher* (*tha snyad ldog pa*), whereas its definition, "that which is able to perform a function," is its *meaning distinguisher* (*don ldog*).

The discussion above concerns the *meaning distinguisher* and the *designated distinguisher* of suffering (*sdug bsngal*). "Suffering" is the *designated distinguisher* or object being defined, and suffering's definition, or what suffering is, qualifies as the *meaning distinguisher* (*don ldog*) of suffering. Our body is a very good example. Since our body has samsara's nature and samsara's nature is suffering, therefore, our body has the nature of suffering. Why? We will realize this once we understand the *meaning distinguisher* (*don ldog*) or definition of suffering. The definition of suffering is "that which is produced by karma and mental afflictions"[42] as given in the text above. So, whatever is produced by the power of karma and mental afflictions must have a suffering nature. In this way we can see how the qualities of this definition are what "distinguish" suffering.

We can use another example for illustration. Fire, for instance, is the *designated distinguisher* (*tha snyad*) or object being defined. Its *meaning distinguisher* (*don ldog*) or definition is "that which is hot and burns" (*tsha shing sreg pa*). In the same way, every single thing has its own specific defining quality. Let's see. Why is this incense slowly turning to ash? This incense is turning to ash because the power of fire is acting upon it. Because heat is the nature of fire and fire carries the power (*stobs shugs kyis*) to burn we can realize why this incense is being consumed by the hot and burning nature of fire. By understanding fire's nature through its definition we realize why it is that this incense is being transformed into ash. To understand this first we must learn the definition or *meaning distinguisher* (*don ldog*) of fire. If we have a clear understanding of fire's definition –that which is hot and

---

[42] *las nyon gyis 'dus byas pa*

burning– we will clearly understand its *designated distinguisher* (*tha snyad*) or thing being defined, in this case, fire.

In like fashion, comprehension of why our body has the nature of suffering requires an understanding of the definition of suffering. Our body has the nature of suffering because it was produced by karma and mental afflictions. Karma and mental afflictions, themselves being the nature of suffering, can only produce results that have the same nature, which is suffering. For example, if we plant chili seeds, since the nature of the cause itself is spicy, when its result comes out as a chili and we taste it, it will likewise be spicy and burn our tongue. Given that a cause and its effect have the same continuum, the effect will have the same quality as its cause. Since karma and mental afflictions are themselves a form of suffering and act as the causes that produced this life and body of ours, as their effect, these will likewise have a suffering nature. It would be impossible for a cause to have the nature of suffering and its effect lack that nature since they belong to the same continuum.

Perhaps right now it may seem that you have understood this material and that by tomorrow morning when you're having breakfast you will have forgotten it entirely, but…

དེ་ངེས་ཟིན་མ་བརྗེད་པ་དང་།

What was understood is not forgotten...

This means that once we have understood something through applying logic that understanding will not disappear but will stay in our mind.

འཆི་ཁའི་ལས་སྲེད་ལས་རིགས་འདྲ་ཕྱི་མ་མཚམས་སྦྱོར་བ་རྗེས་
དཔག་གིས་གྲུབ་པ་ན།

If we understand through inference that the karma of a person on the verge of death will join [this life's mental continuum to] a future life's mental continuum similar in kind by virtue of craving desire...

The karma of a dying person (*'chi kha'i las*) joins the last moment of mind to the first moment of the next life's mind through the power of desire (*sras las*). *Craving desire* here refers to the eighth limb (*sred pa*) and ninth limb or *grasping* (*len pa*) of the Twelve Limbs of Dependent Origination or Wheel of Life. Both of these are forms of "choosing karma," that is, what chooses the next life. What do these forms of karma choose? They choose a "maturation karma" represented by the tenth limb or *existence* (*bcu pa srid pa*).[43] The main quality of the eighth and ninth limbs is desire, which chooses the next life or *existence* (*srid pa*) —the stained, ripened result.

We can perceive *through inference* (*rjes dpag gis*) how karma and the mental afflictions join (*mtshams sbyor*) the mind of this life to the mind of the next life as one continuum since they are *similar in kind* (*rigs 'dra*).

---

[43] The definition of existence found in the twelve limbs of dependent origination is that which has the powerful karmic ability to produce the ripened heaps of a future rebirth fostered by craving or grasping. (*yan lag bcu gnyis kyi nang tshan du gyur pa'i sred len gang rung gis gsols btab pa'i yang srid phyi ma'i rnam smin gyi phung po 'grub byed kyi las nus pa mthu can yan lag bcu gnyis kyi nang tshan du gyur pa'i srid las kyi mtshan nyid*); *Supplementary Texts for the Study of the Perfection of Wisdom at Sera Mey Tibetan Monastic University* (p. 536, vol. 2).

རིགས་འདྲ་ཕྱི་མ་དེ་ཉིད་ལས་དང་ཉོན་མོངས་པའི་གཞན་དབང་ཅན་
དུ་གྲུབ་པས་

Because that future life['s mind], being alike in kind, is produced involuntarily under the power of karma and mental afflictions...

The very first moment of our next life's body and mind is produced involuntarily by the power of karma and mental afflictions and as such is entirely dependent upon karma and the mental afflictions.

Buddha Shakyamuni, who was born in India twenty-five hundred years ago, on the contrary, had a voluntary birth. It was his choice to take rebirth. Before being conceived, he checked and then determined, "Now it's time for me to take rebirth in the world." At that time he chose to be reborn as a prince in a royal family of that particular kingdom together with all the other attendant circumstances that surrounded his rebirth. Therefore, his birth was not like ours. Since ours is controlled by the power of mental afflictions and karma we completely lack the power to choose our next rebirth and, owing to that, are subjected to wherever our karma propels us. It is in this way that all our life's power and conditions rely solely upon karma and mental afflictions. This is what it means above by *produced involuntarily* (*gzhan dbang can du grub pas*). Because our life was produced in dependence upon mental afflictions and karma our body and mind have the nature of suffering. Naturally we don't wish to get older or get sick and if we had the power to control the circumstances of our life we would most definitely hold back our aging and stay healthy and strong as long as possible, for eons even. But, obviously, we cannot do that because our life is dominated by the power of karma and mental afflictions, which causes our condition to constantly change and forces us to experience suffering all the time. This changing condition that we have is a very serious form of suffering and one that is not easy to realize unless we study and think about it profoundly.

སྡུག་བསྔལ་གྱི་དོན་དང་ཐ་སྙད་གཉིས་ཀ་གྲུབ་པར་འགྱུར་བ་ཡིན་ནོ།

...[our future life] will be both the defining characteristics of suffering and what is being defined by those characteristics.

In this way we can realize that our body and mind are of a suffering nature and how they came to be that way. In fact, this should be our motivation when listening to Dharma teachings. We should try to apprehend the real suffering quality of our nature through investigating its origin. We should realize that our life is controlled by mental afflictions and karma. Karma for its part is under the control of the many mental afflictions. The strongest two ministers of the mental afflictions are hatred and desire. These two ministers are also under the power of the king of the mental afflictions, which is ignorance or self-grasping (*bdag 'dzin*). Ignorance, the king, is the worst wrong view and most erroneous mind, which has been influencing our mental continuum from beginningless time and will accompany our continuum until we finally achieve nirvana and Buddhahood. Since ignorance holds that which doesn't exist as if it did, it is the worst wrong view and what produces all the mental afflictions and karma, which in turn nicely arrange our samsaric life. Once we get such a samsaric life, every kind of suffering will naturally follow in its train.

།འོ་ན་གང་ཟག་གི་བདག་འཛིན་དངོས་པོའི་གནས་ལུགས་ལ་ལོག་
པར་ཞུགས་པ་ཡིན་པར་གང་གིས་སྒྲུབ་ཅེ་ན།

Well then, how can I prove that this self-grasping of person perceives my real nature in the wrong way?

Well then (*'o na*) introduces an objection or qualm and means, "if that were the case, then what about such and such...." *Self-grasping of person* (*gang zag gi bdag 'dzin*) is the ignorance or wrong view that grasps at "you" as a non-reliant, independent person. Here we are not discussing the real nature (*gnas lugs*) of things in general, but the real nature of "you" as a person in particular. So, how can I prove to my mind that my ignorance is holding my real nature in the wrong way?

དེ་ནི་གང་ཟག་གི་བདག་མེད་པར་ངེས་པ་ལས་འགྲུབ་པ་ཡིན་ནོ།

།ཞེས་དང་།

It is proven through the ascertainment of the lack of a self-existent person.

A *self-existent person* (*gang zag gi bdag*) can refer to a self-existent listener, a self-existent practitioner, and so forth, all of which are the object of a subjective mind—ignorance. To be a self-existent person is to be an independent person who exists without relying on anything else. This subjective mind of ignorance is holding its object in the wrong way. The opposite of such a person is a self-existent*less* person, which means the emptiness of being a self-existent person, and the subjective mind that perceives its object correctly is wisdom. Therefore, there are two kinds of subjects or subjective minds: the one, ignorance, views its object –the person– as self-existent, thereby holding its object in the wrong way; the other is wisdom that views its object –the person– as self-existent*less*, thereby holding its object correctly.

Is there an elephant on this table? No. You can see that there is no elephant here. Yet it is possible that someone might have an erroneous mind and see an elephant here on this table. A correct or valid subjective mind will not see such a creature here on this table. The mind that holds a person as self-existent is the subject or perceiver (*'dzin stangs*). When the subjective mind no longer perceives its object (*'dzin stangs kyi yul*) in an erroneous way, once it loses its object that subjective mind will likewise automatically disappear. Once we realize clearly that there is no elephant on this table –an erroneous object– the erroneous mind perceiving that wrong object –an elephant on the table– will disappear. In the same way, when the subjective mind that holds a person as self-existent loses its object –an independent person– through realizing that no such person could possibly exist, that erroneous object will automatically disappear.

A synonym for *self-existentless person* is emptiness (*stong pa nyid*) or *shunyata* in Sanskrit, signifying the real nature of the person. In pursuit of this real nature, we might examine our nature by using the following line of reasoning: "Because I was born and my life was given to me by my parents I am not a self-existent person. If I had had no parents I would not have been born, so it is quite clear that my life depends upon them. If my life depends upon them for its existence I am not an independent, self-existent person." Our real nature is self-existentless or the emptiness of self-existence. Once we perceive this real nature, the ignorance that holds the wrong object –self-existence– cannot be sustained and will be forced to disappear. Upon perceiving our own true nature, we will realize that ignorance is a wrong mind. This is what it means above when it says *it is proven through the ascertainment of the lack of a self-existent person.*

ཡང་ཚུལ་དེ་དེ་ལྟ་བུའི་སྒོ་ནས་གཉེན་པོའི་སྟོབས་ཀྱིས་སྡུག་བསྔལ་གྱི་རྒྱུན་མ་ལུས་པར་ཟད་པ་ཡོད་པར་དངོས་སྟོབས་ཀྱི་ཚད་མས་གྲུབ་ཅིང་སྡུག་བསྔལ་གྱི་རྒྱུན་མ་ལུས་པར་ཟད་པའི་འགོག་པ་དེ་ཉིད་ལ་ཐར་པ་མྱ་ངན་ལས་འདས་པ་ཞེས་བྱ་བ་ཡིན་པས་ཐར་པ་ཡོད་པར་དངོས་སྟོབས་ཀྱིས་ལེགས་པར་གྲུབ་པ་ཡིན་ནོ།

It is proven by valid cognition through the power of things that suffering's continuum can be utterly destroyed by a powerful antidote and that that very cessation which is the complete destruction of suffering's continuum is what is called "liberation, the state beyond suffering." Therefore, it is well proven through the power of things that liberation exists.

The powerful antidote referred to here is the wisdom that perceives our real nature. *Suffering's continuum* (*sdug bsngal gyi rgyun*) is the continuum of our body and mind. If we come to understand our emptiness through continued practice, at some point we will be able to perceive our real nature directly with direct valid perception. If we continue to make progress in this perception eventually we will be able to abandon our self-grasping mind (*bdag 'dzin*) completely and cut ignorance at its root. This is how we can gain the cessation of that ignorance, which is known as "liberation" or "nirvana."

IT IS WELL PROVEN THROUGH THE POWER OF THINGS THAT LIBERATION EXISTS

The word "nirvana" currently has become very popular and we use it very casually, but we really don't know anything about it or how to achieve it. That is why this logic text endeavors to teach it in some detail and offers so many correct logical reasons to establish it.

Since a reason by the power of things (*dngos po stobs zhugs kyis rigs pa*)[44] was described earlier it will suffice to give just an illustration of it here: "Consider sound, it is impermanent, because it is produced." This kind of reason is a general reason of nature (*rang bzhin gyi rtags*).

CONTEMPLATING OUR SUFFERING NATURE TO FIND ITS ANTIDOTE

The main key is this. I am suffering in samsara. My body has a suffering nature. Why? Because it was produced by karma and mental afflictions. Since the producer or cause itself is suffering, the results likewise are suffering. Can this suffering be stopped or not? This is the main question. We might think, "I don't like the fact that I will have to suffer continually life after life. Still I can see no end to it. Maybe there's no chance ever to put an end to it. If there is no end to this suffering what then can I do?" Again, practitioners should apply this to their own condition as in "My suffering nature," and not just speculate about it in the abstract as if they were mere words. If we only think of others' nature and situation without thinking of our own, Dharma teachings won't help us much.

"I don't like to suffer; but is there any way this suffering can come to an end?" Of course there is. How can we prove it?

---

[44] The definition of a "reason by the power of things" is as follows: *If the reason exists, then the object to be proved also exists; and if something is that reason, it must also be that object to be proved. It is the reason used to prove the essence or basic nature of things, a nature which characterizes both the reason and the object to be proved, without their being just nominally ascribed* (*dngos po stobs zhugs kyi rtags, rtags de yod na bsgrub bya de yod pa dang, rtags de yin na bsgrub bya de yin dgos pa ming gis bzhag pa tzam min par rtags dang bsgrub bya gnyis kyi dngos po rang gi chos nyid dang gshis la grub pa'i rtags kyi sbyor ba'o*).

Through applying a valid proof through the power of things (*dngos stobs kyi tshad mas grub pa*). Ignorance has a powerful antidote that can eventually eliminate it if applied. However, if we want to keep our self-grasping ignorance as our treasurer, our main assistant, and don't apply an antidote against it, it will never go away. Once we are aware of this the method for putting an end to suffering becomes extremely meaningful for us.

The status of having completely gotten rid of all suffering is cessation or nirvana. We can't go to the store and buy nirvana by the pound as if we were purchasing a big pumpkin—"Oh, look, let's get that one; it's the biggest nirvana!" It's not something tangible that can be exhibited. When we have become completely free from the power of mental afflictions and suffering we have achieved nirvana. This is the status of cessation whereupon samsara has been finally abandoned.

Above, three synonyms are given for nirvana: liberation (*thar pa*), cessation (*'gog pa*), and the state beyond suffering (*mya ngan las 'das pa*). The main thesis, however, is to understand that nirvana exists. What is its quality? How can you achieve it? You have to learn these one by one. If someone were to ask you, "Can you prove that nirvana exists?" now you can confidently say, yes. "Can you give me some proof?" Yes. Nirvana will come when the roots of samsara have been destroyed. Again, this is proven by the power of things (*dngos stobs kyi grub*). How can you destroy the root of samsara? You can destroy it by applying its specific powerful antitdote. If it has a powerful antidote such an opposing force will definitely be able to destroy it at some point. If that were not the case, what would be the use of turning on a heater to get rid of the cold in winter or an air conditioner to get rid of the heat in summer or a light to get rid of the darkness when you want to read? That is very easy to understand. To remove your hunger you go to McDonald's to eat a big hamburger; you apply food, which is hunger's own antidote. These small examples are also very useful in acquiring understanding of this topic.

།ཚུལ་དེས་ཀུན་མཁྱེན་ཡོད་པར་སྒྲུབ་པའི་རིགས་པ་ཡང་ཤེས་པར་བྱ་སྟེ། འདི་ལྟར་གང་རིགས་ལ་གནོད་བྱེད་སྟོབས་ལྡན་ཡོད་པ་དེ་ལ་རང་གི་རིགས་གཉེན་པོའི་སྟོབས་ཀྱིས་རྒྱུན་ཟད་པ་ཡོད་པས་ཁྱབ་སྟེ། དཔེར་ན། མེ་སྟོབས་ཆེན་ཉེ་བས་གྲང་རེག་རྒྱུན་ཆད་པ་མཐོང་བ་བཞིན། ཆོས་ཀྱི་བདག་ཏུ་འཛིན་པའི་རིགས་ལ་ཡང་གནོད་བྱེད་སྟོབས་ལྡན་ཡོད་དོ།

We should also know that the reason proving the existence of omniscience may be applied in the same way. Whatever has a powerful agent to destroy its kind will necessarily have its continuum [which is the same in kind] destroyed by its own powerful antidote. For example, just as when there is a powerful fire nearby we see that the continuum of cold cannot remain likewise this kind of grasping at an inherently existent self of phenomena also has a powerful antidote that can destroy it.[45]

Omniscience (*kun mkhyen*) is a mind that can perceive all objects. Why can't we see all objects directly? Because the

---

[45] The kind of reason being used here is described by Kaydrup Je in *Ocean of Reasoning* as follows: "For example, just as we see the exhaustion of the continuum that causes goosebumps, which are the effect of cold, comes about when we see a powerful agent destroying that cold, similarly, we can see that there is a powerful agent that can destroy the cause of these contaminated heaps. The kind of reason used here is a perfect reason of the power of things through observation of the opposite. (p. 404)

power of our eyes and mind is limited or obstructed by obstacles. Buddha, though, practiced for many eons to remove such obstacles by applying their antidotes until he succeeded in overcoming all of them. Because he removed all obstacles he can see all objects directly without any difficulty or obstruction. This is omniscience or a Buddha's mind. We can also prove that this kind of mind exists in the same way as we proved that nirvana exists, that is to say, through the use of correct reasons.

The text above is saying that any object –whether it be a hard metal or some liquid substance, and so forth– that has a powerful antidote which can destroy it, at some point will definitely be destroyed if that antidote is applied. For example, we perceive that the cold immediately disappears when we approach a powerful fire since the heat of that fire –as the cold's direct antidote– puts an end to it; that is, cold's continuum is broken (*rgyun chad pa*) since it cannot abide the heat. We can observe many such examples.

Ignorance can be classified into two kinds: grasping at a self of person (*gang zag gi bdag 'dzin*) and grasping at a self of phenomena (*chos kyi bdag 'dzin*). Of these two the most subtle root of ignorance is grasping at a self of phenomena. This also has its own powerful agent that can destroy it (*gnod byed stobs ldan yod*), which is the most subtle wisdom. Of course the most subtle wisdom is capable of destroying the most subtle ignorance.

།ཞེས་བྱ་བ་ནི། དངོས་པོ་སྟོབས་ཞུགས་ཀྱི་རྟགས་ཡང་དག་ཡིན་ཞིང་།
འདིའི་ཕྱོགས་ཆོས་སོགས་སྒྲུབ་ཚུལ་ཡང་སྔ་མ་ཉིད་ལས་དཔགས་ཏེ་
ཤེས་པར་བྱ་ཞིང་། དེ་ལྟ་བུའི་རྟགས་ལས་ཤེས་བྱའི་སྒྲིབ་པ་མ་ལུས་

པ་སྤངས་པ་ཡོད་པར་གྲུབ་པ་ན་ཀུན་མཁྱེན་དངོས་པོ་སྟོབས་ཞུགས་
ཀྱིས་ལེགས་པར་གྲུབ་པ་ཡིན་ལ། ཞེས་དང་།

This reason is called "a perfect reason through the power of things" and we should know that it is also the reason that [allows us to] infer from previous lives a way of proving the property of the subject and so forth of the aforementioned proofs. If by using such a reason we prove that each and every obstruction to omniscience can be completely abandoned we can viably prove through the power of things that omniscience exists.

Each of these –the existence of previous lives and the existence of future lives– is a thesis that we must prove to our mind by using correct reasons. In order to qualify as a correct reason it must have the property of the reason in the subject (*phyogs chos*) and entailment (*khyab pa*), which are logic terms. If I teach you this without giving you a little more detailed explanation you won't be able to understand it nicely and will get lost like Alice in Wonderland. If you understand logic, then it is very easy.

The property of the subject or *reason's relevance to the subject* (*phyogs chos*) can be explained this way. For example, in the statement: "Consider sound, it is impermanent, because it is produced," we have to prove to ourselves that sound is produced by causes. That is, we have to prove that the subject of the statement, "sound," has the quality of the reason, "being a product." *Entailment* (*khyab pa*) means that if it is produced it must necessarily be impermanent. If that reason –"because it is produced"– holds true, it must apply in every instance to all impermanent phenomena, which is the thesis or quality to be proved, about the subject, sound.

The text mentions *obstacles to omniscience* (*shes sgrib*). You have to recall the difference between the two major divisions of obstacles: obstacles to liberation (*nyon sgrib*) and obstacles to omniscience (*shes sgrib*). The older students should know these, but as it says in the logic text: "forgetting is the opposite of knowing" (*brjed na shes pa dang 'gal lo*), meaning that if you've forgotten something, then you don't know it. You cannot say you know something but have forgotten it. To say "I know" means that the knowledge is still fresh in your mind. This is how rigorous logic can be. If you have forgotten it, you don't know it, even though you may be a senior, senior student.

Each of these two types of obstacles has its own unique characteristics. The term *nyön drip* refers to both the mental afflictions and bad karma. *Nyön* means mental afflictions; *drip* means obstacles. These are the obstacles to nirvana, and of course, ultimately to Buddhahood. The main characteristic of *nyön drip* is to block the achievement of nirvana. The main characteristic of *she drip* is to block the achievement of omniscience or Buddhahood. "Main" here refers to their principal function.

Obstacles to omniscience or *she je drip pa* (*shes bya'i sgrib pa*) can be explained in two parts. *She ja* means object of knowledge, which encompasses all phenomena. *Drip pa* means obstacles, or that which obstructs the direct perception of all phenomena. Buddha's omniscience (*kun mkhyen*) or Buddhahood, is a perceiver of all phenomena (*thams cad mkhyen pa*). There are many levels and varying degrees of knowledge—rough, medium, and subtle. Due to this the Bodhisattva's path is comprised of ten levels or *bhumis* on which he has to practice by applying the various antidotes to remove the different levels of obstacles.

Here the text is trying to prove that we can achieve cessation as well as abandon each and every obstacle to perceiving all phenomena directly, or omniscience, and thereby achieve Buddhahood. If that is the case, of course cessation exists, as does omniscience and Buddhahood. We will understand this very well if we employ good reasons through the power of things.

It is most essential to realize that we can achieve nirvana and Buddhahood. Well then, how can we realize this? The reason, given negatively, is because their biggest obstacles, the obstacles to liberation (*nyon sgrib*), and the most powerful subtle obstacles to achieving omniscience or Buddhahood (*shes sgrib*), are perishable since they have their own powerful antidote that can destroy them. Once those obstacles are destroyed we will achieve the status of nirvana and Buddhahood respectively.

OMNISCIENCE CAN ALSO BE PROVEN BY REASONING

We can also apply a positive reason. We can practice love and compassion for the purpose of achieving wisdom and thereby eventually gain Buddhahood. Therefore, both ways, positively and negatively, one is sure to achieve nirvana and Buddhahood. So, what is it that we are lacking? We are lacking in knowledge, faith, and effort. The last one –effort– is what we lack most.

ཡང་བརྩེ་བ་དང་ཤེས་རབ་སོགས་ཆོས་ཅན། ཁྱོད་གོམས་པར་བྱས་ན་སེམས་ལ་རང་གི་ངང་གིས་འཇུག་པར་འགྱུར་ཏེ། ཁྱོད་གོམས་པར་བྱས་པ་ན་བློའི་རིགས་འདྲ་རེ་རེ་བསྐྱེད་པ་ལ་སྔར་དང་འདྲ་བའི་འབད་རྩོལ་རེ་རེ་མི་དགོས་པར་འབད་རྩོལ་གཅིག་ལས་ཀྱང་རིགས་འདྲ་དུ་མ་རྒྱུན་ལྡན་དུ་སྐྱེ་བའི་སེམས་ཀྱི་ཡོན་ཏན་ཡིན་པའི་ཕྱིར།

Consider compassion and wisdom and so forth, if we become accustomed to them they will function naturally in our mind. Once we have grown accustomed to them it will not be necessary to expend effort each time [we meditate on them] to reach a level of mind similar to the one before, since, on the contrary, it is an excellent quality of mind to be able to generate a continuum of many like minds from a single effort.

AN EXCELLENT QUALITY OF MIND IS THE ABILITY TO GENERATE A CONTINUUM OF MANY LIKE MINDS THAT GATHER STRENGTH FROM A SINGLE EFFORT

At the beginning of this text there is mention of *excellence of intention* (*sbyor ba phun tshogs*), or preparation for achieving Buddhahood, which is practicing compassion (*brtse ba*) and wisdom (*shes rab*). The definition of compassion is "a type of mind that when observing any suffering sentient being generates the wish to free them from suffering."[46] So, the practice of compassion means that whenever we see a suffering being this kind of compassionate mind will arise automatically because it has grown accustomed to doing so through practice. The general way to measure the strength of compassion is to compare it with the kind of compassion a mother feels toward her only child. Whenever her child has a problem she immediately thinks about how she can remove that problem. This is a description of general compassion. We have to develop this kind of mind and make it a hundred times stronger until it becomes great compassion only to be compared with the compassion of a high Bodhisattva like Avalokiteshvara. The definition of great compassion is "a kind of mind that when observing any suffering sentient being spontaneously feels an authentic wish

---

[46] *sdug bsngal can gyi sems can gang la dmigs kyang sdug bsngal dang bral 'dod kyi blo*

to free them from that suffering with the same intensity that a mother feels for her only child."[47]

There are two classifications of the strong wish to remove the suffering of beings (*bral 'dod kyi blo*). The first is a wishful compassion that wants to remove the suffering of all beings (*bral 'dod kyi snying rje*); and the second is a wishful compassion that not only wishes to remove their suffering but makes the firm decision to take responsibility for freeing them from their suffering (*skyob 'dod kyi snying rje*). A synonym for this is "the supreme intention" (*lhag bsam rnam dag*) or what is known as "Mahayana compassion." The first is the compassion that the Hinayana and the Mahayana share in common.

There are many kinds of wisdom (*shes rab*). The wisdom that is the main antidote to ignorance is the wisdom that perceives the real nature of all phenomena, including our real nature, the real nature of our mind, and so forth. There are also many levels of knowledge, which are referred to above by the words *and so forth* (*sogs*). These are the basis of the argument (*chos can*) that are being used to illustrate the thesis: *If we become accustomed to* compassion and wisdom insofar as they form part of our daily practice, *they will function naturally in our mind*. Once we grow used to them our mind will travel almost automatically to compassion and wisdom like water being channeled into a field with good irrigation. Eventually we will gain real compassion and wisdom. After generating these minds the first time, the second time, the third time, *they will arise at every moment in our mind* (*blo'i rigs 'dra re re bskyed pa la*). Due to our having put forth strong

ANALOGY OF ANGER TO SHOW HOW MIND INCREASES

[47] *sdug bsngal can gyi sems can gang la dmigs kyang ma bu gcig pa la btse bas tshod tsam du sdug bsngal dang bral bar 'dod pa'i blo bcos ma min pa rang gi ngang gis skye ba'i blo snying rje chen po'i mtshan nyid*

effort of meditation and contemplation about compassion and wisdom initially, these minds will produce their own continuum almost automatically so we won't have to strive with special effort each time over and over again to achieve them (*sngar dang 'dra ba'i 'bad rtsol re re mi dgos par*). If we strive very hard at the beginning to generate them (*'bad rtsol gcig las kyang*) this creates one cause for their continuation.

The second cause for their continuation comes from the nature of the mind itself. Since a flowing continuum of like minds is a quality of the mind these moments of mind do not have to be produced each time with special effort (*rigs 'dra du ma rgyun ldan du skye ba'i sems kyi yon ten yin pa'i phyir*). It is also mind's nature such that its object will increase and gradually grow stronger and stronger. How do we know this? For example, if we have a short temper and get angry very easily, we don't have to think about our enemies and their bad activities toward us and ponder over them, since they come almost automatically without effort. The fact that we easily get angry reveals that there is a continuum of anger in our mind that never stops but grows and grows until we finally overpower it with the proper antidotes. Why does this happen? Because that is the nature of mind.

WHY IT IS POSSIBLE TO ACHIEVE BUDDHAHOOD

Fortunately, the opposite kinds of mind such as wisdom and compassion have that nature as well, which will increase once our mind grows used to them. It is just that we have grown so used to getting angry and becoming upset that these negative minds arise so easily. Why? Because this is a special quality of mind. In a similar way, if our mind should grow accustomed to compassion and wisdom and continue to strengthen, why wouldn't they eventually turn into ultimate compassion and ultimate wisdom? There is no reason why they shouldn't. This is one very good reason that contributes to the proof of why it is possible to achieve nirvana and Buddhahood.

The method for learning logic and listening to general lectures are completely different. When you are listening to lectures on general subjects other than Dharma you might think: “Yes, it’s definitely like that because that is what he said.” This indicates that you have not acquired your own knowledge and cannot decide for yourself by using your own ability to reason. When you hear something, all you can do is shrug your shoulders and say, “I guess that’s right. Sure. I guess so.” However, if you learn logic your knowledge will become very firm and steady in your mind so that you’ll be more apt to think like this: “That reasoning is not perfect logic since it doesn’t make sense.” You can begin to make your own decisions through using logic. The main purpose of logical debate is not to shut other people up and gain glory for yourself. The main purpose rather is to defeat your own wrong views and doubts, to make your mind clearer and clearer so that your knowledge will eventually become perfect.

དཔེར་ན། མེ་ལ་སོགས་པས་ཤིང་དག་ལ་ཐལ་བར་སོང་གི་བར་
དུ་ངང་གིས་འཇུག་པ་དང་།

For example, fire will naturally burn a piece of wood until it turns to ash ...

When you make a fire, initially you have to have wood and a source of fire. Once the wood catches fire you don’t have to keep lighting it over and over again to keep it going. The fire will continue to burn of its own accord (*ngang gi*) until the wood being used for fuel eventually turns to ash once it’s been consumed. The point is that the fire will continue to burn without effort since that is what it does by nature. Similarly, when trying to habituate your mind to compassion and wisdom, from the outset you have to generate some effort and start with your motivation and contemplation. However, after genuinely generating these you don't need to apply effort all the time, once and again, since the continuum of mind that has become habituated to them will continue naturally and even increase. This is just one example.

> དངུལ་ཆུ་དང་གསེར་ལ་སོགས་པར་འདུལ་སྦྱོང་ལེགས་པར་བྱས་ཟིན་པ་རང་གི་ངང་གིས་གཡའ་དང་བྲལ་བའི་རིགས་འདྲ་ཕྱི་མ་བསྐྱེད་པར་ནུས་ཀྱི། ཡང་དྲི་མ་དག་པར་བྱེད་པའི་རྫའི་ཁ་སྦྱར་གཉིས་པ་ལ་ལྟོས་མི་དགོས་པ་བཞིན་ནོ། །ཞེས་དང་།
>
> *Just as when such metals as silver and gold have been thoroughly purified they will keep on being completely free of impurities of their own accord so it is not necessary to put them in clay vessels and subject them to the purifying process a second time.*

In purifying silver and gold, first you have to subject the stones to intense heat so that the precious metals liquefy and then separate easily from the stone. This is one method used to purify metals. If this has been done well (*legs par byas zin pa*) the purity of the metal will continue being pure naturally (*rang gi ngang gis*) day after day with the same quality today, tomorrow, and thereafter without having to be purified newly every day. Once purified, it will remain completely free of stains and will go on like that naturally in a continuum (*rigs 'dra phyi ma*).

Formerly in India, they customarily used clay pots (*rdza'i kha sbyar*) in which they put the metals in order to purify them. Once inside they would cover the pot and then subject it to intense heat so that the metal would melt and any impurities would be separated out. If the metal had been well purified the first time it was not necessary to follow this process a second time (*gnyis pa la ltos mi dgos pa*).

ཡང་གོམས་པ་དེ་དག་ལས་སྐྱེས་པའི་བརྩེ་བ་ལ་སོགས་པ་དེ་ཆོས་ཅན། རྟེན་བརྟན་པ་ཡིན་ཏེ། སེམས་ཀྱི་ངོ་བོ་ཉིད་དུ་སྐྱེས་པའི་ཡོན་ཏན་ཡིན་པའི་ཕྱིར། ཞེས་དང་།

> *Consider a mind like compassion, which has arisen as a result of habituation, its continuum relies upon a moment [of like mind] supporting the next, because that is one attribute of the nature of mind.*

COMPASSION AND WISDOM CAN GROW CONTINUALLY IN THE MIND DUE TO THE INTERDEPENDENCE OF MOMENTS OF MIND

Our mind can become used to compassion and wisdom through the practice of meditation. When we become used to them their continuum will grow continually in our mind. This continuum is made up of moments of like kind that have a relationship of support and supported (*rten brtan pa*). What does this mean? For example, I am supported by this chair; the chair is the support and I am that which is being supported. Without this chair's support I would not be able to sit here in this position, so I rely upon it to support me. Similarly, the previous moment of mind supports the subsequent moment of mind in a continuum of support and supported whereby the mind's object grows of its own accord by its own momentum once the mind has grown accustomed to it. The nature of mind is such that both its good qualities as well as its bad qualities will develop naturally and grow stronger and stronger. This is one of mind's features (*yon tan*) whereby it can foster either good knowledge or bad knowledge.

ཡང་ཚད་མར་གྲུབ་ཚུལ་ནི། བཅོམ་ལྡན་འདས་ཆོས་ཅན། གྲོལ་བ་དོན་གཉེར་ལ་ཚད་མའི་སྐྱེས་བུ་ཉིད་ཡིན་ཏེ། གང་གི་ཕྱིར་ན། བརྩེ་བ་ཆེན་པོ་མཐར་ཕྱིན་པས་གདུལ་བྱ་ལ་ལེགས་པ་འབའ་ཞིག་གསུངས་པ་དང་། ཡེ་ཤེས་ཁྱད་པར་གསུམ་ལྡན་ལས་བདེན་པ་ཕྱིན་ཅི་མ་ལོག་པ་འབའ་ཞིག་གསུང་བར་མཛད་ལ། དེ་དག་གི་སྒྲུབ་བྱེད་སྙིང་རྗེ་ཆེན་པོ་དང་བཅས་པའི་བདེན་བཞིའི་གནས་ལུགས་དེ་གསུང་པའི་ཆེད་དུ་མངོན་པར་སྦྱོར་བ་དང་ལྡན་པའི་ཐབས་ཤེས་མཐར་ཕྱིན་པར་མཛད་པ་དེས་ནའོ།

Also, a way to prove how one becomes perfect is the following: Consider the Buddha, the Transcendent Victor, he is perfectly valid for those seeking liberation. Why? Through his having completed the practice of great compassion he was able to teach only a perfect method to disciples and due to his possessing omniscience comprising the three characteristics he was able to teach only the unerring truth. The proof that he had these qualities is that in order to be able to teach the true nature of reality expounded in the Four Arya Truths and to have great compassion, he first had to have perfected authentic practices of method and wisdom.

We often hear people talk about others and say such things as, "He's a very good person," or "He's a terrible person," and so forth. How do they know that? Why should we believe what they say? If we have some logical ability and experience we can check these statements by testing them with good reasons to see whether they are true or not. We always have to inquire and ask "why is this so?" In the same vein we might hear someone say for instance, "Buddha Shakyamuni is an infallible person, a real leader and protector. He is the most precious and holy of beings!" However, these words alone are not sufficient reason to bring logicians to generate belief in their mind. We need good reasons to prove the truth of such statements. What is a good reason we can use to prove this?

When we study Buddha's speech and think about it and acquire a certain level of understanding we realize that whatever we read is perfect and entirely consistent –at the beginning, in the middle, and at the end– whether Sutra teachings or Tantric teachings. Why is his speech perfect? It is perfect because he teaches only what is true and only for the purpose of benefiting beings and not to harm them in the slightest way. We can know this both through reasons and experience. All his speech is internally consistent without one part being in contradiction with another. All the scriptures from beginning to end are taught only to benefit us and make our understanding clearer and never to render even the minutest harm. Therefore, by reading these scriptures and gaining knowledge through them we can believe that the Buddha is a real leader, a real teacher, a real protector since he teaches only that which helps beings to become free from their suffering and obstacles. We gain this belief in Buddha by experience and not by merely subjecting ourselves to what others say about him and blindly following their words.

What does *to prove how one becomes perfect* mean? The term "*tse ma*" (*tshad ma*) means right cognition, whether it pertains to the eye, the ear, or other consciousnesses when perceiving their object without error. Although we cannot perceive all objects directly we can realize some indirectly without error. For example, why are the buds on the trees opening up and the grass on the lawn turning green? Because causes have gathered together –warmth, moisture, soil, light, and so forth– to bring that about, which is an indication that the power of the elements is getting stronger. That is real and not false. The cognition that perceives such things unerringly we call "*tse ma*" or valid cognition. In this case, we are talking about someone who gained that quality, someone who became valid. Buddha Shakyamuni, needless to say, is not a mind but a person. Mind and person are completely different. Nevertheless, he is still *valid* insofar as he is an infallible, authoritative person (*tshad ma'i skye bu*), someone upon whom we can completely rely. Once we prove this to ourselves we can gain trust in him as an infallible teacher.

The text above is trying to prove that the Transcendent Victor, Buddha Shakyamuni, is an infallible person. The term used here "*chom den de*" (*bcom ldan 'das*) can be explained this way. "*Chom*" means to destroy and signifies that he destroyed all obstacles. "*Den*" means possessing and refers to his possessing the two major qualities of cessation and omniscience. "*De*" means beyond and refers to the status beyond that of an Arhat; that is, not only did he achieve nirvana but he achieved Buddhahood, the highest nirvana, as well. In fact, only the Buddha has the characteristic of having achieved the status beyond samsara and the two types of nirvana (*srid zhi gnyis kyi mtha' las 'das pa*), which means that he is both beyond samsara and the peace of the Listener Arhat's nirvana and that of the Solitary Realizer Arhat's nirvana.

Those seeking liberation (*grol ba don gnyer*) refers to those practitioners who have a very strong aspiration to become free from samsara and all its obstacles and want to achieve liberation. These are the ones who need a perfect, infallible instructor, someone who can guide them and help them to achieve that goal. Only Buddha Shakyamuni is an infallible instructor for them (*tshad ma'i skyes bu nyid yin*). *Disciples* (*gdul bya*) refers to those who want to achieve liberation. Every single word Buddha teaches is only for their benefit. How do we know? This is evident because he achieved both ultimate compassion (*brtse ba chen po*) and ultimate wisdom (*ye shes*), which has the threefold extraordinary characteristics (*khyad par gsum ldan*).

The first of these three characteristics is that his mind perceives the real nature of phenomena directly (*de kho na nyid mkhyen pa*). The second is that his mind does not only perceive the real nature once or just occasionally, it perceives it continually without interruption (*mkhyen pa bstan pa*). Even though we may achieve direct perception once, we may even forget it. Buddha's omniscience is not like that but remains firm and steady until the end of samsara. The third characteristic of omniscience is that it perceives the real nature of each and every phenomenon without excluding a single one (*ma lus par mkhyen pa*).

Why did Buddha teach the unerring truth? Because his great compassion urged him to teach those beings who want to become liberated. It is for this reason that he taught the real nature (*gnas lugs*) of the Four Arya Truths. *Method* (*thabs*) and *wisdom* (*shes*) refer to the two major kinds of knowledge: the first consisting of loving kindness, compassion, and bodhichitta, and the second of wisdom. Having practiced these with boundless effort he finally achieved their ultimate result (*mthar phyin par mdzad pa*).

ཊཱི་ཀ་ཆེན་ལེའུ་དང་པོ་ལས། ཡིད་ཆེས་ཀྱི་སྦྱོར་བ་ནི། སྦྱིན་པས་
ཡོངས་སྦྱོང་ཁྲིམས་ཀྱིས་བདེ།

In the first chapter of the Great Commentary it says: A correct logical reason of trusting faith is the following:

> *Consider the scriptural quotation [of Nagarjuna in* Precious Garland] *"From generosity comes wealth; from morality, higher rebirth...,"*

Actually these words come from Sutra and were selected by Arya Nagarjuna and incorporated in his text *Ratnamala. Yi che kyi jor wa* (*yid ches kyi sbyor ba*), one among several types of correct logical reasons, is an inferential cognition based on trust. *Jor ba* is synonymous with *rik pa* meaning reason. To understand this we have to go into a little more detail.

Once we have gained a validating ascertainment (*nges shes*) about the existence of our past and future lives through logical reasoning, this will compel us to believe in karma and strengthen our understanding and resolve to practice Dharma. We will begin to think about what good karma has brought us and what it is going to bring us in the future. Generally speaking, we can say that our having achieved an excellent human being's life is an excellent karma that was arranged primarily by our former lives through our having kept morality.

Thinking this way we acquire a portrait of our life, of our particular abilities and aptitudes, and so forth. We can have direct cognition of some of these, what we call *tong wa ngön gyur* (*mthong ba mngon gyur*), meaning that we can see these qualities directly since they are objects of our direct perception. However, objects such as our mind, our impermanent nature, the impermanent nature of our activities and the like are all slightly hidden (*cung zad lkog gyur*) phenomena. We cannot see these directly but can perceive them through logical reasoning or indirect cognition (*rjes dpag tshad ma*). Given that we cannot perceive our impermanent quality with direct perception, we have to realize it through logical reasoning. This is also true in regard to our real nature or emptiness of inherent existence. These objects are called "hidden" for the very fact that they are not patently evident to our mind and so we are not able to perceive them directly.

As practitioners, accordingly we have to examine our own impermanent nature, our own real nature of emptiness, which we cannot perceive directly right now. We have an excellent human being's life this time, which was produced by a variety of good karma. We have to think, "What kind of karma did I collect in my past life? How did I collect it?" Karma itself is a much deeper subject than emptiness. We can try to meditate on our emptiness and at some point come to realize and perceive it directly. But the system or workings of karma is much, much deeper and harder to fathom and many times more profound than *shunyata*. Therefore, we call it "extremely hidden" (*shin tu lkog gyur*). Since it is not a direct object for us, how can we learn about karma's system? Who can show us how it works? Who is capable of teaching us about such a deep and subtle subject? Only Buddha can teach us. Why is it that only Buddha and no one else can teach us? He is the only one qualified to do so because only Buddha is an infallible person (*tshad ma'i skye bu*). How can we tell that Buddha is an infallible person? Because he was born as a result of two excellent causes – causes of intention and causes of practice– which were mentioned at the beginning of this teaching.

In Acharya Dignaga's verse of homage he states: "The one who wishes to benefit beings/ The Teacher (*'gro la phen bzhed pa / ston pa*)," the first part indicates excellence of intention or compassion as a motivational cause (*rgyu bsam pa phun tshogs*); "Teacher" (*ston pa*) indicates excellence of practice or wisdom (*sbyor ba phun tshogs*), which Buddha cultivated for kalpas and kalpas in order to benefit all sentient beings. Once he finally completed that practice, this resulted in his becoming an infallible person (*tshad ma'i skye bu*). What kind of qualities does an infallible person have? An infallible person has the two excellent results produced by those two excellent causes. The two excellent results are the excellent qualities for oneself (*rang don phun tshogs*) and the excellent qualities for others (*gzhan don phun tshogs*).

The excellent qualities for oneself (*rang don phun tshogs*) can also be divided into two: cessation and omniscience. Buddha abandoned all obstacles by practicing both compassion and wisdom and thereby achieved cessation, which in its turn has three excellent qualities: he abandoned those obstacles well (*legs par spangs pa*), he abandoned them in such a way that they cannot ever return again (*lar mi ldog par spangs pa*), and he abandoned not only one kind of obstacle but every single one (*ma lus par spangs pa*). He also achieved omniscience that perceives the real nature of all sentient beings and all other phenomena. Once he achieved these two excellent qualities – cessation and omniscience– for his own benefit, he was able to accomplish excellent activities that are for the benefit of other beings, which include protecting all sentient beings from their suffering and problems and thereby liberating them.

There is a phrase that is very useful for remembering these qualities: *pang tok tar chin rang gi dön* (*spangs rtogs thar phyin rang gi don*). *Pang* means cessation; *tok* means omniscience; *tar chin* means finishing or achieving them; *rang* means self and refers to the excellent qualities that are for the benefit of oneself. *Dro wa dröl wa shen gyi dön* (*'gro ba sgrol ba gzhan gyi don*). *Dro wa* means sentient beings; *dröl wa* means to liberate; *shen gyi dön* means for the benefit of others. Therefore, this means the excellent qualities that are for the benefit of others.

Because Buddha possesses these qualities of completion – the excellent qualities for the benefit of himself and the excellent qualities for the benefit of others– there are absolutely no obstacles in his teachings; every single detail is real and, precisely for this reason, we can believe him and put our trust in him.

We can also determine the truth of his teachings by other logical means such as indirect cognition. One type of indirect cognition, which we mentioned before is *indirect perception through the power of things* (*dngos stobs rjes dpag*). Let's use this table as our subject (*chos can*). Is this table perishable?

Yes. Why is it perishable? Did you just say "yes" without having a reason? It is perishable because somebody made it with materials. This means that it was produced. If it was produced, if somebody made it, of course various causes and qualities gathered together to produce it. Also, at some point, due to other bad causes that were gathered together eventually it will disappear. Now, all things (*dngos po*) are perishable since that is their nature. Since this table is a thing it is perishable. We realize this by using the logical reason of indirect cognition through the power of things (*dngos stobs rjes dpag*).

Am I perishable? Of course I am. This we can realize very easily with logic. Now, what kind of karma gave me this life? Where is that karma? When did I collect it? When did it ripen? How many times did I collect it? These same questions can be asked about everyone. Although all of these are extremely hidden objects, nevertheless they are still objects and, if something is an object, it must exist. If it is an object, there must be a subject to know it. Without a subject there can be no object. Without an object there can be no subject, since subject and object are mutually related.

Yi che kyi jor wa[48] (*yid ched kyi sbyor ba*) in the phrase given above means a good reason based on trust. When dealing with such things that cannot be apprehended either by direct perception or indirect cognition through the power of things, they have to be realized by this kind of reason based on trust. How do we understand such extremely hidden phenomena? We can gain an understanding of them through trusting what the Buddha taught about them. For example, by trusting the validity of statements found in the Buddha's teachings we can learn about the system of karma, as in the quotation that

---

[48] Among the three principal types of inferential cognition "an inferential cognition based on trust" is an infallible awareness of extremely hidden comprehensible phenomena based on a perfect reason of trust.

appears in Arya Nagarjuna's work *Precious Garland*: "*From generosity comes wealth; from morality, higher rebirth.*" Wealth comes from practicing the perfection of giving. By practicing the perfection of morality we will attain a higher realm's *happiness* like the kind of human being's life we have at present.

Now, although somebody has achieved an excellent human being's life he may still be poor. What is wrong? How can that be? This is possible due to his having failed to practice *dana paramita*, or the perfection of giving, well. There are other cases where someone may be very wealthy but also be extremely stupid or crazy. What is wrong there? In his former life he practiced the perfection of giving nicely but failed to practice the other perfections.

I will try to explain this succinctly. All of Buddha's teachings are completely infallible, undeceptive speech; the subject matter he taught is completely pure without error; his method of teaching is also completely infallible. After eons and eons of searching, Buddha found the best way to eliminate obstacles and to overcome suffering. It is because of this that he became victorious and why he is called "victor" (*rgyal ba*). Once he became victorious, he taught us what he had discovered, what he himself had gained and perceived, exactly what he himself had achieved. It is for this reason that his teachings and his method of leading followers to this same status of Buddhahood are infallible and undeceptive.

Here we are discussing logic, which in some ways seems to be similar to science. Though I don't know much about science it appears to be the act of putting together many things and finding new ways to produce useful, powerful and often dangerous objects. One puts together different things to get a different result. Logic's objective and the objective of science, Buddhadharma's objective, religion's objective, and the objective of philosophy are the same; they only differ in their method. The system of logic looks for the truth and tries to separate what is correct from what is not correct. Its result is to discover what is exactly correct and to discard what is faulty. How? It does this by putting different things together and producing a new result. It employs reasoning by asking "why" whenever it confronts a difficulty. This method of inquiring by asking "why" is the meaning of logic. Logic does not mean "He says yes and I say no" or "They agree, but I disagree… ". Logicians are looking for the same object, the same truth, the same reality.

What does the scriptural quotation "*From generosity comes wealth; from morality, higher rebirth*" above mean? Generosity (*sbyin pa*) is the act of giving to beings what they are lacking; a form of charity. Through practicing giving we will receive a similar result in the future. What is that? Whatever we need we will acquire easily, like becoming rich. Becoming rich means that if we practice giving one dollar with a good motivation, with a good manner, and the person to whom it is being given is in need and a proper object of giving, due to that in the future we will become very rich. This shows the nature and result of practicing charity.

By practicing morality (*khrims kyis*), that is, through taking great care to guard our morality well, the result in the future will be that we achieve a higher realm's life (*bde*), especially that of an excellent human being. This is the basic result that has to be kept in mind and a major topic of our concern. So, it says in scripture that by practicing charity we will become rich and by practicing morality we will achieve an excellent human being's life in the future. Why are we to believe that? How can we trust what it says? We have to verify it through using logic.

This is a lighter. This is incense. This is smoke. This is a table. This is a clock. You can see all of these directly with your eye consciousness. It is for this reason that these objects are called *tong wa ngön gyur* (*mthong ba mngon gyur*) or directly perceptible, because they can be directly seen, heard, tasted, touched, or smelled. Buddha's speech is such that whatever perceptible objects it describes directly cannot be damaged, contradicted, or refuted by other forms of direct perception. What does this mean? If someone's eye faculty, for example, is perfect, he will see a yellow color as yellow, red as red, and so forth. However, some people do not see the same as others but rather see things differently. In Tibet, the best example given is that of a snow mountain. A snow mountain normally should be white. Those who have a problem with their eye faculty will see snow-covered mountains as blue rather than white. However, any eye consciousness that sees a snow mountain as white damages or refutes those mistaken consciousnesses that see those mountains as blue. When someone with a healthy eye faculty and someone with a faulty eye faculty are both looking at the same object and discussing its color, the one will say that the mountain is white and the other will say the color of that snow-covered mountain is blue. This discrepancy does damage both to the subject, or perceiver, and to the object, or the object of perception. Why? Because it shows that there is something wrong with the eye faculty of one of the perceivers, which does not perceive the color of the object correctly. We describe this by saying that the correct perception *does damage to* (*gnod byed*) the incorrect perception.

Buddha mentioned how a poor person who needs help is a visible object for everyone to see. His necessity is visible. He was not only referring to the need for food or clothing but for knowledge –Dharma wisdom– as well. We can easily say that it is true that they are poor since everyone can see that. No one can object to this correct cognition nor can it be contradicted by someone else's observation. Also everybody can see the act of giving and what is being given, for example, when we see relief crews unloading food from trucks and distributing it among many people. These are all manifest objects of direct perception (*mngon gyur*). Practitioners can also be an object of sight. Everybody can see their activities directly and comment about them and say, "They are very good practitioners of the perfection of giving." The same can be said of practicing morality—not taking another being's life, not stealing another being's property, and so forth. The subject and the object can both be seen since they too are objects of direct perception. It is also possible to see directly without error whatever it is they have stolen and from whom they have stolen it. These are examples of objects of direct perception (*mngon gyur*) that cannot be contradicted by another's direct perception or true speech.

As for the perfection of giving, the receiver of the gift, the motivation of the one giving, and what is given should all be proper. For example, the giving of a dollar to a poor person should be given in a respectful manner and not as if one were giving something to a hungry dog. The motivation of the one giving the money should be to remove the poverty of the recipient. All of these actions are a little subtle. Now, are all of these –the one giving, the recipient, and the gift– permanent or impermanent? Their quality is impermanent. If they were permanent or unchanging, the one practicing charity with one dollar would have to continue practicing that way for eons and eons and the receiver of the gift would remain permanently poor. If they were all permanent and unchanging, why would this not be the case? The one giving and the recipient need to have gathered many good causes for this charity to occur. All of these more subtle objects are slightly hidden objects (*cung zad lkog gyur*) because their quality is not so readily apparent but a little deeper and more hidden. Nevertheless, we are still dealing with the same objects: someone who gives, a recipient, and a gift. The quality of all of these is impermanent.

Without studying logic this may be difficult to understand. The subject, object, activities are all impermanent. Why? They are impermanent because they are produced. If something is produced by something else it must be impermanent. For example, in order for smoke to arise from this incense holder there has to be a gathering of fire to act as agent and incense to act as object, to produce this result. All of these are dependent arisings; all are produced by something else. It is for this reason –because they are produced by other things– that they are impermanent. This is not automatically apparent just from seeing the smoke but can be discerned by using logic. When you see smoke you have to think about it and ask, "Where does it come from? What is burning? What is the cause? What is the effect?" The coming together of an incense stick and fire allows the burning of the incense, which thereby produces the smoke that gives off a pleasant aroma. In this way we can see how everything relies upon something else, which is how Buddha explained the practice of charity and the practice of morality. No logical knowledge can refute these teachings since they are logically proven.

This smoke is produced by the gathering of fire and an incense stick. Since these –the smoke, fire, and the stick of incense– are objects you can see directly, that cognition which sees them as cause and effect bears witness and can prove them: "That's true, I saw it." You can prove the functioning of cause and effect by the power of that direct perception. This is not the same as the creation of all phenomena from some primordial nature (*spyi gtso bo*) or by a separate universal (*spyi don gzhan*), which are similar. Such is the philosophical belief according to the Samkhya (*grangs can pa*) system, or the Ennumerators. Formerly in India there were many schools of philosophy propounding different tenets. The most famous of these believed in what is known as *chi tso wo* (*spyi gtso bo*) or a primordial nature. For them smoke is an impermanent product that arises from a permanent creator or nature. According to their philosophy causes are *rang shin* (*rang bzhin*) or nature, while their effects are *nam gyur* (*rnam 'gyur*) or manifestations. They believed that this primordial nature is only a cause or producer and not a result, which implies that this primordial nature itself does not have its own cause. That which does not have its own cause must be permanent and unchanging. Generally, if something is a thing, a phenomenon, it must be impermanent. This is why Buddha indicates that the subject, object, and action of any moral action such as the act of giving are all produced by something else and therefore dependent and impermanent. So there can be no argument or contradiction in that regard.

As logicians you should have this phrase in your mind: "Whatever scripture teaches about manifest visible objects cannot be refuted by direct valid perception" (*mthong ba mngon gyur bstan pa'i cha la mgnon sum tshad mas gnod pa med pa*). This means that they cannot be damaged by any direct valid perception of any of the consciousnesses such as correct eye consciousness, nose consciousness, ear consciousness, tongue consciousness, body consciousness, or mind consciousness. Instead of doing damage to what is taught there these direct valid consciousnesses will verify it. Even without logic we can still see the validity of these things. So our direct perception will not harm what that teaching indicates.

With regard to those things that are taught in scripture that are a little bit subtle (*cung zad lkog gyur*), for example, the impermanent nature of subject, object, and action, no indirect cognition can refute them either. Instead of doing them harm all indirect cognition will verify them. For instance, we might say that those things are impermanent precisely because they were produced by something else. If causes do not gather together, their effect cannot arise. If we have a stick of incense but no fire, smoke cannot arise from it. Fire has to be applied to a stick of incense in order for smoke to be produced. In this way the production of smoke requires the gathering of its own unique causes. If its own unique causes are not present, smoke will not arise. So, by this logic we can safely say that all of these –the smoke, the fire, and the incense– are dependent and consequently impermanent.

The perfection of giving and the perfection of morality have an aspect of extreme subtlety (*shin tu lkog gyur*). Although difficult to perceive, it is not impossible. The three –subject, object, and action– all have the three aspects of being manifest, a little subtle, and extremely subtle. Buddha's speech can indicate these three different aspects at once.

What are these three aspects? With regard to the practice of giving, the first we call "perceptible by direct perception." We can see the practitioner, the action of giving, and to whom the object is being given. The second we call "inferable through the power of things" since we can gain an understanding of them through the use of correct reasons and logic. Although we can see manifestly who is breaking morality and who is guarding it, in order to perceive the impermanent nature of the subject, object, and action, we need to apply logic via correct reasons to understand it. The third, "the extremely subtle," also has an object. If there is an object there must be a subject; if there is a subject, there must also be an object. These are mutually established. What aspect about the practice of giving is extremely subtle? We might see a person with a good motivation practicing charity, giving a fresh, new dollar –not one that has just gone through the washing machine!– to someone in a respectful manner. That person who gives it in that way will be very rich in the future. Now, how do we know that? We cannot know that through direct perception since the result is certainly not something we are able to see directly. Also, we cannot understand it through indirect cognition of the power of things. So then, how can we know it? We are able to know it through "inference based on trust" (*yid ched rjes dpag*). "Trust" here indicates that we have a firm belief in something. "Inference" means understanding something through the use of correct reasons. We can gain this kind of cognition through examining the teachings of the Buddha.

Of course we cannot believe everybody's speech since not every kind of speech is trustworthy or infallible. Buddha's speech, however, is trustworthy. Why? Because Buddha achieved that ultimate status and knowledge through abandoning telling lies for eons and eons and practiced hard for such a long time in order to achieve Buddhahood. After having achieved his main goal –Buddhahood– why ever would he tell us lies unless he was crazy? There is absolutely no logical reason for him to do that. If what he teaches is entirely free of lies it must be true, even though we may not be able to understand it right away. Hence, when he teaches that through practicing giving and guarding morality we will achieve inconceivably good results in the future, we can trust that such speech is infallible and undeceptive.

།ཞེས་པའི་ལུང་ཆོས་ཅན། རང་གི་བསྟན་བྱའི་དོན་ལ་མི་སླུ་སྟེ། དཔྱད་པ་གསུམ་གྱིས་དག་པའི་ལུང་ཡིན་པའི་ཕྱིར། །དཔེར་ན། བདེན་བཞི་སྟོན་པའི་གསུང་རབ་བཞིན། ཞེས་དང་།

Consider the scriptural passage that says [from giving, wealth; from morality, higher rebirth], the meaning of what it teaches is infallible because it is scripture that has been tested by the three examinations as, for example, the teachings on the Four Arya Truths.

SCRIPTURE, TESTED BY THE THREE EXAMINATIONS LIKE THE TEACHINGS ON THE FOUR ARYA TRUTHS

The phrase "*jin pe long chö trim gyi de*" (*sbyin pas longs spyod khrims kyis bde*), is our subject of discussion (*chos can*). "It is infallible speech" (*mi slu te*) is the object to be proved (*bsgrub bya'i chos*). How can we prove that? By using the reason (*rtags*) that all of Buddha's speech can be "tested by those three examinations" or three kinds of cognition (*dpyad pa gsum gyis dag pa'i lung yin pa'i phyir*), which we mentioned above—by direct perception, inference through the power of things, and inference based on trust. By examining Buddha's speech with these three kinds of cognition we find that it is not damaged by any of them but, on the contrary, is verified as true and trustworthy speech. This is the reason used to prove the thesis that his speech is infallible, trustworthy, and correct. What is an example (*dper na*)? The Four Arya Truths that the Buddha taught (*bden gzhi ston pa'i gsung rab bzhin*). Buddha's teaching on the Four Arya Truths is infallible speech, as is the quotation from Nagarjuna's work.

What are these three examinations (*dpyad pa gsum*)? For the first one we can review the earlier illustration of the practice of giving things. The act of giving itself can be seen by others. The things given can be seen, and so too can the recipient of the gift. The gift that is given has to benefit others. To the hungry we give food. To the poor we give money. To those who are cold we give clothing. To the thirsty we give something to drink. There are many things we can give, all of which can serve as objects of our direct perception. Hence, there is no way to argue about them since they can be easily verified.

The second examination concerns those things that can be verified by inference through the power of things (*dngos stobs rjes dpag*). Buddha taught the Four Arya Truths in which he describes the nature of suffering and the source of suffering. We can see that people get sick, have various problems, get older, die, and the like. Why does this happen? We can realize why this happens by our inference through the power of things. Things have samsara's nature in general. If they have samsara's nature, the result of having that nature will eventually show; that is not unusual. We can tell that certain things will happen because they have such a nature; that is, by the very power of a thing's nature it will bring about a specific kind of result. Some non-Buddhist schools, as we mentioned, have a different way of going about explaining cause and effect and thereby introduce the idea of a permanent creator creating impermanent effects, or effects that occur without a cause, and so forth. The Buddhist view, contrarily, rather relies on observation and reasoning.

The third type of examination is inference based on trust (*yid ched rjes dpag*). When Buddha taught the Four Arya Truths he taught about karma's system, whereby essentially he describes the many different results of karma. The Four Arya Truths must be classified into two parts. The first consists of one kind of cause and its effect, and the second part describes another set of cause and effect. The causes and effects of the first part pertain to samsara's side; those of the second pertain to beyond samsara.

We can explain it this way. I'm getting older. I'm beginning to experience many different kinds of sickness and problems. I can't hear nicely; I can't see nicely; I can't taste nicely; I can't remember nicely. Why? What happened? This is happening because suffering is the nature of samsara; this is its quality. Consequently all of these difficulties will come to me sooner or later. I cannot avoid them because that is samsara's nature. Wherever there is fire there will also be heat and burning. When a wolf comes along he will be accompanied by growling and gnashing of teeth. That is its nature. These troubles are simply results that pertain to samsara's side of the Four Arya Truths.

The causes of this suffering are karma and mental afflictions. Buddha taught us that there are many kinds of suffering. If we don't like this suffering, if we don't like samsara, there is a way to become free from its causes and effects. Without purifying the causes of samsara's side we cannot stop these sufferings. This is why Buddha taught the effects of samsara and its source. If we don't like these effects, there is a way we can avert them. There is a status of freedom from samsara's side of causes and effects, which is the status of cessation or nirvana. Nirvana is an effect achieved beyond samsara's side. To achieve it Buddha taught us how to practice the paths. These are the cause and effect he described in the Arya Truths that pertain to the side beyond samsara.

On the first day, just seven weeks after he had achieved Buddhahood, Buddha began to teach Dharma starting with this teaching on the Four Arya Truths. Like this teaching, all of his teachings are infallible because his speech is perfectly valid (*tshad ma*). How do we know that Buddha, the teacher, is an infallible, authoritative person whom we can trust (*tshad ma'i skye bu*)? We can reach this conclusion the scholar's way and gain definitive certainty by testing his teachings through using the three examinations. What Buddha taught was only for the purpose of benefiting beings and not a single word is harmful to them. When we think about his qualities and achievements, we will definitely gain faith in the Buddha.

By listening to Dharma teachings in class you can gain "listening wisdom" (*thos byung gi shes rab*) or a kind of understanding derived from your hearing something being described to you. If you don't forget what you've heard in class, for example, that "Buddha is an infallible teacher," and you contemplate it on your cushion once you get home, you can gain some wisdom. When you begin to think about why he is an infallible teacher you will rememeber the reasons: "He is an infallible teacher because he teaches only to benefit beings and not to harm them in even the slightest way with a single word." This kind of understanding is derived from indirect valid cognition. "How did he become an infallible teacher?" He became an infallible teacher by virtue of his having completed the practices of loving kindness, compassion, and wisdom and having achieved the ultimate goal. As a result he no longer has any problems. Also, because he gained all knowledge and power he is an authority, an infallible teacher, and leader. This kind of cognition you can gain by contemplating good reasons.

It is very important that your inferential cognition about all we have been studying become very firm. Once it is pretty firm and steady in your mind, if somebody were to come along and tell you that there are no future or past lives or that karma and its results don't exist, even though you may not be able to perceive any of these directly, still your understanding of them will be more stable after having investigated them with sound reasons and you will be more equipped to determine whether or not they are true.

You should also gain firm inferential cognition with regard to Buddha's speech. "If Buddha said that then I can trust it since I have examined it with my reasoning. Even though I cannot perceive it directly, since Buddha taught it that way it is trustworthy. There must be previous and future lives. There must be an unwavering system of karma. Since this is Buddha's main teaching, I can believe it." This kind of belief and cognition gained about Buddha's speech through reading, studying, and listening is what is meant by the term "a correct reason based on trust" (*yid ched kyi sbyor ba*) stated above.

Now look. Why is there no smoke coming from this incense holder? There is no smoke coming from here because there is no incense burning inside. We can tell that pretty easily. To give these kinds of reasons we don't have to come armed with quotations and a lot of study, since we can perceive directly the absence of smoke. If there were smoke we would perceive it. However, valid perception about the effects of good and bad karma and about the existence of past and future lives is not achieved in the same way. When farmers see a sprout growing in a field they know that someone has planted a seed; they don't have to study quotations to verify it. They just plant their seeds in a field and wait to get their results. Knowledge of karma's system of former and future lives, on the other hand, cannot be acquired so readily. The only way we can learn about this system is through Buddha's infallible speech and instruction.

Buddha taught the Four Arya Truths three different times. What he taught is the perfect truth. Samsara's nature is suffering. Suffering itself is a result. There are many kinds of suffering—the suffering of the higher realms and the suffering of the lower realms. The suffering of the three higher realms is a little less severe compared with the suffering of the three lower realms. The three lower realms' suffering is almost endless, without respite. The suffering there just gets heavier and heavier for an incredibly long time. That is true suffering. Some of those kinds of suffering, the problems that exist in the animal realm, for example, we can see for ourselves. Sometimes Channel Thirteen presents programs about the animal realm where they show how smaller creatures serve merely as food for the larger ones. Even though some animals have a little wisdom to protect themselves, still they lack the power to do so effectively. Their power only consists of becoming a little bit stronger than other animals so that they can catch and eat them without much trouble. Sometimes while hunting their prey the smaller creature gets away. That's pretty good, but still it is a kind of suffering, or why else would they run away? They know that they were just about to be swallowed alive!

In the hells beings are burning all the time without anything to protect them. Everything becomes a compatible cause for them to burn. Conversely, in the cold hells, everything becomes a compatible cause for them to freeze and there are absolutely no causes, none whatsoever, to create heat to help the beings there keep warm. Such suffering continues this way for many, many kalpas. We are extremely lucky for not having reached there this time. Yet we have the perfect causes to go there. It's not so very difficult ... actually it's rather easy! What is it that keeps us from reaching those hells immediately? Only our next breath. If our next breath were not to come we might arrive there instantly. The kind of birth required to be born there is a miracle birth; it doesn't require a long period of gestation and birth from the womb as it does for human beings. So, reaching there is only a short step away.

How can we learn about these kinds of situations? We can learn about them only through the words of the Buddha, by what he taught. He taught about true sufferings. Who arranged these horrendously long periods of suffering from intense cold and unbearable heat? We did, all by ourselves. We are the ones who collected an ungainly number of bad deeds in countless lives in numerous different ways, and whose only result is to bring us endless suffering. The Buddha taught us the truth of samsara's suffering and the truth of the causes of that suffering, its source. Hence, we can have trust in the infallibility of the words taught in the scriptures. This kind of understanding gained through trust in the scriptures is a correct inferential reason based on trust (*yid che kyi sbyor ba*).

We are surely very rich in bad deeds. Since bad deeds are impermanent entities and we are the ones who have committed them, we have created the causes whose results will come. That is their quality. All the same, even though normally bad deeds do not have any good qualities, they do have one—being impermanent entities and therefore perishable they can be gotten rid of. If we apply the antidote to get rid of them eventually they will disappear. In one way we have to be deeply worried, since we have accumulated a lot of bad deeds. In another way, we don't have to worry if we practice hard to get rid of them. By coming to class we can gain many skills that can benefit us, which can be learned from the mouth of our Dharma teacher.

When listening to these Four Arya Truths, first we learn about the results on samsara's side, which is suffering; then we learn about where this suffering came from, or its source. If we don't like the effect –suffering– we have to find a way to become free from it. In this way we learn about how to do away with all forms of samsaric suffering along with their causes and thereby achieve cessation. How can we achieve cessation or this status of freedom from all of samsara's suffering that Buddha taught? We have to study and practice and gain the truth of the path. The truth of the path and the truth of cessation comprise the second part of the Four Arya Truths that explains what to do to reach the status beyond samsara and completes the two sides that Buddha taught: samsara's side and the side beyond samsara.

Why are they called the "Four Arya Truths"? They are called this because Aryas have perceived the real nature of samsara. Upon gaining that realization Aryas practiced very hard until they abandoned samsara. But we haven't done so yet. When Aryas check samsara they don't find any real happiness anywhere but, on the contrary, they find that everything is only the nature of suffering. We, however, don't see it that way. We think samsara's nature contains the quality of extreme happiness when in fact it is the exact opposite. We may have some small, medium, or big kind of happiness, but actually the real nature of that happiness is suffering. Thinking it is happiness we do whatever we can to achieve it. What we think is happiness Aryas perceive as suffering. This is the real meaning of the Four Arya Truths.

Now, we have to keep in mind the following:

Consider the scriptural statement that says, "From giving comes wealth; from morality, higher rebirth," its meaning is infallible, because it is scripture that has been tested by the three examinations.

If we want to become rich in the future we have to practice giving. However, not all rich beings are necessarily human beings. Some beings of the other realms can become rich as well. Take nagas for instance. Some of them are very rich with lots of jewels and the like as are some demigods. Even though some nagas are very rich they still belong to the animal realm, which is one of the three lower rebirths. It is only through guarding our morality that we gain a higher rebirth. It may seem that the beings of the other higher realms have a comparatively good life, but they cannot practice Dharma, especially Tantra. That is reserved only for human beings. Only they can practice all four levels of Tantra. Therefore, since the unique happiness of a human being's life comes from practicing morality, if we want an excellent human being's life in the future we have to practice and guard our morality.

Why is the statement quoted above true? How can we prove it? To prove it means gaining true cognition by means of a correct reason. When we say "I saw something," this implies our having seen something directly, that we have witnessed something, as in "He is the murderer!" or "He is the thief. I saw him do it." These examples show objects of our direct perception, proving to us that the object is real. Similarly, to prove that the statement expressed above is an infallible statement we have to use a reason to prove it. To prove it we give the reason "because it is scripture tested by the three examinations" (*dpyad pa gsum gyis dag pa'i lung yin pa'i phyir*). These three examinations are very well known on the debate ground.

The above quotation gives an example of such a teaching that can be tested in this way as it says, "Like the teachings on the Four Arya Truths" (*bden gzhi ston pa'i gsung rab bzhin*). The first disciples of the Buddha were very lucky and virtuous since they had a special connection to the Buddha and were able to hear his very first teaching. The conditions had to have been extraordinary for them to be present at the time Buddha was teaching. These first disciples were also quite unusual since they were very mature and ripe for the teachings. When he introduced the first set of truths, the truth of suffering and the source of that suffering, one of the five close disciples immediately achieved the path of insight (*mtong lam*), while the other four achieved the second of the five paths, or the path of preparation (*sbyor lam*). Why did they suddenly achieve those levels? They were able to do so because the teaching on the Four Arya Truths is an infallible teaching. Both the teaching and the teacher are infallible and therefore trustworthy. That is why this is used here as an example.

Buddha's disciples realized that if they did not want to have suffering in the future they had to find the causes of suffering, which are karma and the mental afflictions. The chief of the mental afflictions is ignorance whose main antidote is wisdom. They realized that if they were to gain this they would have a chance to become free from samsara's suffering. So, Buddha taught them about cessation or the abandonment of all of samsara's sufferings, which is a result. If we don't want to suffer in samsara any longer we have to achieve that result, which is cessation, and to achieve that we have to practice true paths. The principal Arya's path is wisdom that perceives samsara's real nature. But just understanding this is not enough of an antidote against samsara since it has to be practiced and developed rigorously to make it firm and stable.

དཔྱད་པ་གསུམ་གྱིས་དག་ཚུལ་ནི། མཐོང་བ་མངོན་གྱུར་སྟོན་པ་ལ་
མངོན་སུམ་གྱིས་གནོད་པ་མེད་པ།

> *The way [scripture] is checked by the three examinations is as follows: 1) when it teaches about manifest visible things it is undamaged by direct perception.*

SCRIPTURE UNDAMAGED BY DIRECT VALID PERCEPTION

How can we prove that this statement "*by practicing charity, wealth; by guarding morality, higher rebirth*" is true? We have to verify it by testing it with the three examinations. In summary, the first is *when it teaches about manifest visible things it is not damaged by direct perception* (*mthong ba mngon gyur ston pa la mngon sum gyis gnod pa med pa*). When debating, this is often phrased in the following way as mentioned before: *tong wa ngön gyur ten pe cha la ngön sum tse me nö pa me pa* (*mthong ba mngon gyur bstan pa'i cha la mngon sum tshad mas gnod pa med pa*). These words should come to our mind effortlessly. This means that the direct valid perception (*mngon sum tshad ma*) of an ordinary person on up to a Buddha cannot see the slightest flaw in what is taught in terms of visible or manifest things. That which it teaches can be verified by our direct valid perception (*mngon sum tshad ma*). *Tong wa* (*mthong ba*) means something perceptible to the sense consciousnesses, for example, something we see directly with our eyes. We cannot find any fault with what is taught there in this regard unless we are crazy. *Ngön gyur* (*mngon gyur*) means an actual object of direct perception; that is, if an actual thing is in front of us we should be able to perceive it. For example, both this clock and those flowers we can see very clearly. We cannot say that they are not here in front of us or that there is something wrong with them unless we are crazy. Similarly, from the direct cognition of ordinary people up to the perfect cognition of a Buddha, no fault can be found (*gnod pa med pa*) with those things that are perceptible to direct valid perception (*mngon sum gyis*), which are taught in scripture (*ston pa la*).

So, again, with regard to the statement "*by practicing giving, wealth; by guarding morality, higher rebirth,*" when practicing the perfection of giving, those who receive our charity such as beggars or the like should be there. We, the ones giving, should also be there, as well as the things that are being given. These three –agent, object, and action– should all be present. Since they are present they are visible to direct valid perception and, since they are perceptible, they are verifiable, hence no one can find fault with them. This represents the first examination of scripture by direct perception.

དཔེར་ན་སྔོན་པོ་མངོན་གྱུར་བསྟན་པ་ལ། མངོན་སུམ་གྱིས་གནོད་པ་མེད་ཅིང་གྲུབ་པ་དང་། གཞན་དག་མངོན་གྱུར་དུ་འདོད་པའི་སྤྱི་དོན་གཞན་སོགས་མངོན་གྱུར་མིན་པ་བསྟན་པ་ལ་མངོན་སུམ་གྱིས་གནོད་པ་མེད་པ་ལྟ་བུ་དང་།

For example, when scripture teaches about a visible blue color, it exists [that way as described] without being damaged by [anyone's] direct perception. When scripture teaches that "separate universals" and such, which others believe to exist as manifest to direct perception, do not exist, such a teaching is not damaged by direct perception.

To explain this let's take the color of those leaves, for example. What color are they? Green. And the color of that mug? Blue (*sngon po*). Since these colors are manifest or visible (*mngon gyur*) we can see them and verify them and safely agree that the color of these leaves is green and the color of that mug is blue. What color is that? When I point to an object and ask you its color, we can all see it at the same time and say, "That is blue" or "That is green." No one can find fault with our direct perception of the quality of the object we have agreed upon (*mngon sum gyis gnod pa med cing*). We can prove that that quality is that way (*grub pa*)—"That is blue;" "That is green." Not only will we not find fault with that perception but we can prove it to be correct by direct perception as when corroborating such statements as "I saw it" or "I heard it."

"*Others*" (*gzhan dag*) in this case refers to the beliefs of certain non-Buddhist scholars. The passages we are studying are primarily based on Dharmakirti's *Commentary to "Valid Cognition"* itself, as the title indicates, a commentary on Dignaga's *Compendium of Means of Valid Cognition*, from which the homage above derives. In India at the time this text was composed there were many logicians, both Buddhist and non-Buddhist, who debated over numerous issues. Here, these passages, written of course from the Buddhist perspective, are exposing and refuting the beliefs of a particular non-Buddhist tenet.

Separate universals (*spyi don gzhan*) is a very famous concept in logic, which is refuted by Buddhist logicians as being non-existent. Because the Buddhists were debating with other schools at the time, and since this concept happened to be this other school's main belief, of course they have to show how that view is incorrect and go about establishing and proving the correctness of their own view in the debate.

The concept of *separate universals* can be described as follows. There are two different kinds of flowers on this table—a rose and a lilac. Both being flowers we can say that they are the particulars of the general category of "flower." Hence, the rose and the lilac are particular types of flower subsumed by the general category of "flower." *Chi* (*spyi*) is the Tibetan word for general. *Dön shen* (*don gzhan*) means separate identities. So *chi dön shen* as a concept means separate identities sharing a general quality. According to their view, however, that general quality is endowed with a permanent, unchanging nature and is a different entity from the particulars.

According to Buddhist belief the general is described as follows. These two flowers are the particulars of the general category "flower." If the general category did not exist, no particular of that category could exist. But mostly, without the particulars that comprise that category, that category itself could not possibly exist. General "flower" covers all particulars of its category. When a particular flower grows and gets bigger, it does so endowed with the general quality of a flower and not of a rock or metal, let's say. This is how the particulars are related to their general category. Therefore, it is not possible for a permanent general category to create impermanet particulars of that category as some other schools maintain. Also, when these non-Buddhist scholars hold this to be their main creator and teach this view, of course they cannot prove that it exists by direct valid cognition since it does not exist at all. Therefore, to teach that "*chi dön shen*" does not exist is also correct and therefore *not damaged by direct perception* (*mngon sum gyis gnod pa med pa*).

མཐོང་བ་ལྐོག་གྱུར་གྱི་དོན་སྟོན་པ་ལ་དངོས་པོ་སྟོབས་ཞུགས་ཀྱི་རྗེས་
དཔག་ཉིད་ཀྱིས་གནོད་པ་མེད་པ། དཔེར་ན་འཕགས་པའི་བདེན་པ་

བཞི་གཏན་ལ་ཕབ་པ་ལ་དངོས་པོ་སྟོབས་ཞུགས་རྗེས་དཔག་གིས་
གནོད་པ་མེད་ཅིང་གྲུབ་ལ། གཞན་དག་ལྐོག་གྱུར་དུ་འདོད་པའི་
བདག་དང་གཙོ་བོ་སོགས་བཀག་པ་ལ་རྗེས་དཔག་གིས་གནོད་པ་
མེད་པ་ལྟ་བུ་དང་།

With regard to teaching the meaning of the hidden nature of visible things, it is not damaged by inferential cognition through the power of things. For example, when establishing the Four Arya Truths, these remain undamaged and are even proven by inferential cognition through the power of things. In like manner, in refuting what others believe to be hidden such as the "self" or a "principal creator," there is no damage by inferential cognition.

The second of the three examinations deals with objects that are slightly hidden or what we call *chung tse gok gyur* (*cung zad lkog gyur*); though not objects of direct cognition they are objects of indirect cognition.

SCRIPTURE UNDAMAGED BY INFERENTIAL COGNITION

You can see these flowers, see their shape and color, smell their odor, feel their softness, and so forth. However, if I were to ask you whether they are permanent or impermanent, you would not be able to verify that by using your direct perception. This question itself is asking about a nature that is a little more subtle and can only be proven by using indirect cognition. "Indirect" means through the use of correct reasons. The nature of these flowers is impermanent. Since you cannot apprehend their impermanent nature through direct perception you have to use your indirect cognition. These flowers are impermanent because they grow from a seed. Someday they will perish. Why? Because they are things (*dngos po*). They arise, they stay, and they disintegrate. Impermanence is their nature. You have to find the reasons why their nature is impermanent. Without their seeds they wouldn't exist since they require certain causes and conditions to bring them about and to make them grow. Once they have grown their power and energy will become exhausted and they will die. That too is their nature. By going through these progressive logical steps you will come to recognize their impermanence. In light of this understanding you will realize that your life, your body, your very quality is the same. Again, your main concern should be your own situation and how what you discover applies to you, in this case, realizing your own impermanent nature. Therefore, we see how this nature is a little subtle and not obvious to direct perception but is a little hidden (*cung zad lkog gyur*).

This life is suffering. There are many kinds of suffering: the suffering of old age, the suffering of suffering, the suffering of change—we have all of them. On top of these there are also many extra kinds of suffering, like various forms of sickness and so forth. In order to comprehend that these are true forms of suffering we often have to check more closely and meditate on them. Even though they are forms of suffering, many people don't believe they are. Once we understand that they are in fact real forms of suffering we will want to know where this suffering comes from. Most often we are prone to thinking that suffering comes from such things as a McDonald's hamburger or a Burger King chicken sandwich that we didn't digest well, but fail to think about the main causes, which are mental afflictions and karma. Those others are only temporary, secondary causes. The actual causes are present in our mind in the form of the stains of the mental afflictions and karma. Once we realize that all suffering comes from this main source we will have established the true cause of our suffering.

Now, if we don't want suffering anymore there is a state of freedom from that suffering and paths to reach that status. This is what Buddha taught and whose truth cannot be disputed or contradicted (*gnod pa med pa*) by inferential cognition; on the contrary, this kind of cognition actually serves to confirm it (*grub la*).

Others (*gzhan dag*) refers to other non-Buddhist scholars and the beliefs they uphold. The adherents of the view referred to here believe in a self (*bdag*) that is a combination of being permanent and impermanent, as well as believe in a principal creator (*gtso bo*) that is a permanent entity with the ability to create impermanent entities as its creation. *Tso wo* (*gtso bo*) is synonymous with *chi dön shen* (*spyi don gzhan*) and *chi tso wo* (*spyi gtso bo*) meaning principal creator. These are just some examples given (*sogs*) of those things that are believed to be slightly hidden rather than readily available to direct perception. However, such things do not exist at all.

To explain this further we need an example. Do you do activities? Do you eat? Do you sleep? Do you think? Yes, of course. Do you come and go? Coming from somewhere and going somewhere is a quality that is specific only to an impermanent entity. Permanent entities do not have that quality. Going there means not being here, and conversely, being here means not being there. However, according to some non-Buddhist school systems they say that a drinker's quality, an eater's quality, a sleeper's quality can be permanent. In their view an entity, a thing, can be both permanent and impermanent simultaneously, without any contradiction. Nothing can have both these qualities at the same time. Nonetheless, some still hold that a person can be both an eater and a permanent entity at the same time, for example. According to this view a person has three qualities: he is an eater, a combination of impermanent and permanent entity, and a non-agent (*za ba po rtag dngos byed po min pa*). Buddhist logic rejects that kind of person (*bkag pa la*), since such a person could not possibly exist. This refutation is not harmed but even proven by indirect cognition (*rjes dpag gyis gnod pa med pa*).

མ་མཐོང་བའི་དངོས་པོ་ཤིན་ཏུ་ལྐོག་ཏུ་གྱུར་པའི་དོན་དེ་དག་ལུང་དེ་ལས་ཇི་ལྟར་བསྟན་པ་ལྟར་ཁས་བླངས་པ་ལ་ལུང་ལ་བརྟེན་པའི་རྗེས་དཔག་གིས་ཀྱང་གནོད་པ་མེད་ཅིང་། རང་ཚིག་སྔ་ཕྱི་དང་འགལ་བ་དང་དངོས་ཤུགས་འགལ་བས་ཀྱང་གནོད་པ་མེད་པ།

With regard to the assertion that what is taught in scripture as extremely hidden refers to those things that are unseen, even those, in reliance upon that scripture, cannot be damaged by inferential cognition nor can they be damaged by former words contradicting later words in that scripture or by a contradiction between what is taught directly and indirectly.

SCRIPTURE UNDAMAGED BY INFERENCE BASED ON TRUST

Here this passage mentions those things that are *extremely hidden* or very subtle. When we practice the perfection of giving and morality, these practices will definitely bring us wealth and rebirth in the higher realms in the future. But are we able to see these practices giving us wealth and an excellent happy future life? No, we cannot. Why? Because the relationship between karma and its results is far too subtle and profound.

Most people think that since shunyata or the real nature of all phenomena is so difficult to perceive it is the most profound object. However, the subtle relationship between karma and its effects is a hundred times more profound than that. The Sravaka Aryas, Pratyeka Aryas, and Mahayana Aryas can perceive their mind's real nature and the real nature of other beings directly during their meditation. Yet they cannot perceive the most subtle relationship between karma and its results. Some meditators, though they may be great Arhats or Bodhisattvas, when it comes to fathoming this most subtle relationship still have to defer to the Buddha. Therefore, karma's system is most subtle and can only be comprehended through inferential reasoning based on trust in reliance upon the infallible speech of the Buddha. We have to believe Buddha's speech since there is no other way we can perceive such subtle phenomena either by direct perception or through the reasoning of indirect cognition.

The *scriptures* (*lung*) referred to here are the teachings on the Four Arya Truths, the Six Paramitas, and so forth. What is indicated in these teachings is not contradicted by any other speech of the Buddha nor is there any contradiction between what is taught directly and indirectly. If we need still more reasons to believe these teachings we can think about how Buddha achieved Buddhahood only for the purpose of other beings. In order to do that he had to be free of telling lies for eons and eons. After achieving Buddhahood through abandoning telling lies for so long, why would he tell us lies? That would not make sense. Therefore, we can use our logic to strengthen our belief. If this is still not clear and our faith remains weak, then we have to try to learn about the extraordinary qualities of Buddha's speech, body, and mind.

དཔེར་ན། ཆགས་སོགས་སྤྱིག་པའི་རྒྱ་བ་ཡང་ཡིན། ཁྲུས་དང་མར་མེ་ལྷུགས་པ་སོགས་ཀྱིས་སྤྱིག་པ་དག་པ་ཡང་ཡིན་པའི་གཞི་མཐུན་བཀག་པ་དང་། སྦྱིན་པ་དང་མི་འཚེ་བ་སོགས་ཆོས་སུ་བཤད་པ་ལ་ནང་འགལ་མེད་པ་སྟེ། དེ་ལྟར་དཔྱད་པ་གསུམ་གྱིས་དག་པ་དེ་ཁྱད་

པར་གསུམ་ལྡན་གྱི་ལུང་འདིའི་རང་གི་བརྗོད་བྱ་ལ་མི་བསླུ་བའི་རྒྱུ་མཚན་ཡང་དག་ཡིན་ནོ།

For example, although desire and such are the root of bad deeds we must reject the idea that we can purify them by washing them away or by licking the flame of a butter lamp. There are no internal contradictions in the Buddha's explanations of Dharma concerning such subjects as practicing the perfection of giving and desisting from harming other beings. Therefore, because it possesses the three qualities tested by the three examinations this is a perfect reason to prove to ourselves that the subject matter of Buddha's speech is not deceptive.

Buddha's speech rejects explanations of contradictory activities such as first believing that the root of bad deeds is desire and then accepting that those bad deeds can be cleansed from the mind by taking a shower and washing them away with soap. This is the first contradiction. The next contradiction is to believe that by licking the flame of a candle or butterlamp we can get rid of our bad deeds. Buddha's speech rejects this kind of activity as well. We can find no such faults of internal contradictions, no faults between direct or indirect cognition, or between the implicit and explicit, within Buddha's speech. His speech is perfect because it has been tested by the three examinations. From this it is evident that the way in which Buddha teaches Dharma and the way non-Buddhist scholars teach is substantially different.

མི་བསླུ་བར་དཔོག་ཚུལ་དེ་ཧེ་ལྷ་བུ་ཞེ་ན། སྣང་བྱའི་དེ་ཉིད་འགོག་བདེན་དང་། ངོར་བྱའི་དེ་ཉིད་སྡུག་བདེན་དང་། འགོག་བདེན་སྣང་

པའི་ཐབས་ལམ་བསྟེན་པ་དང་། སྡུག་བདེན་དོན་པའི་ཐབས་ཀུན་འབྱུང་སྤོང་བ་དང་བཅས་པ་སངས་རྒྱས་ཀྱིས་གསུངས་པ་ལྟར་དངོས་སྟོབས་ཀྱི་ཚད་མས་རབ་ཏུ་ངེས་པ་ཡི་བཙོ་བོའི་དོན་བདེན་བཞིའི་གནས་ལུགས་ལ་སངས་རྒྱས་དེས། ཇི་ལྟར་གསུངས་པ་ལྟར་མི་བསླུ་བ་དངོས་སྟོབས་ཀྱིས་གྲུབ་པའི་ཕྱིར་ན། དེ་ཉིད་མཚུངས་ཆོས་སུ་བྱས་ནས་དཔྱད་པ་གསུམ་གྱིས་དག་པའི་རྟགས་ཀྱིས་གཞན་ཤིན་ཏུ་ལྐོག་གྱུར་ལའང་། སངས་རྒྱས་ཀྱི་གསུང་དེ་ཉིད་མི་བསླུ་བ་རྗེས་སུ་དཔག་པར་བྱ་བ་ཡིན་ནོ། ཞེས་དང་།

We may wonder how we can determine this infallibility. What is to be adopted is the truth of cessation; what is to be abandoned is the truth of suffering. The method for practicing the truth of cessation is to rely on a path; and the method for extricating ourselves from the truth of suffering is by abandoning the source of suffering. The true nature of the Four Arya Truths just as Buddha taught them is the principal meaning to be understood by valid cognition through the power of things. In this regard, because the way Buddha taught reality accords with the way it is established through the power of things, such a teaching is infallible. Hence, having taught a Dharma [specifically the Four Arya Truths] that is in conformity with reality, we can accurately infer that the Buddha's other teachings as well concerning extremely hidden matters, when tested by the three examinations, will be found to be perfectly valid and infallible.

If our main object is to achieve cessation (*blang bya'i de nyid 'gog bden*), how do we go about achieving it? By practicing the paths, which are its main cause. What are we seeking to abandon? Suffering. Both of these –the Truth of Suffering and the Truth of Cessation– are results. To achieve suffering, first we have to have a source or cause of suffering. Similarly, to achieve cessation of suffering we have to have a method that serves as a cause for its attainment, which are the paths. We have to clearly establish in our mind what Buddha taught about this by using inferential cognition through the power of things. These teachings are infallible and therefore valid teachings to follow and practice. We have to examine all of Buddha's other teachings in the same way, both Sutra and Tantra, especially those concerning the most subtle objects like the subtle relationship between karma and its results.

When Buddha was teaching in India there was an old farmer who had worked on his farm for most of his life supporting his wife and many children until he got too old to work. Since he was no longer able to work and support his family they kicked him out of his house. Being so old and unable to work of course it was extremely difficult for him to find food and shelter. So he had a very big problem. One day, while he was sitting by himself on the side of the road dejected and thinking over his troubles, he started crying profusely. Since there is nothing to block Buddha's omniscience Buddha could perceive him directly at that time. So Buddha went there and asked him, "What is the problem? Why are you crying?" And the farmer answered, "Up to now I have worked to raise my family. But since I am too old and weak and unable to work and help my family they have kicked me out onto the street so now I don't have any food or anywhere to go." In reply the Buddha told him, "You don't have to worry. Just come with me." With this the old man followed Lord Buddha to the monastery where they met with two of Buddha's disciples, Shariputra and Maugalyayana.

Buddha instructed Shariputra, his closest disciple, to make the old man a monk. If he became a monk he would have a place to stay and food to eat without any problem. Immediately Shariputra took him to his quarters and proceeded to examine him, checking to see whether he had the special virtue to achieve nirvana in this life or not. This kind of virtue we call *tar pa cha thün gyi ge tsa* (*thar pa cha mthun gyi dge rtsa*), which means the virtue accumulated that gives one the ability to achieve nirvana. Shariputra checked and checked but for the life of him he couldn't find any so, frustrated, he had no choice but to send this old fellow back out into the street as before.

From there the old man went to stay in a non-Buddhist monastery for several months. The first thing that he was given to learn by heart was the mantra "Om buru buru soha." Listening intently, he struggled to get the pronunciation right. When he got a hang of the first part "Om," and had memorized it, he straightaway forgot the second part, "buru buru soha." When he finally learned the second part by heart, he would immediately forget the first part. For three months it went on like this, but he still couldn't recite that entire mantra at one sitting. As a result these non-Buddhist scholars out of exasperation finally kicked him out of their monastery as well. As they were kicking him out of the gate they said, "If we were to allow such a foolish person as you to stay here in our monastery we would certainly become the laughing stock of the community!" With that they shut the gate hard behind him.

Once on the street again the old man began to cry inconsolably as before in sorrow over the desperate situation in which he found himself. Hearing his cries Buddha, a little surprised to see him again on the street went to him and asked, "What happened? Why are you sitting here again crying?" To this the old man responded, "The great Shariputra told me that I didn't have any *tar pa cha thün gyi ge tsa* so that it would be impossible for me to become a monk. Now I really don't have any place to go!" To this Buddha replied, "No, no, that's not so. You do have somewhere to stay. Don't worry. I will make you a monk."

With this Buddha accompanied the old man back to the monastery and told Shariputra once again to ordain him. Shariputra replied, "But he doesn't have any *tar pa cha thün gyi ge tsa*. I checked for a long, long time but I couldn't find any. Without that virtue I cannot make him a monk." To this Buddha replied, "It is true that from beginningless time up to now he has hardly collected any virtue. Yet though it may seem as if he has none, he certainly does have some very slight virtue. In one of his previous lives when he was born as a small black fly he happened to land on a cowpie where he sat for a time enjoying himself. It so happened that that cowpie was at the top of a hill. When it suddenly began to rain, as the water accumulated and began to rush down the hill in a torrent it carried that cowpie along with it. In the valley at the bottom of the hill there was a very nice stupa, which contained many relics of Buddhas and Arhats. As that water rushed into the valley it circled that stupa once and coursed down until it met with the river below. Since the fly was still sitting on that cowpie, he collected some slight amount of virtue because of having circumambulated the stupa, even though he had no intention of doing so. Nevertheless, it was a very fortunate opportunity for him to receive the blessing from the Buddhas' and Arhats' relics and collect some modicum of virtue. That was also a very, very long time ago."

So, from this we can realize how, though accumulated many kalpas ago virtue will not disappear or be destroyed but will remain ever undamaged. That is one quality. Additionally, though that virtue may be very subtle or quite insignificant, it can still ripen into a good result. Therefore, we should try to collect as much virtue as we can no matter how small it may seem. Also, whatever virtue we have collected from previous times will definitely eventually ripen, since the relationship between karma and its results is infallible. This is very important to realize.

ཡང་དེ་ཉིད་ལས། རྣམ་དཔྱོད་དང་ལྡན་པ་དག་གིས་ནི་ལམ་གྱི་ཐོག་མ་སྐྱབས་སུ་འགྲོ་བའི་སྒོ་ཙམ་ཞིག་ལ་ངེས་པ་གཏིང་ཚུགས་པ་ཚོལ་ན་ཡང་། རིགས་པའི་གཞུང་ལུགས་འདི་ཉིད་ལ་ཅི་ནུས་ཀྱང་བརྟེན་པར་བྱ་དགོས་ན། ལམ་གྱི་ལུས་ཡོངས་སུ་རྫོགས་པ་ལ་སྙིང་ནས་སྒྲུབ་པ་ལྷུར་ལེན་པའི་བསམ་པས་གཏིང་ཚུགས་པ་ཞིག་ཚོལ་ན། རིགས་པའི་གཞུང་ལུགས་འདི་ལྟ་བུའི་དོན་ལ་ཐོས་བསམ་གྱི་ཤེས་རབ་ཀྱིས་ངེས་པ་སྐྱེད་པ་མེད་མི་རུང་གི་ཡན་ལག་ཏུ་དགོས་པ་ལྟ་སྨོས་ཀྱང་ཞིག་དགོས་སྙམ་དུ་ཤེས་པར་བྱའོ།

If the wise, in seeking a deep understanding about the practice of refuge that they do at the beginning of every path find it necessary for this particular practice to rely as much as they can on these very logic texts, how much more necessary is it that they rely on them when, rather than just a heartfelt and devoted practice, they are seeking a more profound understanding of the entire body of the path. It would by untenable to think that they wouldn't gain understanding through listening wisdom and contemplation wisdom on the meaning [of Taking Refuge] as found in these logic texts.

Here, reference is being made to "taking refuge" (*skyab su 'gro ba*). All practices in the Buddhist field are based on taking refuge. First we take refuge and then begin to practice at our appropriate level. Fittingly, the first most important thing to do before every practice is to take refuge. In whom do we take refuge? We take refuge in the Buddha, Dharma, and Sangha. These are the objects in which we take refuge, although actual taking refuge is in our mind. Our main goal is to achieve our own three ratnas—Buddha, Dharma, and Sangha. To achieve these we need an infallible instructor or a person who has achieved that status such as Buddha Shakyamuni. Until we actually achieve our own Buddharatna, Dharmaratna, and Sangharatna, receiving instructions from other Buddhas like Buddha Shakyamuni and following them with our practice is like a great river that gets closer and closer to the destination of Buddha's great ocean. Finally, we end up combining with that ocean, which results in our having that very same quality.

When we take refuge we have to have skill, understanding, and knowledge, so that this achievement becomes possible. Everything is there ready and perfect. When students enter college, by practicing and studying every day, day by day, week by week, month by month, their river travels toward the "diploma" ocean. Achieving their diploma is like achieving cessation. Once they gain it, rather than check their knowledge others will ask what degree they have. When they say, "I have such and such a degree," the others will think, "Oh, you must be very knowledgeable." Similarly, once we surpass the earlier sufferings, we won't have to experience them again when we achieve cessation. Since Buddha taught us the method to achieve cessation, everything is ready. So what is missing? What are we lacking? We lack strong faith, effort, and knowledge. The very lack of these is like a strong rope holding us back, as if saying, "I need a foolish person like you to help me. Don't do it; don't do it," as it continues to pull us back.

When the intelligent (*rnam dpyod dang ldan pa*) practice the paths to achieve their goals, at the very beginning they take refuge. Why do they have to take refuge at that time? At the beginning of any practice of Buddhadharma we have to start with taking refuge. The object of taking refuge is our goal. Because this is our goal we have to practice to achieve it. This goal can be divided into three: the Buddha, the Dharma, and the Sangha. The Buddha, Dharma, and Sangha are of two kinds. The first kind is general Buddha, Dharma, and Sangha, which consists of an instructor, the instruction, and those who help us with our practice. The second kind is the practitioner's own goal, our own Buddhahood, or Buddharatna, our own Dharmaratna, and our own Sangharatna. The main purpose is for us as practitioners to achieve our own main goals, our own Three Ratnas. We can understand this logically. If only others achieve Buddhahood and we don't we are going to remain suffering in samsara. So, if we wish to become free we for our part have to achieve our own goals. No one can do this for us.

When we achieve our own Buddhahood of course we won't have any obstacles. When we achieve our own Dharmaratna we will have achieved our own real omniscience and ultimate cessations. When we achieve the Sangharatna we will have achieved the Arya's path and no longer be a *prtagyana*, or ordinary person. To achieve our own Sangharatna we have to perceive our own real nature directly within our meditation. Since these are the practitioner's real goals, any practice we do should be directed toward that purpose.

In order to gain a deep understanding about this and to fortify our belief, first we have to study and try to find out how to achieve this goal. What is the best way to do this? The best way is by studying *logic texts such as these* (*rigs pa'i gzhung lugs*), which is referring here specifically to the great Dignaga's logic text, *Compendium of Means of Valid Cognition* or *Pramanasamuccaya*, and in general to its commentaries composed by Indian and Tibetan scholars. We have to rely on such texts as these to gain a broad and deep understanding. We have to study logic, think about logic, and practice the logical system all the time. How? Through using good reasons to find out whether the object we are pursuing is correct or incorrect, right or wrong.

At the beginning of any practice we have to have a very deep and broad understanding about taking refuge. First we must practice taking refuge and then begin whatever practice we do according to our level. If it is necessary to do this at the beginning of any practice needless to say it is all the more necessary when we are about to begin practicing the generation stage and completion stage practices of Tantra. If we don't have a profound and extensive understanding of taking refuge in our mind before starting all such practices, they will lack their specific result and just be a waste of time. This is a very important point.

Logic texts (*rigs pa'i gzhung lugs*) are those that teach about correct valid reasoning and are the kind of texts we should study. We can gain wisdom gradually first through listening and thereafter through thinking and checking. This way we become absolutely assured (*nges pa rnyed pa*) in our mind about what it is we are practicing and acquire a thorough understanding of our main goal and the entire body of the path (*lam gyi lus yongs su rdzogs pa*). Not only are these texts necessary but without them we won't be able to achieve our goal at all.

Don't forget this instruction. Keep it firmly in your mind as long as possible until you achieve your goal. You cannot hear about a subject like this very often.

གང་གི་ཚེ་ཕྱིའི་གོ་རྒྱུ་ཙམ་གཙོད་པ་དང་།   ཚེ་འདིའི་སྣང་ཤས་འབའ་
ཞིག་ལྷུར་ལེན་པའི་ཐབས་སུ་གཞན་དང་ཁ་གཤགས་འགྱིད་པ་ཙམ་
ཀྱི་ཡན་ལག་ཏུ་རིགས་པའི་གཞུང་ལུགས་དག་ལ་ཐོས་བསམ་གྱིས་
འཇུག་ཅིང་།   སྙིང་ནས་སྒྲུབ་པ་ལྷུར་ལེན་པའི་བསམ་པ་ཅུང་ཟད་

ཅིག་སྐྱེས་པ་དེའི་ཚེ་རིགས་པའི་བརྟག་དཔྱད་དོར་ནས་བླུན་པོ་དག་གི་
ཚིག་ཙམ་ཞིག་སྐྱབས་སུ་བཟུང་སྟེ།

If we contemplate and study such logic texts as these just to gain some limited understanding of logic and devote all our efforts merely toward acquiring the fantasies of this life or solely for the sake of winning in debate with others, and then when we become a little more serious about practicing we all but abandon our endeavors at logical analysis and reasoning, at that point we will just be taking refuge blindly like silly followers of words.

When we study logic our purpose is not just so that we will be able to say, “I know something about logic because I studied it once.” We also don’t study logic just to gather the frivolous benefits of this life (*tshe ’di’i snang shas*), to gain this life’s goals such as to become famous as a debater and so forth, nor should we study in order to get the better of our opponent and win debates with others. Real practitioners should never treat the study of logic in this manner.

By studying and contemplating logic texts at some point we will gain very good knowledge through using good reasons, which will shake our mind and make our understanding very firm and clear. When some people begin to study logic and come to have a pretty good grasp of it, they often realize that they really want to practice Dharma seriously (*snying nas sgrub pa lhur len pa’i bsam pa chung zad cig skyes pa*) and think, “I must achieve the essence of Dharma.” So they begin to devote themselves to practicing renunciation, bodhichitta, and right view. However, once they seriously begin these practices they feel that they can ignore and even abandon logic altogether (*rigs pa’i brtag dpyad dor nas*). In short, when they are about to actually engage in their main practice they give up logic. This is completely wrong and an enormous mistake.

THE FOOLISH BELIEVE THAT LOGIC IS NOT NECESSARY FOR PRACTICE

Some practitioners may even think, "Though I know a little bit of logic, since my teacher never taught it much and rarely mentions it, I don't think it's necessary for my practice. When I meditate I don't have to think about logic." Such words uttered within the field of Buddhism are a display of the utmost foolishness (*blun po dag gi tshig*).

Practicing according to what someone says without having an understanding supported by logic is just blindly following others' words without apprehending the meaning. This does nothing but reveal an utter lack of wisdom. If we practice this way of course we will acquire nothing but a silly result.

ཚད་མས་གནོད་པ་འབའ་ཞིག་གི་དོན་མནོས་ཙམ་གྱིས་ཡིད་ལ་བྱེད་
པའི་སྙིང་རུས་འབའ་ཞིག་གིས་ཐར་པ་དང་ཐམས་ཅད་མཁྱེན་པའི་གོ་
འཕང་ལོ་འམ་ཟླ་བའམ་ཞག་གི་དུས་ཚོགས་ལ།

[If someone were to instruct you] promising that you can achieve the state of liberation and omniscience in a year or a month or even a day just by hard work and perseverance alone through focusing on something that is invalidated by valid cognition...

If something is invalidated by valid cognition it means that it doesn't exist. Why? Because the definition of an existent is that which is validated by valid cognition (*tshad mas grub pa yod pa'i mtshan nyi*). For example, if I were to say that I have horns on my head such a statement can be refuted by valid cognition because I do not have horns on my head. Valid cognition disproves their existence. If I did have horns on my head you would be able to see them, but of course you don't. Therefore they don't exist on my head. Even the words themselves are a little ridiculous. So, the belief that the study of logic only serves those purposes mentioned above but is not necessary when engaging in real practice is rejected by valid cognition (*tshad mas gnod pa*). On the contrary, you most definitely need logic when practicing.

An example of this kind of trust in something that doesn't hold up to logic is the following. When we first arrived in India the Indians would call all the monks "Dalai Lamba" and all the women "Dalai Lambi." In many Indian languages the grammatical rule for the gender of words is very strict so, in this case, they were adding vowels to accord with male or female gender. To call all Tibetan males "Dalai Lamba" and all Tibetan females "Dalai Lambi," when they are not is silly because the words don't accord with reality. Instead of being proved by valid cognition, on the contrary, valid cognition refutes them.

Practicing something that is unacceptable to valid cognition can be characterized by the following. "I don't know whether what I am practicing is correct or not but I heard about it and am just following the words that I heard in order that I might gain something someday." If after examining with logic you find that what you are meditating on doesn't exist but you continue to meditate on it believing that through practicing with strong perseverance (*snying rus 'ba' zhig gis*) following those empty words you will gain the ultimate goal, that is simply nonsense.

མངོན་དུ་བྱེད་པར་ཁས་འཆེ་བའི་རྨོངས་པ་ལུག་ལྟར་ལྐུགས་པ་དག་
གི་ཏ་ཙང་ཡང་མི་འཚམས་པའི་ལོག་པའི་གཏམ་ལ་ཞེས་ལྡན་དག་གི་

རྣ་བ་དགབ་པར་བྱའོ། །ཞེས་ཐམས་ཅད་མཁྱེན་པ་མཁས་གྲུབ་དགེ་ལེགས་དཔལ་བཟང་པོས་གསུངས།

To this the omniscient Kaydrup Je Gelek Pelsang Po said: "He is as foolish as a sheep who promises such a thing. Not only is that foolish instruction, it is also terribly misguided. If you're intelligent and happen to hear such reckless instruction you should cover your ears!"

To say that one doesn't need logic when actually practicing the paths and that just by practicing diligently for several months or years one can definitely achieve nirvana and Buddhahood, is completely erroneous instruction and, whoever teaches such an instruction is completely foolish. How foolish? *As foolish as a sheep* (*lug ltar lkugs pa*). So, what should you do if you have some wisdom and happen to hear someone giving such an instruction? You should cover your ears (*rna ba dgab par ja'o*)! These are the words of one of the greatest of Je Tsong Khapa's disciples, Kaydrup Je.

གངས་རིའི་ཁྲོད་ཀྱི་ཤིང་རྟའི་སྲོལ་འབྱེད་ཆེན་པོ་འཇམ་དབྱངས་མིའི་རྣམ་རོལ་རྗེ་ཐམས་ཅད་མཁྱེན་པ་ཙོང་ཁ་པ་ཆེན་པོས་གསུང་ལས་ཀྱང་། བྱང་ཕྱོགས་འདི་ན་ཚད་མའི་གཞུང་ལུགས་ལ། །སྦྱངས་དང་མ་སྦྱངས་དུ་མ་མགྲིན་གཅིག་ཏུ། །མདོ་དང་སྡེ་བདུན་ཀུན་ལ་བྱང་ཆུབ་ཏུ། །བགྲོད་པའི་ཉམས་ལེན་རིམ་པ་ཡོད་མིན་ཟེར།

> *The great renovator [of the teachings] in the Land of Snow Mountains, Manjushri masquerading in human form, the omniscient Lord Tsong Khapa said as well: "In this northern country of ours [we hear] many people, both schooled in logic and those unschooled, unanimously agreeing that there is no instruction on how to practice the paths and reach Buddhahood in either [Dignaga's]* 'Compendium of Means of Valid Cognition' *or in [Dharmakirti's]* 'Seven Treatises [on Logic].'"

The great renovator (*shing rta'i srol 'byed chen po*) referred to here is Je Tsong Khapa. The Dharma that was taught by Buddha, commented upon by both Nagarjuna and Chandrakirti, and by which many sages achieved Vajradhara's status, initially arrived in Tibet in a very pure state. Later, of course, year after year these teachings got mixed up with other teachings so that they no longer remained pure. This happened time and again in both India and Tibet. These teachings remained impure until the great Je Tsong Khapa came and renewed them, separating the mistaken teachings from the true ones and made them sound once again. Je Tsong Khapa's quality is so extraordinary that he is considered an emanation of Manjushri who appeared in human form as a lama. He is not an ordinary person but *an omniscient Lord*, meaning that all objects appeared to him directly.

Many people study and learn very diligently but nevertheless fail to put the knowledge they acquire into their mind as they would medicine. Je Tsong Khapa is referring here specifically to those practitioners of *the northern country* or Tibet. He is saying that both the scholars of logic and non-scholars agreed unanimously that neither Dignaga's logic work *Compendium of Means of Valid Cognition* (*tshad ma mdo*) nor the famous *Seven Treatises on Logic* by Dharmakirti, which we call *Tsema De Dün* (*tshad ma sde bdun*),[49] the commentaries to the work of Dignaga, treat the subject of how to practice the paths and reach Buddhahood. What does this mean?

In my own experience I also have heard many people say such things as "the study of valid cognition, or logic, is strictly for debate." Formerly in India the prevalent view was that it was only necessary to learn logic in order to defeat other non-Buddhist scholars and that if one really wanted to gain nirvana and Buddhahood the study of logic wasn't necessary. Even many of the great scholars who spread such silly words had studied logic themselves but still made the same foolish noise.

།འཇམ་པའི་དབྱངས་ཀྱིས་ཕྱོགས་ཀྱི་གླང་པོ་ལ། །དངོས་སུ་འདི་བརྩམས་འདི་ནི་མ་འོངས་དུས། །འགྲོ་བ་ཀུན་གྱི་མིག་ཏུ་འགྱུར་རོ་ཞེས། །གསུང་གི་གནང་བ་སྩལ་བའང་ཚད་མར་བྱེད།

Manjushri said directly to Dignaga as encouragement: "You must compose this book [Compendium of Means of Valid Cognition] *for, in the future, it will be of great benefit*

[49] Dharmakīrti's *Seven Treatises on Valid Cognition* include: (1) Analysis of Relations; (2) Ascertainment of Valid Cognition; (3) Commentary on (Dignāga's) "Compendium of Valid Cognition"; (4) Drop of Reasoning; (5) Drop of Reasons; (6) Proof of Other Continua; (7) Reasoning for Debate (1) *'Brel pa brtag pa'i rab tu byed pa* 2) *tshad ma rnam par nges pa* 3) *Tshad ma rnam 'grel gyi tshig le'ur byas pa* 4) *Rigs pa'i thigs pa zhes bya ba'i rab tu byed pa* 5) *gTan tshigs kyi thigs pa zhes bya ba rab tu byed pa* 6) *rGyud gzhan grub pa zhes bya ba'i rab tu byed pa* 7) *rTsod pa'i rigs pa zhes bya ba'i rab tu byed pa*

to many beings and serve as their wisdom eyes." And Tsong Khapa said, "That is what I too believe."

Manjushri directly encouraged Dignaga to compose his logic text saying that it would be of great benefit to many people in the future. Je Tsong Khapa here agrees implying that it corroborates with his own experience.

།དེ་ནི་མི་རིགས་སྨྲ་བའི་ཕྱུལ་བྱུང་དུ། །མཐོང་ནས་ལྷག་པར་ཚུལ་དེར་དཔྱད་པ་ན། །ཚད་མ་ཀུན་ལས་བཏུས་པའི་མཆོད་བརྗོད་དོན། །ཚད་མ་གྲུབ་པར་ལུགས་འབྱུང་ལུགས་ལྡོག་གིས། །རྣམ་གྲོལ་དོན་དུ་གཉེར་བ་བཅོམ་ལྡན་འདས། །ཚད་མར་བསྒྲུབས་ཤིང་དེ་ལས་དེ་ཡི་ནི། །བསྟན་པ་ཁོ་ན་ཐར་འདོད་འཇུག་ངོགས་སུ། །ངེས་པ་གཏིང་ནས་རྙེད་པས་ཐེག་གཉིས་ཀྱི། །ལམ་གྱི་གནད་ཀུན་འདྲིལ་བར་རིགས་ལམ་ནས། །ལེགས་པར་ཐོན་པས་ལྷག་པར་དགའ་བ་རྙེད། །ཚུལ་འདི་བསམས་ཤིང་འདུན་མ་ལེགས་ནས་གདའ། །བཀའ་དྲིན་ཆེའོ་རྗེ་བཙུན་མཁྱེན་པའི་གཏེར། །ཞེས་གསུངས་སོ།

When [Je Tsong Khapa] realized the superb foolishness of such statements that say that these logic texts don't teach about nirvana and Buddhahood and that one doesn't need logic to reach the ultimate goal, he set about diligently examining them and found the meaning in the homage to the Buddha from Compendium of Means of Valid Cognition. *He realized that the Bhagavan is a perfect teacher for those striving to become liberated from samsara, which is shown in forward and reverse manner, and how Buddha became a valid person, how he is an infallible instructor, and how his infallible teachings are the only entry point for those desiring liberation. He understood profoundly that the path of reasoning is what combines a complete instruction of all the crucial points of the two vehicles. In this regard [Je Tsong Khapa] said, "When I realized that all the teachings come nicely through [those logic texts], I was elated and very eager to study and check them. When I think about it I did a very good job toward gaining my ultimate goal and this realization came strictly through the great kindness of Manjushri."*

That (*de ni*) is referring to the idea that when we practice we don't need logic and that the *Compendium of Means of Valid Cognition* and Dharmakirti's *Seven Treatises on Logic* don't in any way teach about nirvana and Buddhahood. This is *the most superb of worst teachings* (*mi rigs smra ba'i phul byung*), which is expressed in a poetically ironic way to mean "this is the worst kind of statement anyone could make!" When Je Tsong Khapa saw this he engaged in a very serious study of the logic texts and examined them thoroughly and found just the opposite to be true. Where did he find this refutation? He *found the meaning in the homage to the Buddha from* Compendium of Means of Valid Cognition (*tshad ma kun las btus pa'i mchod brjod don*). In this homage, as we saw, it mentions how Buddha became a valid person or authority, someone who can be relied on and trusted. Why is Buddha like that? Because he chose to be born in the position he was born in and later turned into a valid person. How? Through excellent causes. For what is he a perfect person? For teaching and leading all beings to Buddhahood. This is what Je Tsong Khapa understood to be the meaning of the homage Dignaga's logic text.

In a forward manner (*lugs 'byung*) means that in the homage "*tse mar gyur pa dro la pen she pa / tön pa de shek kyob la chak tsel te*" each of the qualities of Buddha are described one by one and taught in a successive manner. *Reverse manner* (*lugs ldog*) means that these qualities are described in reverse order by taking the effect and explaining the cause that brought about this result.[50]

Buddha, the Bhagavan (*bcom ldan 'das*) is an infallible instructor *for those who want to achieve liberation* (*rnam grol don du gnyer ba*) from samsara. Why? Because of his teachings on the way things are. Most ordinary people simply follow others' words and have trust in what they hear. For

---

[50] In the *Ocean of Reasoning* it states: "The meaning of 'forward manner and 'reverse manner' is the following: The first is the way to explain the words of the homage to Buddha according to the order of the words as they appear and the latter is the way to explain the same words in reverse order. When explained according to the first way we see that excellence of practice arises from excellence of intention. From that very excellence of intention comes the abandonment that is one's own purpose, which precipitates the *Sugata* possessing the three characteristics. This precipitates the *Protector* who liberates others from their suffering due to the power of having achieved complete cessation. The progression is revealed by presenting the manner in which subsequent results arise from previous causes.

The second mode, that is, the homage to Buddha as explained in reverse order, is as follows: Consider the Buddha Bhagavan, he is a *Sugata* who possesses the three extraordinary qualities of realization, because he is a *Protector* and *Teacher* who taught others all the methods regarding what to abandon and what to adopt in the Four Arya Truths without having to rely upon other teachers. As a way of benefiting others he had to have first completed the excellence of practice, which required that he be utterly habituated for a long time to the wisdom that realizes no-self, thereby gaining the three extraordinary qualities of realization. In order for this to have occurred, he had to have had great compassion that is *dedicated solely for the benefit of all sentient beings*. Due to that great compassion he completed his long-term habituation to the wisdom that realizes no-self for the sake of others. The reverse order is shown by giving reasons beginning with the effects and working backwards. Teaching this way causes us to understand the proof through presenting the preceding causes."

instance, "He said such and such so I believe it." However, this is not in accord with the way of Buddhist belief, which should not come so easily. Is Buddha an infallible teacher or not? If someone were to say, "Buddha is an infallible teacher," we might ask, "How do you know he's an infallible teacher?" They might answer with, "Because he said such and such." That is not proof enough for us since we need some kind of verification supported by good, sound reasons. On the contrary, we have to study deeply, examine carefully, and then begin to practice his teachings. If these teachings award us a perfect result, by that we can realize that the teacher must be a perfect, infallible instructor.

His teachings are the only door for those wishing to achieve liberation (*bstan pa kho na thar 'dod 'jug ngogs*). If we wish to achieve nirvana and Buddhahood we have to have some way to begin, somewhere to enter, some field of teaching and practice. Buddha's field and system of teaching is the perfect entry point for those wishing to achieve liberation. In order to practice these teachings first we have to *gain a deep and firm understanding* (*nges pa gting nas*) about them. How? Such understanding can be acquired especially through the use of logic. When we investigate we come to realize that many people who have followed and practiced Buddha's teachings have achieved the goal of nirvana and Buddhahood. If that's the case, why then shouldn't we also be able to achieve our goal if we practice sincerely and diligently? Everything we need, the complete instruction *of the two vehicles* (*theg gnyis kyi*), all the crucial points of their paths are condensed in the logic texts (*lam gyi gnad kun 'dril bar rigs lam*) and taught in detail without excluding anything. If we want to enter the Hinayana or Mahayana paths, at whatever level, all of the crucial points, complete with instuctions, are in those texts. We can understand all of these through using the path of reasoning. Je Tsong Khapa himself is saying that he gained such knowledge through the path of reasoning. If we study nicely, the meaning of all of those teachings will come through these texts (*legs par thon pas*). When Je Tsong Khapa realized this he became exceedingly delighted to study and examine those logic texts (*lhag par dga' ba rnyed*). Additionally, when he thought further about it he realized that by so doing he had made tremendous strides toward his ultimate goal and had not made a mistake (*'dun ma legs nas gda'*). This is the thought that came to Je Tsong Khapa's mind. How did this happen? *Through the great kindness of Manjushri* (*bka' drin che'o rje btsun mkhyen pa'i gter*). Such is the way that Je Tsong Khapa describes his experience with the logic texts.

Logic is so important. Once you've learned logic you have to use it all the time and examine everything through it. In Tibet, there is an expression that goes: *ge she la la tsö pa ma kyab*, *ka wa la la dun ka ma kyab*, which means "Arguing with a Geshe is like hitting your head against a pillar for you're bound to lose" since they practiced logic a lot. Logic is truly critical. Whenever logicians hear something they immediately think of reasons to verify whether or not what they hear is true.

།མཁས་གྲུབ་གྱི་ཚད་མ་སྡེ་བདུན་ཡིད་ཀྱི་མུན་སེལ་ལས། སྐྱེས་བུ་སྐྱེས་
མ་ཐག་གི་རིག་པ་དེ་ལ་རྒྱུ་མེད་ན། རེས་འགའ་ཡིན་པས་གནོད་ལ།
རྒྱུ་ཡོད་ན། རྟག་པའམ་མི་རྟག་པ་གང་ཡིན། རྟག་དངོས་ཡིན་ན་ཡུལ་
དང་དུས་གང་ལ་ཡང་། །མ་ཁྱབ་པ་མི་སྲིད་པས། འབྲས་བུ་དང་རྗེས་
སུ་འགྲོ་ལྡོག་ངེས་པ་མི་སྲིད་དོ། །ཕྱི་མ་ལྟར་ན། ཐེམ་རིག་གང་རུང་
ལས་གཞན་པའི་དངོས་པོ་ལས་སྐྱེ་བར་མི་འཐད་པས། གང་རུང་ལས་
སྐྱེ་དགོས་ལ། །ཐེམ་པོས་ཉེར་ལེན་བྱེད་ན། དབང་པོ་དང་བཅས་

པའམ། ཕྱི་རོལ་གྱི་བེམ་པོ་ཡིན། དང་པོ་ལྟར་ན། དབང་པོ་ཀུན་
ཚོགས་པ་རྒྱུར་དགོས་སམ། གང་རུང་རེས་ཚོག །དང་པོ་ལྟར་ན།
མིག་དབང་མ་ཚང་ན་ཡང་ཡིད་བློ་མི་སྐྱེ་བར་འགྱུར་ལ། ཕྱི་མ་ལྟར་ན།
མིག་ཤེས་བཞིན་དུ་རྟོག་པས་ཀྱང་གཟུགས་གསལ་བར་འཛིན་པར་
འགྱུར་ཞིང་།

In Clearing Away the Darkness of the Mind: A Commentary to [Dharmakirti's] "Seven Treatises of Logic" *Kaydrup Je says: "If a newly conceived baby's mind had no cause, since mind would arise occasionally there is a logical fault [for whatever arises occasionally is impermanent and therefore must have a cause]. If it does have a cause, is that cause permanent or impermanent? If [that mind] were a permanent entity it would be impossible for it not to be present everywhere at all times. Therefore, the definite relationship between [cause] and effect – contingent upon the presence or non-presence of a cause– would not be possible. If it is the latter [i.e., that newborn mind is an impermanent entity] it is impermissible that it arise from anything other than matter or mind [and not from a non-associated compositional factor, for example]. Given that it must arise from either of these, if matter is its substantial cause, is it sensitive matter accompanied by the sense faculties or external matter [unrelated to the sense faculties]? If it is sensitive matter accompanied by the sense faculties, must all the sense faculties be present as a collection [when it acts as mind's cause] or is a single sense faculty sufficient [since there is no third choice]? If all the sense faculties must be present as a collection, should the eye faculty be faulty in some way, for instance,*

> *then the mental faculty would not arise. Or, if a single sense faculty were sufficient [when it acts as mind's cause], the discursive mind would be able to apprehend form as clearly as if it were the eye consciousness.*

Now we have reached a crucial part in this text. Above is a quotation from Kaydrup Je's work, *Clearing Away the Darkness of the Mind* (*tshad ma sde bdun gyi rgyan yid kyi mun sel*), which is a commentary on Dharmakirti's *Seven Treatises on Valid Cognition* (*tshad ma sde bdun*). In Kaydrup Je's passage he mentions the first moment (*skyes ma thag*) of mind of a newborn baby. Many Westerners and ordinary people of Tibet consider the being that comes out of the womb and begins crying "Waaaa Waaaa!" a new baby. From the Buddhist perspective we consider a new baby a being that has just been conceived in the mother's womb. Just prior to the conception of that ordinary being's mind, that mind was an intermediate state being or *bardo wa*. Before being a *bardo wa* that mind belonged to a previous life. Once that mind takes conception in the mother's womb, the *bardo wa* is no more and has started the next life.

The very first moment of that new being's mind is of course mind and an entity. If that is so, it should have its own causes. There is no such thing as an entity without a cause, since all entities come from their own causes. The quotation asks, does the first moment of that mind have a cause or not? If that mind does not have its own unique cause then it is not acceptable that mind arises sporadically or occasionally (*res 'ga' ba*). What does this mean? Take snowstorms or rainstorms, for example. Do they occur all the time without pause or not? They occur sometimes but not all the time. So, whatever only occurs sometimes, or occasionally, cannot be permanent and unchanging. Why not? Because what is permanent requires no causes for its existence. On the other hand, anything that requires a cause is impermanent as do those things that occur *occasionally*. Since the mind of that newborn being occurs occasionally, insofar as there are times when it appears and times when it does not appear, it must have a unique cause to bring it about. If something occurs *occasionally* (*res 'ga' ba*) it must have its own causes.

You have to keep the subject (*chos can*) of this argument in mind and not lose it. The subject here is "the very first moment of an ordinary new being's mind." If in fact that mind is an occasional or impermanent entity and has a cause, is that cause permanent or impermanent? According to logic there is no such thing as a permanent cause. Whatever is a cause must be impermanent. If mind's cause is impermanent the result, mind, should also be impermanent. If it were possible for there to be a permanent, unchanging result, we would not be able to justify something's being in some places at one time and other places at other times. For example, some people often come here to New Jersey to sell flowers and others occasionally come to buy them; however, these sellers and buyers are not here all the time and in every place, hence, we can say that they are *occasional.*

Relationship (*rjes su 'gro ldog*) can be described this way. Smoke is related to fire. Smoke comes as a result of fire. If there is no fire, there is no smoke. This is the general rule. *Dro* (*'gro*) means that if there is fire smoke will *come*. *Dok* (*ldog*) means that if the *opposite* is the case, if there is no fire, smoke will not come. *That definitive relationship would not be possible* (*rjes su 'gro ldog nges pa mi srid*) if mind's cause were permanent. For example, if smoke's cause –fire– were permanent, we would not be able to determine that smoke is only present when fire is present since, if fire were permanent, both fire and smoke would be permanently present.

Now, if the cause of mind is impermanent is that cause matter (*bem*) or mind (*rig*)? The definition of matter or form is "that which is suitable as form." Matter (*bem*) and form (*gzugs*) are synonyms. The cause of mind must be one or the other. What is it that is other than these two, that is, something that is neither matter nor mind? A non-associated compositional factor (*ldan min 'du byed*). What is an example of a non-associated compositional factor? Me, me, me. I am neither form nor mind, but I eat and drink and walk and sit, and do many other things. If I can act in these ways I must be a thing nevertheless. The genitive, or possessive, case is very useful to illustrate this. Many people say such things as, "*My* mind is not clear." What is the difference between "me" and "my"? "Me" is a noun and "my" shows the possessive or genitive case. Whenever we say "my mind," this implies that I am the basis of mind, but not mind itself. My mind is one of my characteristics, but I am not my mind. My physical body, being form, is the same, as demonstrated by saying "my head," "my limbs" and so forth. These are my characteristics and I am their basis. Basis and characteristics are different. This is a description of a non-associated compositional factor, which is defined as "a thing that is neither form nor mind" (*gzugs shes gang rung ma yin pa'i dngos po*)

There are many kinds of non-asociated compositional factors, which can be illustrated this way. What is today's date? February 15th. Is this date a kind of form or a kind of mind? If you check carefully you will discover that it is neither, because, being a date or time, it has neither form nor is it mental. If you say that time is not real, you would have to agree that the year is not real. If the year is not real then your age is not real. What, you don't have any age? Why ever then would we ask the question, "How old are you?" This is just one example of a non-associated compositional factor. There are many. So, if mind has a unique cause, that cause must be either matter or mind (*gang rung las skye dgos*).

If that mind's unique cause is matter, is it sensitive matter? What does "sensitive" mean here? Some forms are related to the senses, or sensitive, and some are not. "Sensitive" means that if somebody touches that matter there is feeling. So, matter is classified into that which is sensitive and that which is not sensitive. Generally speaking, rocks and wood are not sensitive objects. If somebody were to put their finger in your eye what would you feel? You would immediately say "Ouch!" because that eye is associated with feeling and therefore is a kind of sensitive matter. If the unique cause of mind is sensitive form, then does it arise containing all the five senses or just one? We have five different types of sensitive form: eye, ear, nose, tongue, and body. If mind arises from sensitive form, should all of these sense faculities gather together to produce that first moment of mind or not? If those five sense faculties gather together, they should produce five different kinds of mind. Why wouldn't they? However, there is only one single first moment of mind. If you say that only some of them gather together, but not necessarily all of them, just like a blind person who lacks the eye sense faculty, or a deaf person who lacks the ear sense faculty, in the absence of one of those faculties, how would it be possible to produce a sound mind?

Here we are using a method of logic to determine the exact nature of the cause of that first moment of mind. Accordingly we have determined that the cause of mind must be mental. If the cause that produced that first moment of mind is mental, to whom did that mental cause belong? That mental cause had to have pertained to someone. To whom then? That mental cause of mind pertained to the previous life's mind. Now you have to say, "Wow, now I understand that there must have been a former life!" You have to go step by step in the logical process. If this life had a former life, then that former life must also have had a former life, and so on. Previous lives and previous minds are beginningless. You will never be able to find the very first mind. This is one way of proving the existence of previous lives. Once you discover with logic that you have had a former life you can use the same method to investigate whether or not you will have a future life.

Why should it be so essential to discover whether or not we have had previous lives and will have future lives and whether or not mind is physical, mental, or a non-associated compositional factor? This is essential because it is pertinent to the homage to Buddha that says, "I take refuge in the one who became perfectly valid, to the one who wishes only to benefit beings." Buddha Shakyamuni practiced compassion for eons and eons in many, many lifetimes and finally gained ultimate compassion. We too have to do the same. If we do this we will realize that this life is not useless but very useful in helping us to achieve ultimate compassion in the future.

According to Sutrayana it is impossible to begin such a practice and achieve Buddhahood within this lifetime. Therefore, we have to practice over many lifetimes. If so, we have to have practiced in many former lifetimes and will have to practice in many future lives to accomplish this. If we have that basic knowledge we can perfectly understand the nature of karma. Otherwise, just by using the word "karma" our knowledge will be anything but perfect. We have to practice virtue as much as we can within this life so that our future lives will become better and better, since this is karma's unfailing system. Volcanoes cannot burn our karma; nor can the kalpa-ending fire nor torrents of water nor rivers nor oceans wash it away since karma's system is absolutely firm. Just as good karma is infallible, so too is bad karma. Therefore, we should do as much as we can to collect virtue within this life, which will serve as a great help to our future lives. If we desist from collecting new bad karma and reduce the bad karma we have already collected previously, we will be giving great meaning to our future lives. Our suffering will diminish in the future and our happiness will increase. If we believe in former and future lives and make our belief firm through the use of logic it will definitely help us to understand and trust karma's infallible system and influence the quality of our actions so that they become better and better.

When logicians debate about previous lives and try to prove their existence they use the argument given above, namely, that the cause of the very first moment of mind of a being just conceived in the womb is mental. This is like Congressmen debating in Congress over the Crime Bill, for example. At that time the Crime Bill is the basis of debate (*chos can*) or the subject they are debating. Here our basis of debate is previous lives.

To understand this subject better first we have to know about main causes and main results, secondary causes and secondary results, and about common causes and common results. For example, whereas the main cause is the seed, the secondary causes are fertilizer, heat, water, air, and earth. Fertilizer, for its part, acts as a common secondary cause since it can be used in various fields where different seeds are planted and function in the same way with regard to all of them. Why do we gather different crops from different fields? Although the fertilizer, water, heat, and so forth are the same and used in common with all the fields, the seeds that are planted in the different fields, being the main cause, yield different crops. These different crops are the unique result of the unique causes that are the various seeds. Secondary causes are what help flowers and plants to grow and give their fruit.

In a mother's womb very many different secondary causes gather together. However, if the main cause is not present a new being cannot be conceived. That new baby's first moment of mind is produced only by its unique cause, which is mental. That mental cause creates a mental result. A mental result is produced immediately after the mental cause that precedes it. Unique mental causes should have preceded this mental cause as well since causes and effects proceed in a successive continuum, one moment following the next. This is how the system of cause and effect works. Hence, the unique cause of mental must be mental and not the physical elements or any other such things. A mental result is only preceded by a mental cause.

To whom did that mental cause belong, to the parents or to the new baby's mental continuum? If that mental cause belonged to parents who happened to be very intelligent, that newborn baby's mind should likewise be very intelligent. There is no reason why it shouldn't be like that. However, if the parents are intelligent and the baby turns out to be very stupid or vice versa, which does sometimes happen, how could that be possible? If the previous mind that is the cause of the newborn baby's mind belonged to the parents, did it belong to the father's mind or to the mother's mind? Are the father and the mother the same individual? They cannot be the same since they are different individuals. So, that new baby's mind cannot belong to either the father or the mother. This is how we can understand that the previous mind did not belong to the parents but had its own unique cause, which is a previous mind that belonged to its previous life. Because of this one can say that there is a previous life. That previous life's first mind also came from the mind of its previous life and so on.

By now we should understand that the very first moment of a newly conceived baby's mind was caused by its unique previous life's mind. Why is it of such importance to prove this? Understanding this is a practitioner's main key and principal objective. Why? Do we have hope to achieve nirvana someday? Do we hope to achieve Buddhahood someday? We will easily say, "Of course we do." This hope is a practitioner's main goal. Now, do we hope to achieve nirvana and Buddhahood within this life? This is a little more difficult to answer. Finally, if we cannot achieve nirvana and Buddhahood within this life why then are we struggling so hard and putting so much effort into achieving it? If it were possible to achieve the goals only within this life, all our activities would be wasted if we failed to gain this objective in this life.

This is the main key. We have to know that even though we may not be able to achieve these goals within this lifetime, practicing all the time, day and night, to achieve nirvana and Buddhahood still is not a useless waste of time. We don't necessarily have to achieve these goals within this life but can achieve nirvana and Buddhahood sometime in the future. Therefore, our daily hard struggle to achieve these goals is not just useless effort. In order to achieve nirvana and Buddhahood we have to improve our knowledge and reduce our bad deeds. By so doing, of course at some point we will finally desist from doing bad deeds altogether and will eventually achieve ultimate knowledge. We have to continue to make progress all the time by abandoning bad deeds to achieve that knowledge. Since many Buddhas achieved their goals that way by practicing for eons and eons, it is not useless to practice. Even though we may not achieve our goals within this lifetime we can get better and better and make progress.

If we improve our life now, our future life will be much better and our activities will become much easier to perform. Then, in the life following that one it will get even easier and easier and become better and better. So the basic key is the following: "Since we will have future lives we will have future knowledge and future goals." We can see that having practiced to accumulate good causes in previous lives is not useless since good results have come in this very life. This is what it means to put seeds (*bag chags*) into our mind. At some point those seeds will combine with secondary causes and produce their results and gradually progress. We can tell from this life of ours that our previous life did very well for us.

What will our future life be like? We can tell what kind of life we will have in the future by the kind of thoughts we are thinking and actions we are doing right now; in short, by our motivation and our behavior. How do we go about proving that virtuous practice in this life will help our future life? Since each thing has its own unique quality, so too does mind. The unique quality of mind is such that if we guard it, care for it, and control it, it will get better and better. If we neglect it, it will go astray. That is the nature of mind, the unique quality of what is mental.

We can understand this better through testing it with our experience. For example, if we don't like somebody and consider that person our enemy, initially, whenever that person is nearby our mind becomes unhappy. Gradually that unhappy mind will combine with secondary causes and turn into anger. It is quite easy to "improve" this anger by thinking such thoughts as, "Yeah, that person did that to me last year. Then, just last week he did something else to me. And yesterday he did the very same thing to me again!" That is how we strengthen our anger until it reaches a feverish pitch. Anger also reveals the unique quality of what is mental. Since anger is mental it has the power to develop. Sometimes on TV we see illustrations of how anger gets extremely hot and out of control. For example, there are couples who start out by calling each other "honey." Later that "honey" turns a little bit sour like a lemon. Then that lemon heats up and starts to burn. Along with that come the secondary causes such as guns and kitchen knives and many other weapons until finally they produce a very bad result. We can see from this how anger can grow, and when accompanied by secondary causes, it can increase and get hotter and hotter because that is its nature, that is its natural quality.

In order to reverse this process we have to learn how to avoid anger's secondary causes and focus on this specific quality of mind and on the general nature of samsara. The best way to go about doing this is to practice patience, love, and compassion instead of improving that anger. If we practice this way, of course the mind will gradually get better and better, softer and softer, gentler and gentler until it will render us the temporary result of peace and happiness. The ultimate result is that in future lives we will have genuine love and compassion and become a better person in general. This is how Buddha practiced to achieve compassion and how we too have to develop it and bring it to perfection. Can we be sure that we will progress if we practice this way? Yes, of course, because that is mind's quality, which we understand by logic.

Not only can we gain compassion in this way but in the same fashion we can get rid of suffering. No one likes suffering; everyone likes happiness. Where does suffering come from? Where does happiness come from? They both come from their own unique main causes and secondary conditions. If we don't like suffering we have to try to remove the unique causes of suffering. Even though we may want to remove the unique causes of suffering yet don't know what they are, all we can do is respond to our suffering in the American way by shrugging our shoulders and saying, "I don't know what to do. I don't know what the causes of suffering are."

The unique cause of suffering is self-grasping ignorance (*bdag 'dzin ma rig pa*). Whatever suffering we have, from beginningless time up to now, was arranged strictly by that principal ignorance. Where is this ignorance located? Is it somewhere in this room? If so where? In my mind? In your mind? Every ordinary person has that ignorance in their mind. We have to realize that. Since ignorance is mental and therefore not visible, it is difficult to recognize. If we make a big effort to realize it we may possibly catch it.

If I were to tell you that among the people in this room some of you are very cruel and others are very stupid, the thought immediately will arise in your mind, "Who, me? Me? Me? Does he mean me?" The "me" that immediately comes to mind is the king of ignorance. This implies that one mental event arose in your mind when you had the thought of "me." That "me" is both the subject and the object of that mental event. Even though that "me" never wishes to have suffering and only wants happiness, that "me" acts in a backward way by destroying the causes of happiness as if it were an enemy and even diligently collects the causes for further suffering.

How do we collect the causes for suffering? We collect bad causes by doing things by body, thinking things in the mind, and saying things by speech. If we examine all of these activities carefully we will discover that they are designed and directed exclusively for our own purpose and never motivated toward the purpose of others. We spend all our time thinking only of our own benefit and never thinking about the benefit of others. This kind of mind that arranges affairs for our own benefit and ignores the benefit of others is the main cause of all our suffering. We behave this way all the time, from morning till night, day after day, month after month, year after year, life after life. The one who manages all of them, like their king, is this mental event that incessantly thinks "me, me, me."

Why do we call this mind "ignorance"? We call it ignorance because its main direction, its way of collecting and arranging deeds, are completely wrong and improper. There are times when this ignorance can even seem rather friendly toward us, and other times when it becomes quite brutal and forceful. No matter what we still fall under its control. If we wish to put an end to our suffering we have to fight with this ignorance and eliminate it altogether. Is this possible? If we think about it we will discover that it is indeed very possible. If we try we can eventually destroy that self-grasping ignorance.

Let's take self-grasping ignorance as the subject of debate. How can we destroy it? We have to find a good reason. One reason we can offer for why it can be destroyed is because it has its own powerful antidote. That is a correct reason. Whatever has a powerful direct antidote, when that antidote is present, the two will not be able to abide together in the same place. For example, wherever it is extremely hot we can put an end to that heat by using an air conditioner. Wherever it is very cold we can put an end to that cold by using a heater. Both the heat and the cold are powerful antidotes for eliminating their opposites. In the same way we can also destroy the ignorance in our mind if we practice applying a unique powerful antidote. What powerful antidote is this? Shunyata, or the wisdom that perceives the opposite of ignorance.

What do I have here in my hand? A mala.[51] You can see it quite clearly. Now what do you see? You can't see the mala because I have removed it from your sight. Just by removing the object, the subject, that is, the mind that perceives it, will automatically be removed as well. Similarly, as soon as wisdom refutes the object of that ignorance i.e., the untenable inherently existent self, the subject, or ignorance that holds that erroneous object, will automatically disappear. When the

[51] A string of Buddhist prayer beads.

object is no longer there, the subject can no longer remain. If we remove the object of ignorance that appears to our mind by means of practice and logic, the subject will definitely disappear. Only wisdom can eliminate that ignorance.

Our understanding has to be very firm. If we gain wisdom perceiving the correct object, which is the opposite of ignorance, ignorance will not be able to abide in our mind any longer. If ignorance is no longer there, we have eliminated it through practicing wisdom. Once we have eliminated ignorance through practice we have achieved freedom from ignorance. This is the meaning of nirvana. When we achieve nirvana we automatically become an Arhat, since we have become free of samsara's suffering.

As soon as we understand this vital point, we will realize that freedom from suffering does in fact exist. That freedom, or ultimate peace, is nirvana. By getting rid of ignorance through the practice of wisdom at some point we will complete our practice and become free. Becoming free is the status of cessation. It is in this way that we come to realize that cessation also exists and that it is possible to achieve it. There are perfect causes to achieve wisdom and a proper way to practice it. Hence, nirvana and wisdom are not just mere words but objectives that are actually achievable through practice.

This is how Buddha practiced. He practiced compassion for eons and eons until he finally achieved ultimate compassion, which urged him to help other beings, and then he practiced wisdom for eons and eons, which helped him to serve beings unerringly.

ཕྱི་རོལ་གྱི་ཞེམ་པོས་ཉེར་ལེན་བྱེད་ན། ཡན་ལག་ཅན་གྱི་རྫས་ཀྱིས་
སམ། རྡུལ་ཕྲན་གྱིས་བྱེད། དང་པོ་ལྟར་ན། ཡན་ལག་ཅན་གྱི་
རྫས་ཆ་བཅས་ཆ་མེད་གཉིས་ལས། ཆ་བཅས་ཀྱིས་ཉེར་ལེན་བྱེད་

ནེ། ཆ་ཐམས་ཅད་ཚོགས་པ་རྒྱུར་དགོས་སམ། གང་རུང་རེས་ཆོག་ཅེས་པ་གོང་གི་རིགས་པའི་ཚུལ་གྱིས་ཁེགས་ལ། ཡན་ལག་རྣམས་ལས་རྫས་ཐ་དད་པའི་ཡན་ལག་ཅན་ཆ་མེད་ཀྱིས་ཉེར་ལེན་བྱེད་ན། གདོང་གོས་ཀྱིས་བསྒྲིབས་ན། ཡན་ལག་གཞན་རྣམས་ཀྱང་གོས་ཀྱིས་བསྒྲིབས་པ་དང་། གཞན་མ་བསྒྲིབས་ན་བསྒྲིབས་མ་བསྒྲིབས་ཆ་གཉིས་སུ་ཡོད་པར་འགྱུར་བ་དང་། བསྒྲིབས་མ་བསྒྲིབས་ཆ་གཉིས་ཡན་ལག་རྣམས་ལ་ཡོད་ཀྱི་ཡན་ལག་ཅན་ལ་མེད་ན། གདོང་གོས་ཀྱིས་བསྒྲིབས་པའི་ཚེ་ཡན་ལག་ཅན་གྱི་གདོང་གསལ་བར་མཐོང་བར་ཐལ་ལ། དེ་བཞིན་དུ་གཡོ་མི་གཡོ་དང་། ཁ་བསྒྱུར་མ་བསྒྱུར་སོགས་ལ་སྦྱར་བའི་རིགས་པ་རྣམས་ཀྱིས་གནོད་དོ། །རྡུལ་གྱིས་ཉེར་ལེན་བྱེད་ན། རེ་རེ་བས་ཀྱང་ལྟོས་མེད་དུ་སྐྱེ་ན། ཡིད་རྟོག་དུ་མ་ཅིག་ཅར་སྐྱེ་བར་འགྱུར་ལ། ཀུན་ཚོགས་དགོས་ན། རྡུལ་ཕྲན་གཅིག་མ་ཚང་ན་ཡང་མི་སྐྱེ་བར་འགྱུར་རོ། །མཐའ་གཞན་འགོག་པའི་རིགས་པ་དེ་དག་ལ་བརྟེན་ནས་ཤེས་པས་ཉེར་ལེན་བྱེད་པར་གྲུབ་ལ། དེ་ལ་ཡང་རང་རྒྱུད་ཀྱིས་བསྡུས་པ་དང་། གཞན་རྒྱུད་ཀྱིས་བསྡུས་པ་གཉིས་ལས། གཞན་རྒྱུད་ཕ་མ་ལྟ་བུའི་ཤེས་པས་

དངོས་ཀྱི་ཉེར་ལེན་བྱེད་ན། ཕ་བཟོ་མཁས་པ་དང་བླུན་པ་སོགས་ཀྱི་བུ་ཡང་དེ་ལྟར་ཐལ་བའི་སྐྱོན་འབྱུང་བས། རང་རྒྱུད་ཀྱི་རིག་པ་སྔ་མ་ཁོ་ནས་ཉེར་ལེན་བྱེད་པར་འགྱུར་ལ། དེ་ལྟར་ན་རིག་པའི་ཡ་མཐའ་དང་མ་མཐའ་ཐུག་པ་མེད་པ་དང་། སྐྱེ་བ་སྔ་ཕྱི་ཡོད་པ་ལེགས་པར་གྲུབ་པ་ཡིན་ནོ། །ཞེས་དང་།

Now, if external matter [that is unrelated to the sense faculties] is the substantial cause [of mind], is it a substance that is a discrete whole or is it made up of subtle particles? If the first is the case, does that discrete whole have parts or is it partless? If that discrete whole having parts were the substantial cause [of mind], then either each part would be the cause of the collection of all those parts or it would be enough to have any one or a combination of them to make up the whole, an argument which has already been refuted above concerning things that arise sporadically. If a partless whole which is a different substance from that which makes it up were to serve as the substantial cause [of mind], then if I were to cover my front with my robe, would my other parts be covered as well? If my other parts are not covered, then there would have to be two parts; that is, the part not covered and the part covered. If that which has two parts –covered and not covered– has no parts, it would follow that whenever my front part was covered I would still be able to see my front part clearly. Just as applied to covered and uncovered things, all other opposite things would be damaged by the same reasoning, for example, with regard to moving and not moving or turning your face and not turning it, and so forth.

Now, if the substantial cause [of mind] is made up of subtle particles, many conceptions would arise simultaneously since each of those particles would not rely on the others. If they must all arise as a complete collection, should one of those particles fail then the whole could not arise. In proving the substantial cause of consciousness by relying upon this kind of reasoning that refutes all other extremes [we might ask], is [this mind] a part of our own continuum or is it a part of others' continuum? If the direct substantial cause of consciousness comes from another's continuum, let's say from the continuum of our father or mother, there would arise the faulty consequence that the child would have to be either intelligent or foolish in accord with its father's [or mother's] mind, for instance. So, if it is the case that the substantial cause of consciousness is only a previous mind of its own continuum, given that this continuum is endless insofar as there is a lack of any break between later moments and earlier moments of mind, we can confidently prove that former and future lives exist.

ཡང་དེ་ཉིད་ལས། བཅོམ་ལྡན་འདས་ཀྱིས། དགེ་སློང་དགེ་གམ་མཁས་རྣམས་ཀྱིས། །བསྲེགས་བཅད་བརྡར་བའི་གསེར་བཞིན་དུ། །ལེགས་པར་བརྟགས་ལ་ང་ཡི་བཀའ། །བླང་བར་བྱ་ཡི་གུས་ཕྱིར་མིན། ཞེས་བཀའི་དོན་ཀུང་ཚད་མས་བསྒྲུབ་དགོས་པར་གསུངས་པའི་ཕྱིར་དང་།

Again, in the same text Kaydrup Je quotes the Buddha Bhagavan as saying, "Those monks are virtuous and intelligent who thoroughly examine my speech in the same way one would test gold by burning and cutting. Do not accept my teachings only out of respect for me!" From this [we can see how] Buddha taught the necessity of establishing the meaning of his speech by valid cognition.

རྗེ་བཙུན་བྱམས་པས་ཀྱང་། ཆོས་ བཟང་ རིགས་ པས་ རྣམ་ དཔྱད་ བསམ་པ་ཅན། །རྟག་ཏུ་བདུད་ཀྱིས་བར་ཆད་བྱེད་པ་མེད། །ཅེས་ གསུངས་ཤིང་། དབུ་མ་བསྟན་བཅོས་ལ་འཇུག་པ་ལས་ཀྱང་། སོ་ སོ་སྐྱེ་བོ་རྣམས་ནི་རྟོག་པས་བཅིངས། །མི་རྟོག་རྣལ་འབྱོར་པ་ནི་གྲོལ་ འགྱུར་བས། །རྟོག་རྣམས་ལོག་པར་གྱུར་པ་གང་ཡིན་དེ། །རྣམ་པར་ དཔྱོད་པའི་འབྲས་བུར་མཁས་རྣམས་གསུངས། །ཞེས་གསུངས་ལ།

Also, as the reverend Maitreya says, "It is good philosophical technique to examine everything you learn with logical reasoning. Should you do that you will never fall under the influence of demons." As [Chandrakirti] also states in his treatise Entering the 'Middle Way,' *"Ordinary people are bound by discursive thought. / Since yogis see [the real nature of reality] directly, they will become liberated. / Whatever erroneous thoughts there are, / Scholars agree that [the discovery of their real nature is] a result of careful logical examination.*

According to Maitreya's quotation, whenever we study and practice it is very good Dharma practice (*chos bzang*) to examine everything with logical reasoning and continually ask, "Why is this so? What is the reason for that?" Whenever we engage in analyzing something, first we have to ask the question "why?" and proceed to draw accurate conclusions by finding correct reasons. We have to establish everything we've learned through correct reasoning (*rigs pas rnam dpyad bsam pa can*). If we establish everything through sound logical reasoning, demons will never be able to influence and obstruct us through their harmful blessings (*rtag tu bdud kyis bar chad byed pa med*); they will not be able to change our mind, because we have established everything with sturdy logic.

This use of sound logical reasoning is further upheld by Chandrakirti in his Madhyamika text. To understand this quotation first we have to know the difference between conceptual (*rtog pa*) and non-conceptual (*rtog med / mi rtog*). The conceptual can in general be classified into two: correct conceptual and incorrect conceptual. "Conceptual" mind means a kind of subjective mind that grasps its object indirectly and not directly. For example, do you know who President Clinton is? Yes, of course you do. The type of mind that "knows" President Clinton is conceptual. This type of mind is what we call a *dön chi* (*don spyi*) or general mental image that conceives something indirectly. A general image is an appearance to the mind, in this instance, the image of President Clinton. If I were to say "Mr. Clinton," immediately a general image of him comes to your mind appearing in his form. However, that image is not actually President Clinton since he is not really standing here in front of you. He just appears to your mind as if he were real. Nevertheless, you have a perception of him *through* that appearance. This conceptual mind is valid insofar as there is a President Clinton that exists as you perceive him. If you were to go to Washington and visit the White House and see President Clinton directly, the perception you have upon meeting him is a direct perception (*mngon sum*) and is no longer conceptual (*rtog pa*), since you are seeing him directly. Therefore, "non-conceptual" (*rtog med / mi rtog*) means that it is direct perception (*mngon sum*).

The basic thesis here is that if we want to become free from samsara and thus from every kind of suffering, we have to be able to perceive our real nature. Without perceiving our real nature we cannot become free from our samsara's sufferings. The wisdom we gain when studying or when contemplating after class and trying to perceive our real nature are classified into two kinds of wisdom: listening wisdom and checking wisdom. These two wisdoms we can acquire right now in class and after class. They are forms of conception (*rtog pa*), that is, we can perceive our real nature indirectly through a general mental image.

If I ask you individually, "Are you a self-existent person?" you will think, "He is asking me, me." You have to use your wisdom: "I cannot be a self-existent person because, in the first place, I have parents. Since without my parents I could not exist and be here as this person, I am reliant upon them." This means that your real nature is reliant upon other things for its existence and so is not self-existent. Hence, your real nature is the opposite of being a self-existent person since it is dependent. Therefore, your real nature is the emptiness of being a self-existent person. You can prove this by using the logical reason that you are reliant upon other things for your existence and due to that you cannot be a self-existent person. Your real nature is the opposite of being a self-existent person, that is, you are empty of being self-existent.

If you try to go a little deeper, following the Madhyamaka method, it will protect you from falling into one extreme. If you go still a little deeper it will protect you from falling into the other extreme. Madhyamaka means "center," standing in the middle between two extremes. One way of being free from self-existence is being free of the following extreme view: "If it is not self-existent, then it cannot exist." That is one extreme. To refute this we have to think: "I am an emanation of my real nature. My real nature appeared as 'me.' I can talk, listen, eat, and do many things. I am an appearance of my real nature and so I exist. I am real." By understanding this you do not fall into the one extreme of nihilism. Now, even though you are right here acting as a listener, an eater, a doer, a worker, a goer, and so forth, you are still not self-existent but free of self-existence. Self-existentlessness is your real nature, which emanates you as a goer, an eater, a worker, and so forth. You are still produced from causes and therefore not a permanent, unreliant entity. This is how we gain the meaning of Madhyamaka, which, as I said, means standing in the middle of these two extremes.

Now, if I were to ask you, "Do you realize your real nature?" You will see that you have gained knowledge just now in this class. The kind of knowledge you have just gained is a conceptual understanding (*rtog pa*) of your real nature. Although you may not be able to perceive your real nature directly at present, you can understand it by means of a general mental image and through using the reason that your real nature relies upon other things for its existence and so is empty of self-existence. Even though it is empty of self-existence, you are still a worker, a listener, a thinker, and the like.

Try not to forget this general mental image and go meditate on it to perceive your emptiness. In your meditation you will gradually get closer and closer to your real nature until finally you will perceive your real nature directly without that mental image in the same way as you might see the President directly by going to the White House. When you perceive your real nature in this way while meditating, you will have gained a non-conceptual image (*mi rtog*).

Practitioners such as yogis (*rnal 'byor pa*) become liberated from samsara by putting an end to that general mental image and gaining a direct perception of their real nature. Great scholars and sages unanimously agree that becoming liberated from samsara's suffering and achieving the ultimate happiness is the result of examining their real nature through the use of logic and profound meditation, until at some point they perceive it directly.

རིགས་པ་ལ་མི་བརྟེན་པར་ཚིག་ཙམ་གྱི་རྗེས་སུ་འབྲང་བ་དག་དབང་པོ་རྟུལ་པོ་དད་པའི་རྗེས་སུ་འབྲང་བ་ཞེས་འཕགས་པའི་གང་ཟག་ཐམས་ཅད་ལ་གྲགས་པའི་ཕྱིར།

It is very well known among Aryas that those who don't rely on reasoning are just followers of words. Such dull-minded practitioners are the so-called "Followers through faith."

FOLLOWERS THROUGH FAITH

Among scholars there are two very famous expressions: followers through faith (*dad pa'i rjes 'brang ba*) and followers of Dharma (*chos kyi rjes 'brang ba*). The first may be described as follows. If we had heard that someone was a very noble, well-educated person, and we believed those words without checking with logic to determine whether or not that person truly did have those qualities, we would be considered "followers through faith." Such are the practitioners who believe in something, practice it, and try to achieve its goal without examining it thoroughly but simply by following a mere description. This kind of follower is described above as *followers of dull faculties* (*rjes su 'brang ba dag dbang po rtul po*). These gain belief by following other people's words rather than checking what they hear with their own logical knowledge. In contrast, the person with sharp wisdom will not follow another's words so easily, but will rely upon his own wisdom.

བླང་དོར་གྱི་གནས་ལ་རིགས་པས་རྣམ་པར་དཔྱོད་པ་ནི། ཆོས་ཀྱི་རྗེས་སུ་འབྲང་བ་ཞེས་མཁས་པས་བསྔགས་པ་ཡིན་ནོ།

Those who carefully examine the points of what to do and what not to do with logical reasoning are so-called "Followers through Dharma" and the ones the scholar-sages praise.

We call such a person who does not just follow another's words but investigates his object with reasoning and his own wisdom "a person of sharp faculties (*dbang po rno ba*)." Dharma (*chos*) here refers to what these persons of sharp faculties establish in their own mind, namely, the correct object of their pursuit, through using their wisdom and logical power of reasoning (*blang dor gyi gnas la rigs pas rnam par dpyod pa*). In this way they are able to realize what they should practice and what activities they should give up. Both of these objects must be correct, otherwise it can prove to be a little funny. For example, we might be trying very hard to abandon compassion and be diligently endeavoring to develop our anger, finely honing it so that it gets worse and worse. Therefore, the object we are striving after should clearly be the correct one. In short, we should definitely be like the latter practitioners of sharp faculties and not like the followers through faith. This is how the term "blind faith" arises. Blind faith implies that we don't know what the object of our pursuit is. Scholars praise the one who has the ability to check with wisdom and logic the object to be abandoned and the object to be practiced.

FOLLOWERS THROUGH DHARMA

།དེ་ཉིད་ཀྱི་ཕྱིར་རིགས་པས་དཔྱོད་པ་ལྷུར་ལེན་པ་ནི་རྟོག་གེའི་ཚུལ་ཡིན་པས། གྲོལ་བ་དོན་གཉེར་ལ་མཁོ་བ་མ་ཡིན་ནོ། །ཞེས་བྱ་

བའི་བདུད་ཚིག་ལ་ཤེས་ལྡན་དག་གིས་རྣ་བ་དགབ་པར་བྱོས་ཤིག
།ཞེས་དང་།

For that reason be diligent and examine [everything] with logical reasoning. This is the way of debaters. Whenever you hear someone say: "You don't need logic to attain liberation," know these are a demon's words. So, Wise Ones, cover your ears!

Many people say that studying, learning, and practicing logic is useless especially for practitioners of meditation. On the contrary, those practitioners who lack logical knowledge merely practice by closing their eyes like a chicken or standing dead-still like a rabbit. Such practitioners can remain very still for a long time without focusing on a main object of practice or any correct goal. This kind of meditation is nothing but a complete waste of time. They even go so far as to say, "If you want to become liberated, all you have to do is meditate. You can become liberated by that alone. You don't need logic." That kind of statement is nothing but *a demon's words* (*bdud tshig*). *So, Wise Ones, cover your ears* (*shes ldan dag gis rna ba dgab par byos shig*). Should you ever hear anyone say such things to you, you have to tell them, "Please, be quiet!"

Okay, thank you. We will stop here.

[*Note: Given that Rinpoche gave no further teachings on this text from this point on, in deference we have chosen to leave the remainder untranslated and include the original at the end of this volume for those knowledgeable in Tibetan who would like to read it in its entirety.*]

******

།འདི་ནི་བློ་དམན་འགའ་རེ་ལ་ཕན་ཕྱིར་དུ། དགེ་བའི་བཤེས་གཉེན་ཆེན་པོ་སྐྱོར་དཔོན་རིན་པོ་ཆེ་ནས་རྗེ་ཡབ་སྲས་ཀྱི་གསུང་རྣམས་ལས་བཏུས་ཏེ་ཕྱོགས་བསྒྲིགས་སུ་མཛད་པ་དགེ་ལེགས་འཕེལ།

In order to benefit those of lesser ability this text was compiled from the collection of works of the spiritual father and sons –Je Tsong Khapa, Gyeltsab Je, and Kaydrup Je– by the great spiritual friend Kyorbön Rinpoche.

May this be a cause for the increase of virtue.

ROOT TEXT

༄༅། །ཐར་འདོད་རྣམས་ལ་སྙིང་ལྟར་གཅེས་པའི་ཉེར་མཁོ་འགའ་ཞིག་བཞུགས་སོ། ། །།

ལེའུ་གཉིས་པའི་རྒྱ་ཆེར་བཤད་པ་རིགས་པའི་རྒྱ་མཚོ་ལས། ཚད་མ་མདོར། ཚད་མར་གྱུར་པ་འགྲོ་ལ་ཕན་བཞེད་པ། །སྟོན་པ་བདེ་གཤེགས་སྐྱོབ་ལ་ཕྱག་འཚལ་ཏེ། །ཞེས་གསུངས། ཕྱག་འཚལ་ཞེས་བྱ་བ་བཤད་པའི་གཞིའོ། །གང་ལ་ན་ཚད་མ་ལའོ། །ཚད་མ་ཇི་ལྟ་བུ་ལ་ཞེ་ན། །རྒྱུ་མེད་རང་བྱུང་གི་ཚད་མ་མ་ཡིན་གྱི། །རྒྱུ་ཕུན་སུམ་ཚོགས་པ་ལས་ཚད་མར་འཁྲུངས་པར་གྱུར་པ་ཞིག་ལའོ། །རྒྱུ་ཇི་ལྟ་བུ་ལས་ཚེད་མ་ཇི་ལྟ་བུའི་ངོ་བོར་འཁྲུངས་པ་ལ་ཞེ་ན། །རྒྱུ་བསམ་སྦྱོར་ཕུན་སུམ་ཚོགས་པ་ལས། འབྲས་བུ་དོན་གཉིས་ཕུན་སུམ་ཚོགས་པའི་ཚད་མར་འཁྲུངས་པ་ལའོ། །དེ་ཡང་རྒྱུ་བསམ་པ་ཕུན་སུམ་ཚོགས་པ་ནི། འགྲོ་ལ་ཕན་བཞེད་པ། ཞེས་པས་བསྟན་ཏེ། འགྲོ་བ་མཐའ་དག་སྡུག་བསྔལ་ལས་སྒྲོལ་བར་བཞེད་པའི་ཐུགས་རྗེ་ཆེན་པོའོ། །རྒྱུ་སྦྱོར་བ་ཕུན་སུམ་ཚོགས་པ་ནི། སྟོན་པ།

ཞེས་པས་བསྟན་ཏེ། བདག་མེད་མངོན་སུམ་དུ་རྟོགས་པའི་ཤེས་
རབ་འཁོར་དང་བཅས་པའོ། །འབྲས་བུ་རང་དོན་ཕུན་སུམ་ཚོགས་
པ་ནི། བདེ་གཤེགས། ཞེས་པས་བསྟན་ཏེ། དེ་ཡང་། ལེགས་
པར་སྤངས་པ་དང་། སླར་མི་ལྡོག་པར་སྤངས་པ་དང་། མ་ལུས་པར་
སྤངས་པ་སྟེ། ཁྱད་པར་གསུམ་ལྡན་གྱི་སྤངས་པ་ངོ་བོ་ཉིད་ཀྱི་སྐུ་
དང་། དེ་ཁོ་ན་ཉིད་མཁྱེན་པ་དང་། མཁྱེན་པ་བརྟན་པ་དང་། མ་
ལུས་པ་མཁྱེན་པ་སྟེ། ཁྱད་པར་གསུམ་ལྡན་གྱི་རྟོགས་པ་ཟག་པ་
མེད་པའི་ཡེ་ཤེས་གཉིས་ལ་བདེ་བར་གཤེགས་པ་ཞེས་བརྗོད་དོ།
།འབྲས་བུ་གཞན་དོན་ཕུན་སུམ་ཚོགས་པ་ནི། སྐྱོབ་ཅེས་པས་
བསྟན་ཏེ། རང་གིས་གཟིགས་པའི་མངོན་པར་མཐོ་བ་དང་། ངེས་
པར་ལེགས་པའི་ལམ་མཐའ་དག །རང་ཉིད་ཀྱིས་ཇི་ལྟར་གཟིགས་
པ་ལྟར་གཞན་ལ་བསྟན་པའི་སྒོ་ནས། འགྲོ་བ་སྡུག་བསྔལ་ལས་
སྒྲོལ་བའི་ཕྱིར་སྐྱོབ་པ་ཞེས་བྱའོ། ཞེས་དང་། ཡང་དཀོན་མཆོག་
གསུམ་ལ། ཚད་མས་དྲངས་པའི་ངེས་པ་རྙེད་པ་དེ་ཉིད་ནས་

བཟུང་སྟེ། སྐྱབས་སུ་འགྲོ་བ་ལན་ཅིག་ཙམ་བསྒོམ་པ་ཡན་ཆད་ཀྱང་། སྲིད་པའི་རི་བོ་ཕྱིར་བསྐྱིལ་བ་ལ་མཐུ་དང་ལྡན་པ་འགྱུར་གྱི་གཞན་དུ་ན། ཇི་སྲིད་དཀོན་མཆོག་གསུམ་གྱི་ཡོན་ཏན་ལ་གཞན་གྱི་ཚིག་ཙམ་གྱིས་རྗེས་སུ་འབྲངས་ནས་དད་པ་བསྒོམ་པ་དང་། དཀོན་མཆོག་གསུམ་ལ་ཡོན་ཏན་དེ་ལྟ་བུ་ཡོད་པའི་རྒྱུ་མཚན་རྙེད་པ་ལྟ་ཞོག །དཀོན་མཆོག་གསུམ་པོ་དེ་ཉིད་སྤྱིར་ཤེས་བྱ་ལ་ཡོད་པ་ཙམ་གྱི་རྒྱུ་མཚན་གང་ཡང་མ་མཐོང་བཞིན་དུ། ནན་གྱིས་སྐྱབས་སུ་འགྲོ་བའི་ཚིགས་སུ་བཅད་པ་དགྲངས་ཀྱི་ང་རོ་དྲག་པོས་དུས་ཚིགས་མང་པོའི་བར་དུ་བསྒྲགས་ཤིང་། རྒྱུ་མཚན་གང་ཡང་བཤད་དུ་མེད་པའི་མིག་གི་ཆུ་རྒྱུན་ནམ་མཁའི་ཆར་ལྟར་བབ་ཀྱང་། མཚན་བརྗོད་པ་ཙམ་ཞིག་གི་ཕན་ཡོན་འབྱུང་བ་ཟད་ཀྱི། སྐྱབས་འགྲོའི་དོན་གང་ཡང་ཚང་བ་མ་ཡིན་ནོ། །ཞེས་དང་།

ཡང་སྐྱེ་བ་སྔ་ཕྱི་མེད་དོ་ཞེས་གྲུབ་པའི་མཐའ་བཅས་ནས་སྨྲ་བའི་སྒྲོ་འདོགས་ཀུན་བཏགས་མངོན་གྱུར་རྒྱང་ཕན་སོགས་ཕྱི་རོལ་པ་ཁ་

ཅིག་མིན་པ་ལ་མེད་ཀྱང་། སྒྲོ་འདོགས་དེ་ཉིད་ཀྱི་ས་བོན་སོ་སོ་སྐྱེ་བོ་ཕལ་ཆེ་བ་ལ་ཡོད་དེ། སྔོན་སྐྱེ་བ་གཞན་དག་ཏུ་རྒྱང་ཕན་སོགས་ཀྱི་གྲུབ་པའི་མཐའ་དང་། གཞུང་ལུགས་ཐོས་པའི་སྟོབས་ཀྱིས་བག་ཆགས་བཞག་པར་གྱུར་པའོ། །དེ་ལྟ་མ་ཡིན་ན། གྲུབ་མཐས་བློ་མ་བསྒྱུར་བའི་སོ་སོ་སྐྱེ་བོ་དག་གི་རྒྱུད་ལ་མཐོང་སྣངས་གཏན་ནས་མེད་པ་ཐལ་བར་འགྱུར་རོ། །གཞན་ཡང་སོ་སོ་སྐྱེ་བོ་ཐ་མལ་པ་ཕལ་ཆེ་བ་དག་གི་རྒྱུད་ལ་སྐྱེ་བ་སྔ་ཕྱི་འཛལ་བའི་མངོན་སུམ་ཚད་མ་མི་སྲིད་ཅིང་། ཇི་སྲིད་སྐྱེ་བ་སྔ་ཕྱི་ཡོད་པར་སྒྲུབ་པའི་རྟགས་ཡང་དག་མ་མཐོང་བ་དེ་སྲིད་དུ་རྗེས་དཔག་ཀྱང་མི་སྲིད་ལ། དེ་ཉིད་འཛལ་བའི་ཚད་མ་རྣམ་པ་གཉིས་གང་ཡང་རྒྱུད་ལ་མ་སྐྱེས་པར། །དེ་ཉིད་ངེས་པའི་ངེས་ཤེས་སྐྱེ་མི་སྲིད་པའི་ཕྱིར། སྐྱེ་བ་སྔ་ཕྱི་མེད་པར་འཛིན་པའི་སྒྲོ་འདོགས་མངོན་གྱུར་ཡང་སྐྱེ་བ་ལ་འགལ་བ་མེད་པ་ཡིན་ནོ། །དེ་ལྟར། སྐྱེ་བ་སྔ་མ་དང་ཕྱི་མ་ཡོད་པའི་ངེས་ཤེས་རྒྱུད་ལ་མ་སྐྱེས་པ་དེ་སྲིད་དུ། བདག་ཉིད་ཀྱི་སྐྱེ་བ་དུ་མར་

སྙིང་རྗེ་ལ་སོགས་པའི་ལམ་བསྒོམས་པ་ལ་ངེས་པ་རྒྱུད་ལ་སྐྱེ་མི་སྲིད་ཅིང་། དེ་དག་སྐྱེ་བ་དུ་མར་བསྒོམས་པ་མི་སྲིད་པའི་སྒྲོ་འདོགས་གཅོད་མི་ནུས་ལ། དའི་ཕྱིར། ཇི་སྲིད་སྐྱེ་བ་སྔ་ཕྱི་ཡོད་པར་སྒྲུབ་པའི་རྟགས་ཡང་དག་ལ་བརྟེན་ནས་ངེས་པ་མ་རྙེད་པ་དེ་སྲིད་དུ། བདག་གིས་སེམས་ཅན་ཐམས་ཅད་ཀྱི་དོན་དུ་སངས་རྒྱས་ཐོབ་པར་བྱའོ་སྙམ་པའི་སེམས་བསྐྱེད་ཀྱང་རྣལ་མ་སྐྱེ་མི་སྲིད་ཅིང་། དེར་མ་ཟད། ཚེ་ཕྱི་མ་ངན་སོང་དུ་ལྟུང་གིས་དོགས་པ་དང་ལྷ་མིའི་གོ་འཕང་ཐོབ་པར་བྱ་བའི་ཕྱིར་དུ། དགེ་སྡིག་ལ་བླང་དོར་བྱེད་པའི་ཚུལ་ལ་ཡང་། ངེས་པ་རྣལ་མ་སྐྱེ་མི་སྲིད་པས། ཇི་སྲིད་སྐྱེ་བ་སྔ་ཕྱི་ཡོད་པར་རིགས་སྟོབས་ཀྱིས་མ་ངེས་པ་དེ་སྲིད་དུ། མངོན་པར་མཐོ་བ་དང་ངེས་པར་ལེགས་པའི་ལམ་ཐམས་ཅད་ཀྱི་སྒོ་འགགས་ཏེ་འདུག་པ་ཡིན་ནོ། །དེས་ན། འདི་ཉིད་ལ་ངེས་པ་རྙེད་པ་དང་། སྐྱེ་བ་སྔ་ཕྱི་མེད་པའི་སྒྲོ་འདོགས་ཆོད་པ་ནི། ལམ་སྒོམ་པ་ལ་ཐོག་མ་ཉིད་དུ་ཆེས་ཆེར་གལ་ཆེ་ཞིང་། ཞེས་དང་།

ཡང་སྐྱེ་བ་སྔ་ཕྱི་ཡོད་པའི་སྒྲུབ་བྱེད་དགོད་པ་ནི། ཐ་མལ་པ་སྐྱེས་མ་ཐག་གི་རིག་པ་དང་པོ་ཆོས་ཅན། རང་རྒྱུ་རིག་པ་སྔ་མ་སྔོན་དུ་སོང་སྟེ། རིག་པ་ཡིན་པའི་ཕྱིར། དཔེར་ན། ད་ལྟའི་རིག་པ་འདི་བཞིན་ཞེས་པའི་རྟགས་ལས། ཐ་མལ་པ་སྐྱེས་མ་ཐག་གི་རིག་པ་དང་པོ་ལ། རང་རྒྱུ་རིག་པ་སྔ་མ་སྔོན་དུ་སོང་བ་འགྲུབ་པས་སྐྱེ་བ་སྔ་ལ་ཡོད་པར་འགྲུབ་ཅིང་། དེ་ལྟར་གྲུབ་པ་ན་སྐྱེ་བ་སྔ་མ་ནས་འདི་ཉིད་དུ་མཚམས་སྦྱོར་བའི་ནུས་པ་དང་ལྡན་པ་མཐོང་བ་གང་ཡིན་པ་དེ་ལ། རྒྱུ་ལྷག་པོ་ཅི་ཞིག་ཡོད་པར་གྱུར་ཅིང་རྒྱུ་གང་ཞིག་མེད་པའི་རྒྱུ་མཚན་གང་གིས། ཐ་མལ་པའི་འཆི་སེམས་ཐ་མས་ཕྱི་ནས་རིགས་འདྲ་ཕྱི་མ་མཚམས་སྦྱོར་བ་མེད་པར་འདོད་པ་ཡིན་ཏེ། དེས་ན་རྒྱུ་ཚོགས་ཁྱད་པར་མེད་པའི་ཕྱིར་ཐ་མལ་པའི་འཆི་སེམས་ཐ་མས་ཀྱང་། རང་འབྲས་རིག་པ་ཕྱི་མ་མཚམས་སྦྱོར་བ་ཡོད་པར་གྲུབ་པ་ཡིན་ནོ། །ཞེས་དང་། ཡང་ཤེས་པ་སྔ་མ་ལ་ལྟོས་མི་དགོས་པར་འབྱུང་བ་ཁོ་ན་ལས་ཤེས་པ་སྐྱེ་བ་ཡིན་ན། གང་དུ་རྡོད་གཤེར་

ལ་སོགས་པ་སྐྱེ་བོ་སྐྱེ་བར་མི་འགྱུར་བའི་ས་སོགས་ཆ་དེ་འགའ་
ཡང་མེད་པར་འབྱུང་བ་ཡོད་ཙམ་གྱིས་ཤེས་པ་སྐྱེ་དགོས་པ་དེའི་
ཕྱིར། ས་སོགས་ཐམས་ཅད་སེམས་ཀྱི་བདག་ཉིད་ཀྱི་ས་བོན་དུ་
ཐལ་བར་འགྱུར་རོ། ཞེས་དང་། ཕྱི་མ་ཡོད་པའི་སྒྲུབ་བྱེད་ནི།
ཐ་མལ་པ་འཆི་ཁའི་བློ་རྟོག་པ་ཆོས་ཅན། རིག་པ་ཕྱི་མ་མཚམས་
སྦྱོར་ཏེ། སྲེད་པ་དང་བཅས་པའི་རིག་པ་ཡིན་པའི་ཕྱིར། ཐ་མལ་
པ་འཆི་ཁའི་དབང་པོ་ཐ་མ་ཆོས་ཅན། དབང་པོ་ཕྱི་མ་གཞན་
མཚམས་སྦྱོར་ཏེ། ལུས་ལ་སྲེད་པ་དང་བཅས་པའི་དབང་པོ་ཡིན་
པའི་ཕྱིར། འཁོར་བ་ཐོག་མ་མེད་པ་སྒྲུབ་པ་ནི། འདོད་ཆགས་དང་
ཞེ་སྡང་ལ་སོགས་པ་ཆོས་ཅན། རིགས་འདྲ་སྔ་མ་སྔོན་དུ་སོང་སྟེ།
རང་ཉིད་གོམས་པ་ལས་གོང་ནས་གོང་དུ་རང་གི་ངང་གིས་ཆེས་
གསལ་བར་སྐྱེ་བ་མཐོང་བའི་ཕྱིར། ཞེས་དང་། ཡང་འཁོར་བ་ཐོག་མ་
མེད་པར་གྲུབ་སྟེ། སེམས་ཅན་མིན་པ་སེམས་ཅན་དུ་གསར་དུ་
སྐྱེས་པའི་རིག་པ་མེད་པའི་ཕྱིར། དེར་ཐལ། རྣམ་ཤེས་ཀྱི་རྫས་

མིན་པ་རྣམ་ཤེས་ཀྱི་ཉེར་ལེན་དུ་རུང་བ་མིན་པའི་ཕྱིར། ཞེས་དང་། ཡང་དངོས་པོ་སྟོབས་ཞུགས་ཀྱི་རྟགས་ཀྱིས་ཐར་པ་སྒྲུབ་པའི་རིགས་པ་གཞུང་གི་ཆ་གོང་འོག་དག་ལས་གསུངས་པ་དག་གི་དོན་བསྡུས་པ་ནི་འདི་ཡིན་ཏེ། གང་རང་གི་རྒྱུའི་རིགས་ལ་གནོད་བྱེད་སྟོབས་ལྡན་དང་བཅས་པ་ཡིན་ན། རང་གི་རྒྱུན་གཉེན་པོའི་སྟོབས་ཀྱིས་ཟད་པ་ཡོད་པས་ཁྱབ་སྟེ། དཔེར་ན། གྲང་རེག་ལ་གནོད་བྱེད་སྟོབས་ལྡན་མཐོང་བས་གྲང་འབྲས་སྤུ་ལོང་བྱེད་ཀྱི་རྒྱུན་ཟད་པ་མཐོང་བ་བཞིན། ཟག་བཅས་ཀྱི་ཕུང་པོ་འདིའི་རྒྱུའི་རིགས་ལ་ཡང་གནོད་བྱེད་སྟོབས་ལྡན་མཐོང་བ་ཡིན་ནོ། །ཞེས་བྱ་བ་ནི། འགལ་ཟླ་དམིགས་པའི་དངོས་པོ་སྟོབས་ཞུགས་ཀྱི་རྟགས་ཡང་དག་གོ འདིའི་ཁྱབ་པ་མངོན་སུམ་ཚད་མས་གྲུབ་ལ། ཕྱོགས་ཆོས་སྒྲུབ་པ་ནི། གང་དངོས་པོའི་གནས་ལུགས་ལ་ལོག་པར་ཞུགས་པ་དེ་ལ། དེའི་རིགས་ལ་གནོད་བྱེད་སྟོབས་ལྡན་ཡོད་པས་ཁྱབ་སྟེ། དཔེར་ན་དུ་བ་དང་ལྡན་པའི་ལ་ལ་མེ་མེད་པར་འཛིན་པའི་བློ་འདོགས་

བཞིན། གང་ཟག་གི་བདག་ཏུ་འཛིན་པ་འདི་ཡང་དངོས་པོའི་གནས་ལུགས་ལ་ལོག་པར་ཞུགས་པའི་བློ་ཡིན་ནོ། ཞེས་བྱ་བའོ།

།གང་ཟག་གི་བདག་འཛིན་ལ་གནོད་བྱེད་མཐོང་བས་སྡུག་བསྔལ་གྱི་རྒྱུ་ལ་གནོད་པར་གང་གིས་འགྲུབ་ཅེ་ན། དེ་གཉིས་རྒྱུ་འབྲས་སུ་ངེས་པར་བྱེད་པའི་ཚད་མ་ལས་འགྲུབ་སྟེ། གོང་དུ་བཤད་པ་ལྟར། གང་ཟག་གི་བདག་ཏུ་འཛིན་པ་ལས་བདག་དང་མི་འབྲལ་བར་འདོད་པའི་སྲེད་པ་རང་སྟོབས་ཀྱིས་འདྲེན་པ་མངོན་སུམ་གྱིས་འགྲུབ་ལ། དེ་ལས་བདག་གི་བདེ་བ་ལ་སྲེད་པ་དང་། དེ་ལས་བདག་གི་བདེ་བ་སྒྲུབ་བྱེད་ད་ལྟར་གྱི་དབང་སོགས་དང་། ཕྱི་རོལ་གྱི་ཟས་གོས་ལ་སྲེད་པ་དང་། དེ་ལས་བདག་གི་བདེ་བ་སྒྲུབ་པའི་ཆེད་དུ་སྒོ་གསུམ་གྱི་ལས་མངོན་པར་འདུ་བྱེད་པ་དང་། དེ་ལས་འདོད་པའི་དོན་མ་ཐོབ་པ་དང་། མི་འདོད་པའི་དོན་ཐོབ་པའི་ཚོར་བ་སྡུག་བསྔལ་སྐྱེ་བ་མངོན་སུམ་ཚད་མས་གྲུབ་པའི་ཕྱིར། ཚེ་འདིའི་སྡུག་བསྔལ་དང་བདག་འཛིན་རྒྱུ་འབྲས་སུ་མངོན་སུམ་ཚད་

མས་གྲུབ་ལ། འཆི་ཁའི་སྲེད་པ་ལས་རིགས་འདྲ་ཕྱི་མ་མཚམས་སྦྱོར་བ་དངོས་སྟོབས་རྗེས་དཔག་གིས་གྲུབ་པ་ན། མཚམས་སྦྱོར་བའི་རིགས་འདྲ་ཕྱི་མ་དེ་ཉིད་ཀྱང་སྡུག་བསྔལ་ཞེས་ཐ་སྙད་དུ་བྱ་བ་ཡིན་པས་ཕྱི་མའི་སྡུག་བསྔལ་དང་རྒྱུ་འབྲས་སུ་དངོས་སྟོབས་རྗེས་དཔག་གིས་ངེས་སོ། རིགས་འདྲ་ཕྱི་མ་དེ་དོན་ལ་སྡུག་བསྔལ་ཡིན་ཡང་། ཚེ་འདིའི་ལས་ཉོན་དང་དེ་གཉིས་རྒྱུ་འབྲས་སུ་ངེས་པ་ཙམ་གྱིས་དེའི་སྟེང་དུ་སྡུག་བསྔལ་ལ་གྱི་ལྡོག་པ་དངོས་སྟོབས་ཀྱིས་ཇི་ལྟར་ངེས་ནུས་ཞེ་ན། ལས་ཉོན་གྱིས་འདུས་བྱས་པ་སྡུག་བསྔལ་གྱི་དོན་ལྡོག་ཏུ་དངོས་སྟོབས་ཀྱི་ཚད་མས་ངེས་ནུས་ལ། དེ་ངེས་ཟིན་མ་བརྗེད་པ་དང་། འཆི་ཁའི་ལས་སྲེད་ལས་རིགས་འདྲ་ཕྱི་མ་མཚམས་སྦྱོར་བ་རྗེས་དཔག་གིས་གྲུབ་པ་ན། རིགས་འདྲ་ཕྱི་མ་དེ་ཉིད་ལས་དང་ཉོན་མོངས་པའི་གཞན་དབང་ཅན་དུ་གྲུབ་པས་སྡུག་བསྔལ་གྱི་དོན་དང་ཐ་སྙད་གཉིས་ཀ་གྲུབ་པར་འགྱུར་བ་ཡིན་ནོ། །འོ་ན་གང་ཟག་གི་བདག་འཛིན་དངོས་པོའི་གནས་ལུགས་

ལ་ལོག་པར་ཞུགས་པ་ཡིན་པར་གང་གིས་སྒྲུབ་ཅེ་ན། དེ་ནི་གང་ཟག་གི་བདག་མེད་པར་ངེས་པ་ལས་འགྲུབ་པ་ཡིན་ནོ། །ཞེས་དང་། ཡང་ཚུལ་དེ་དེ་ལྟ་བུའི་སྒོ་ནས་གཉེན་པོའི་སྟོབས་ཀྱིས་སྡུག་བསྔལ་གྱི་རྒྱུན་མ་ལུས་པར་ཟད་པ་ཡོད་པར་དངོས་སྟོབས་ཀྱི་ཚད་མས་གྲུབ་ཅིང་། སྡུག་བསྔལ་གྱི་རྒྱུན་མ་ལུས་པར་ཟད་པའི་འགོག་པ་དེ་ཉིད་ལ་ཐར་པ་མྱ་ངན་ལས་འདས་པ་ཞེས་བྱ་བ་ཡིན་པས་ཐར་པ་ཡོད་པར་དངོས་སྟོབས་ཀྱིས་ལེགས་པར་གྲུབ་པ་ཡིན་ནོ། །ཚུལ་དེས་ཀུན་མཁྱེན་ཡོད་པར་སྒྲུབ་པའི་རིགས་པ་ཡང་ཤེས་པར་བྱ་སྟེ། འདི་ལྟར་གང་རིགས་ལ་གནོད་བྱེད་སྟོབས་ལྡན་ཡོད་པ་དེ་ལ་རང་གི་རིགས་གཉེན་པོའི་སྟོབས་ཀྱིས་རྒྱུན་ཟད་པ་ཡོད་པས་ཁྱབ་སྟེ། དཔེར་ན། མེ་སྟོབས་ཆེན་ཉེ་བས་གྲང་རེག་རྒྱུན་ཆད་པ་མཐོང་བ་བཞིན། ཆོས་ཀྱི་བདག་ཏུ་འཛིན་པའི་རིགས་ལ་ཡང་གནོད་བྱེད་སྟོབས་ལྡན་ཡོད་དོ། །ཞེས་བྱ་བ་ནི། དངོས་པོ་སྟོབས་ཞུགས་ཀྱི་རྟགས་ཡང་དག་ཡིན་ཞིང་། འདིའི་ཕྱོགས་

ཆོས་སོགས་སྒྲུབ་ཚུལ་ཡང་སྔ་མ་ཉིད་ལས་དཔགས་ཏེ་ཤེས་པར་བྱ་
ཞིང་། དེ་ལྟ་བུའི་རྟགས་ལས་ཤེས་བྱའི་སྒྲིབ་པ་མ་ལུས་པ་སྤངས་
པ་ཡོད་པར་གྲུབ་པ་ན་ཀུན་མཁྱེན་དངོས་པོ་སྟོབས་ཞུགས་ཀྱིས་
ལེགས་པར་གྲུབ་པ་ཡིན་ལ། ཞེས་དང་། ཡང་བརྩེ་བ་དང་ཤེས་
རབ་སོགས་ཆོས་ཅན། ཁྱོད་གོམས་པར་བྱས་ན་སེམས་ལ་རང་
གི་ངང་གིས་འཇུག་པར་འགྱུར་ཏེ། ཁྱོད་གོམས་པར་བྱས་པ་ན་
བློའི་རིགས་འདྲ་རེ་རེ་བསྐྱེད་པ་ལ་སྔར་དང་འདྲ་བའི་འབད་རྩོལ་
རེ་རེ་མི་དགོས་པར་འབད་རྩོལ་གཅིག་ལས་ཀྱང་རིགས་འདྲ་དུ་མ་
རྒྱུན་ལྡན་དུ་སྐྱེ་བའི་སེམས་ཀྱི་ཡོན་ཏན་ཡིན་པའི་ཕྱིར། དཔེར་ན།
མེ་ལ་སོགས་པས་ཤིང་དག་ལ་ཐལ་བར་སོང་གི་བར་དུ་ངང་གིས་
འཇུག་པ་དང་། དངུལ་ཆུ་དང་གསེར་ལ་སོགས་པར་འདུལ་སྦྱོང་
ལེགས་པར་བྱས་ཟིན་པ་རང་གི་ངང་གིས་གཡའ་དང་བྲལ་བའི་
རིགས་འདྲ་ཕྱི་མ་བསྐྱེད་པར་ནུས་ཀྱི། ཡང་དྲི་མ་དག་པར་བྱེད་
པའི་རྫའི་ཁ་སྦྱར་གཉིས་པ་ལ་ལྟོས་མི་དགོས་པ་བཞིན་ནོ། །ཞེས་

དང་། ཡང་གོམས་པ་དེ་དག་ལས་སྐྱེས་པའི་བརྩེ་བ་ལ་སོགས་པ་དེ་ཆོས་ཅན། རྟེན་བརྟན་པ་ཡིན་ཏེ། སེམས་ཀྱི་ངོ་བོ་ཉིད་དུ་སྐྱེས་པའི་ཡོན་ཏན་ཡིན་པའི་ཕྱིར། ཞེས་དང་། ཡང་ཚད་མར་གྲུབ་ཚུལ་ནི། བཅོམ་ལྡན་འདས་ཆོས་ཅན། གྲོལ་བ་དོན་གཉེར་ལ་ཚད་མའི་སྐྱེས་བུ་ཉིད་ཡིན་ཏེ། གང་གི་ཕྱིར་ན། བརྩེ་བ་ཆེན་པོ་མཐར་ཕྱིན་པས་གདུལ་བྱ་ལ་ལེགས་པ་འབའ་ཞིག་གསུངས་པ་དང་། ཡེ་ཤེས་ཁྱད་པར་གསུམ་ལྡན་ལས་བདེན་པ་ཕྱིན་ཅི་མ་ལོག་པ་འབའ་ཞིག་གསུང་བར་མཛད་ལ། དེ་དག་གི་སྒྲུབ་བྱེད་སྙིང་རྗེ་ཆེན་པོ་དང་བཅས་པའི་བདེན་བཞིའི་གནས་ལུགས་དེ་གསུང་བའི་ཆེད་དུ་མངོན་ པར་ སྦྱོར་ བ་ དང་ ལྡན་ པའི་ ཐབས་ ཤེས་ མཐར་ ཕྱིན་ པར་ མཛད་པ་དེས་ནའོ། ཊཱི་ཀ་ཆེན་ལེའུ་དང་པོ་ལས། ཡིད་ ཆེས་ ཀྱི་ སྦྱོར་བ་ནི། སྦྱིན་པས་ལོངས་སྤྱོད་ཁྲིམས་ཀྱིས་བདེ། །ཞེས་པའི་ལུང་ཆོས་ཅན། རང་གི་བསྟན་བྱའི་དོན་ལ་མི་སླུ་ཏེ། དཔྱད་པ་གསུམ་གྱིས་དག་པའི་ལུང་ཡིན་པའི་ཕྱིར། །དཔེར་ན། བདེན་

བཞི་སྟོན་པའི་གསུང་རབ་བཞིན། ཞེས་དང་། དཔྱད་པ་གསུམ་གྱིས་དག་ཚུལ་ནི། མཐོང་བ་མངོན་གྱུར་སྟོན་པ་ལ་མངོན་སུམ་གྱིས་གནོད་པ་མེད་པ། དཔེར་ན་སྔོན་པོ་མངོན་གྱུར་བསྟན་པ་ལ། མངོན་སུམ་གྱིས་གནོད་པ་མེད་ཅིང་གྲུབ་པ་དང་། གཞན་དག་མངོན་གྱུར་དུ་འདོད་པའི་སྤྱི་དོན་གཞན་སོགས་མངོན་གྱུར་མིན་པ་བསྟན་པ་ལ་མངོན་སུམ་གྱིས་གནོད་པ་མེད་པ་ལྟ་བུ་དང་། མཐོང་བ་ལྐོག་གྱུར་གྱི་དོན་སྟོན་པ་ལ་དངོས་པོ་སྟོབས་ཞུགས་ཀྱི་རྗེས་དཔག་ཉིད་ཀྱིས་གནོད་པ་མེད་པ། དཔེར་ན་འཕགས་པའི་བདེན་པ་བཞི་གཏན་ལ་ཕབ་པ་ལ་དངོས་པོ་སྟོབས་ཞུགས་རྗེས་དཔག་གིས་གནོད་པ་མེད་ཅིང་གྲུབ་ལ། གཞན་དག་ལྐོག་གྱུར་དུ་འདོད་པའི་བདག་དང་གཙོ་བོ་སོགས་བཀག་པ་ལ་རྗེས་དཔག་གིས་གནོད་པ་མེད་པ་ལྟ་བུ་དང་། མ་མཐོང་བའི་དངོས་པོ་ཤིན་ཏུ་ལྐོག་ཏུ་གྱུར་པའི་དོན་དེ་དག་ལུང་དེ་ལས་ཇི་ལྟར་བསྟན་པ་ལྟར་ཁས་བླངས་པ་ལ་ལུང་ལ་བརྟེན་པའི་རྗེས་དཔག་གིས་ཀྱང་གནོད་

པ་མེད་ཅིང་། རང་ཚིག་སྔ་ཕྱི་དང་འགལ་བ་དང་དངོས་ཤུགས་འགལ་བས་ཀྱང་གནོད་པ་མེད་པ། དཔེར་ན། ཆགས་སོགས་སྡིག་པའི་རྒྱུ་བ་ཡང་ཡིན། ཁྲུས་དང་མར་མེ་ལྷུགས་པ་སོགས་ཀྱིས་སྡིག་པ་དག་པ་ཡང་ཡིན་པའི་གཞི་མཐུན་བཀག་པ་དང་། སྦྱིན་པ་དང་མི་འཚེ་བ་སོགས་ཆོས་སུ་བཤད་པ་ལ་ནང་འགལ་མེད་པ་སྟེ། དེ་ལྟར་དཔྱད་པ་གསུམ་གྱིས་དག་པ་དེ་ཁྱད་པར་གསུམ་ལྡན་གྱི་ལུང་འདིའི་རང་གི་བརྗོད་བྱ་ལ་མི་བསླུ་བའི་རྒྱུ་མཚན་ཡང་དག་ཡིན་ནོ། མི་བསླུ་བར་དཔོག་ཚུལ་དེ་ཇི་ལྟ་བུ་ཞེ་ན། བླང་བྱའི་དེ་ཉིད་འགོག་བདེན་དང་། དོར་བྱའི་དེ་ཉིད་སྡུག་བདེན་དང་། འགོག་བདེན་བླང་པའི་ཐབས་ལམ་བསྟེན་པ་དང་། སྡུག་བདེན་དོན་པའི་ཐབས་ཀུན་འབྱུང་སྤོང་བ་དང་བཅས་པ་སངས་རྒྱས་ཀྱིས་གསུངས་པ་ལྟར་དངོས་སྟོབས་ཀྱི་ཚད་མས་རབ་ཏུ་ངེས་པ་ཡི་བཙོ་བོའི་དོན་བདེན་བཞིའི་གནས་ལུགས་ལ་སངས་རྒྱས་དེས། ཇི་ལྟར་གསུངས་པ་ལྟར་མི་བསླུ་བ་དངོས་སྟོབས་ཀྱིས་གྲུབ་པའི་ཕྱིར་ན། དེ་ཉིད་མཚུངས་

ཆོས་སུ་བྱས་ནས་དཔྱད་པ་གསུམ་གྱིས་དག་པའི་རྟགས་ཀྱིས་གཞན་ཤིན་ཏུ་ལྐོག་གྱུར་ལའང་། སངས་རྒྱས་ཀྱི་གསུང་དེ་ཉིད་མི་བསླུ་བ་རྗེས་སུ་དཔག་པར་བྱ་བ་ཡིན་ནོ། ཞེས་དང་། ཡང་དེ་ཉིད་ལས། རྣམ་དཔྱོད་དང་ལྡན་པ་དག་གིས་ནི་ལམ་གྱི་ཐོག་མ་སྐྱབས་སུ་འགྲོ་བའི་སྒོ་ཙམ་ཞིག་ལ་ངེས་པ་གཏིང་ཚུགས་པ་ཚོལ་ན་ཡང་། རིགས་པའི་གཞུང་ལུགས་འདི་ཉིད་ལ་ཅི་ནས་ཀྱང་བརྟེན་པར་བྱ་དགོས་ན། ལམ་གྱི་ལུས་ཡོངས་སུ་རྫོགས་པ་ལ་སྙིང་ནས་སྒྲུབ་པ་ལྷུར་ལེན་པའི་བསམ་པས་གཏིང་ཚུགས་པ་ཞིག་ཚོལ་ན། རིགས་པའི་གཞུང་ལུགས་འདི་ལྟ་བུའི་དོན་ལ་ཐོས་བསམ་གྱི་ཤེས་རབ་ཀྱིས་ངེས་པ་རྙེད་པ་མེད་མི་རུང་གི་ཡན་ལག་ཏུ་དགོས་པ་ལྟ་སྨོས་ཀྱང་ཞིག་དགོས་སྙམ་དུ་ཤེས་པར་བྱའི། གང་གི་ཚེ་ཕྱིའི་གོ་རྒྱ་ཙམ་གཙོད་པ་དང་། ཚེ་འདིའི་སྣང་ཤས་འབའ་ཞིག་ལྷུར་ལེན་པའི་ཐབས་སུ་གཞན་དང་ཁ་གཤགས་འགྲེད་པ་ཙམ་གྱི་ཡན་ལག་ཏུ་རིགས་པའི་གཞུང་ལུགས་དག་ལ་ཐོས་བསམ་གྱིས་འཇུག་ཅིང་།

སྙིང་ནས་སྒྲུབ་པ་ལྷུར་ལེན་པའི་བསམ་པ་ཙུང་ཟད་ཅིག་སྐྱེས་པ་
དེའི་ཚེ་རིགས་པའི་བརྟག་དཔྱད་དོར་ནས་བླུན་པོ་དག་གི་ཚིག་ཙམ་
ཞིག་སྐྱབས་སུ་བཟུང་སྟེ། ཚད་མས་གནོད་པ་འབའ་ཞིག་གི་དོན་
མཐོས་ཙམ་གྱིས་ཡིད་ལ་བྱེད་པའི་སྙིང་རུས་འབའ་ཞིག་གིས་ཐར་
པ་དང་ཐམས་ཅད་མཁྱེན་པའི་གོ་འཕང་ལོ་འམ་ཟླ་བའམ་ཞག་གི་
དུས་ཚིགས་ལ། མངོན་དུ་བྱེད་པར་ཁས་འཆེ་བའི་སྨྲོངས་པ་ལུག་
ལྟར་གླུགས་པ་དག་གི་ཧ་ཅང་ཡང་མི་འཚམས་པའི་ལོག་པའི་
གཏམ་ལ་ཤེས་ལྡན་དག་གི་རྣ་བ་དགབ་པར་བྱའོ། །ཞེས་ཐམས་
ཅད་མཁྱེན་པ་མཁས་གྲུབ་དགེ་ལེགས་དཔལ་བཟང་པོས་གསུངས།
གངས་རིའི་ཁྲོད་ཀྱི་ཤིང་རྟའི་སྲོལ་འབྱེད་ཆེན་པོ་འཇམ་དབྱངས་
མིའི་རྣམ་རོལ་རྗེ་ཐམས་ཅད་མཁྱེན་པ་ཙོང་ཁ་པ་ཆེན་པོས་གསུང་
ལས་ཀྱང་། བྱང་ཕྱོགས་འདི་ན་ཚད་མའི་གཞུང་ལུགས་ལ། །སྦྱངས་
དང་མ་སྦྱངས་དུ་མ་མགྲིན་གཅིག་ཏུ། མདོ་དང་སྡེ་བདུན་ཀུན་ལ་
བྱང་ཆུབ་ཏུ། །བགྲོད་པའི་ཉམས་ལེན་རིམ་པ་ཡོད་མིན་ཟེར།

།འཇམ་པའི་དབྱངས་ཀྱིས་ཕྱོགས་ཀྱི་གླང་པོ་ལ། །དངོས་སུ་འདི་
བརྩམས་འདི་ནི་མ་འོངས་དུས། །འགྲོ་བ་ཀུན་གྱི་མིག་ཏུ་འགྱུར་
རོ་ཞེས། །གསུང་གི་གནང་བ་བསྐུལ་བའང་ཚད་མར་བྱེད། །དེ་
ནི་མི་རིགས་སླ་བའི་ཡུལ་བྱུང་དུ། །མཐོང་ནས་ལྷག་པར་རྩལ་དེར་
དཔྱད་པ་ན། །ཚད་མ་ཀུན་ལས་བཏུས་པའི་མཆོད་བརྗོད་དོན།
།ཚད་མ་གྲུབ་པར་ལུགས་འབྱུང་ལུགས་ལྡོག་གིས། །རྣམ་གྲོལ་
དོན་དུ་གཉེར་བ་བཅོམ་ལྡན་འདས། །ཚད་མར་བསྒྲུབས་ཤིང་དེ་
ལས་དེ་ཡི་ནི། །བསྟན་པ་ཀོ་ན་ཐར་འདོད་འཇུག་ངོགས་སུ།
།ངེས་པ་གཏིང་ནས་རྙེད་པས་ཐེག་གཉིས་ཀྱི། །ལམ་གྱི་གནད་ཀུན་
འབྲེལ་བར་རིགས་ལམ་ནས། །ལེགས་པར་ཐོན་པས་ལྷག་པར་
དགའ་བ་རྙེད། །རྩལ་འདི་བསམས་ཤིང་འདུན་མ་ལེགས་ནས་
གདའ། །བཀའ་དྲིན་ཆེའོ་རྗེ་བཙུན་མཁྱེན་པའི་གཏེར། །ཞེས་
གསུངས་སོ། །མཁས་གྲུབ་ཀྱི་ཚད་མ་སྡེ་བདུན་ཡིད་ཀྱི་མུན་སེལ་
ལས། སྐྱེས་བུ་སྐྱེས་མ་ཐག་གི་རིག་པ་དེ་ལ་རྒྱུ་མེད་ན། རེས་འགའ་

ཡིན་པས་གནོད་ལ། རྒྱུ་ཡོད་ན། རྟག་པའམ་མི་རྟག་པ་གང་ཡིན།
རྟག་དངོས་ཡིན་ན་ཡུལ་དང་དུས་གང་ལ་ཡང་། །མ་ཁྱབ་པ་མི་
སྲིད་པས། འབྲས་བུ་དང་རྗེས་སུ་འགྲོ་ལྡོག་ངེས་པ་མི་སྲིད་དོ། །ཕྱི་
མ་ལྟར་ན། བེམ་རིག་གང་རུང་ལས་གཞན་པའི་དངོས་པོ་ལས་སྐྱེ་
བར་མི་འཐད་པས། གང་རུང་ལས་སྐྱེ་དགོས་ལ། །བེམ་པོས་ཉེར་
ལེན་བྱེད་ན། དབང་པོ་དང་བཅས་པའམ། ཕྱི་རོལ་གྱི་བེམ་པོ་
ཡིན། དང་པོ་ལྟར་ན། དབང་པོ་ཀུན་ཚོགས་པ་རྒྱུར་དགོས་སམ།
གང་རུང་རེས་ཆོག །དང་པོ་ལྟར་ན། མིག་དབང་མ་ཚང་ན་ཡང་
ཡིད་བློ་མི་སྐྱེ་བར་འགྱུར་ལ། ཕྱི་མ་ལྟར་ན། མིག་ཤེས་བཞིན་
དུ་རྟོག་པས་ཀྱང་གཟུགས་གསལ་བར་འཛིན་པར་འགྱུར་ཞིང་།
ཕྱི་རོལ་གྱི་བེམ་པོས་ཉེར་ལེན་བྱེད་ན། ཡན་ལག་ཅན་གྱི་རྫས་ཀྱིས་
སམ། རྡུལ་ཕྲན་གྱིས་བྱེད། དང་པོ་ལྟར་ན། ཡན་ལག་ཅན་གྱི་
རྫས་ཆ་བཅས་ཆ་མེད་གཉིས་ལས། ཆ་བཅས་ཀྱིས་ཉེར་ལེན་བྱེད་
ན། ཆ་ཐམས་ཅད་ཚོགས་པ་རྒྱུར་དགོས་སམ། གང་རུང་རེས་

ཆོག་ཅེས་ཕ་གོང་གི་རིགས་པའི་ཚུལ་གྱིས་ཁེགས་ལ། ཡན་ལག་རྣམས་ལས་རྫས་ཐ་དད་པའི་ཡན་ལག་ཅན་ཆ་མེད་ཀྱིས་ཉེར་ལེན་བྱེད་ན། གདོང་གོས་ཀྱིས་བསྒྲིབས་ན། ཡན་ལག་གཞན་རྣམས་ཀྱང་གོས་ཀྱིས་བསྒྲིབས་པ་དང་། གཞན་མ་བསྒྲིབས་ན་བསྒྲིབས་མ་བསྒྲིབས་ཆ་གཉིས་སུ་ཡོད་པར་འགྱུར་བ་དང་། བསྒྲིབས་མ་བསྒྲིབས་ཆ་གཉིས་ཡན་ལག་རྣམས་ལ་ཡོད་ཀྱི་ཡན་ལག་ཅན་ལ་མེད་ན། གདོང་གོས་ཀྱིས་བསྒྲིབས་པའི་ཚེ་ཡན་ལག་ཅན་གྱི་གདོང་གསལ་བར་མཐོང་བར་ཐལ་ལ། དེ་བཞིན་དུ་གཡོ་མི་གཡོ་དང་། ཁ་བསྒྱུར་མ་བསྒྱུར་སོགས་ལ་སྦྱར་བའི་རིགས་པ་རྣམས་ཀྱིས་གནོད་དོ། །རྡུལ་གྱིས་ཉེར་ལེན་བྱེད་ན། རེ་རེ་བས་ཀྱང་ལྟོས་མེད་དུ་སྐྱེ་ན། ཡིད་རྟོག་དུ་མ་ཅིག་ཅར་སྐྱེ་བར་འགྱུར་ལ། ཀུན་ཚོགས་དགོས་ན། རྡུལ་ཕྲན་གཅིག་མ་ཚང་ན་ཡང་མི་སྐྱེ་བར་འགྱུར་རོ། །མཐའ་གཞན་འགོག་པའི་རིགས་པ་དེ་དག་ལ་བརྟེན་

ནས་ཤེས་པས་ཉེར་ལེན་བྱེད་པར་གྲུབ་ལ། དེ་ལ་ཡང་རང་རྒྱུད་ཀྱིས་བསྡུས་པ་དང་། གཞན་རྒྱུད་ཀྱིས་བསྡུས་པ་གཉིས་ལས། གཞན་རྒྱུད་ཕ་མ་ལྟ་བུའི་ཤེས་པས་དངོས་ཀྱི་ཉེར་ལེན་བྱེད་ན། ཕ་བཟོ་མཁས་པ་དང་བླུན་པ་སོགས་ཀྱི་བུ་ཡང་དེ་ལྟར་ཐལ་བའི་སྐྱོན་འབྱུང་བས། རང་རྒྱུད་ཀྱི་རིག་པ་སྔ་མ་ཁོ་ནས་ཉེར་ལེན་བྱེད་པར་འགྱུར་ལ། དེ་ལྟར་ན་རིག་པའི་ཡ་མཐའ་དང་མ་མཐའ་ཐུག་པ་མེད་པ་དང་། སྐྱེ་བ་སྔ་ཕྱི་ཡོད་པ་ལེགས་པར་གྲུབ་པ་ཡིན་ནོ། །ཞེས་དང་། ཡང་དེ་ཉིད་ལས། བཅོམ་ལྡན་འདས་ཀྱིས། དགེ་སློང་དག་གམ་མཁས་རྣམས་ཀྱིས། །བསྲེགས་བཅད་བདར་བའི་གསེར་བཞིན་དུ། །ལེགས་པར་བརྟགས་ལ་ང་ཡི་བཀའ། །བླང་བར་བྱ་ཡི་གུས་ཕྱིར་མིན། །ཞེས་བཀའི་དོན་ཀྱང་ཚད་མས་བསྒྲུབ་དགོས་པར་གསུངས་པའི་ཕྱིར་དང་། རྗེ་བཙུན་བྱམས་པས་ཀྱང་། ཆོས་བཟང་རིགས་པས་རྣམ་དཔྱད་བསམ་པ་ཅན། །རྟག་ཏུ་བདུད་ཀྱིས་བར་ཆད་བྱེད་པ་མེད། །ཅེས་གསུངས་ཤིང་། དབུ་མ་བསྟན་

བཙོས་ལ་འཇུག་པ་ལས་ཀྱང་། སོ་སོ་སྐྱེ་བོ་རྣམས་ནི་རྟོག་པས་བཅིངས། །མི་རྟོག་རྣལ་འབྱོར་པ་ནི་གྲོལ་འགྱུར་བས། །རྟོག་རྣམས་ལོག་པར་གྱུར་པ་གང་ཡིན་དེ། །རྣམ་པར་དཔྱོད་པའི་འབྲས་བུར་མཁས་རྣམས་གསུངས། །ཞེས་གསུངས་པ་ལ། རིགས་པ་ལ་མི་བརྟེན་པར་ཚིག་ཙམ་གྱི་རྗེས་སུ་འབྲང་བ་དག་དབང་པོ་རྟུལ་པོ་དད་པའི་རྗེས་སུ་འབྲང་བ་ཞེས་འཕགས་པའི་གང་ཟག་ཐམས་ཅད་ལ་གྲགས་པའི་ཕྱིར། སྔང་དོར་གྱི་གནས་ལ་རིགས་པས་རྣམ་པར་དཔྱོད་པ་ནི། ཆོས་ཀྱི་རྗེས་སུ་འབྲང་བ་ཞེས་མཁས་པས་བསྔགས་པ་ཡིན་ནོ། །དེ་ཉིད་ཀྱི་ཕྱིར་རིགས་པས་དཔྱོད་པ་ལྟར་ལེན་པ་ནི་རྟོག་གེའི་ཚུལ་ཡིན་པས། གྲོལ་བ་དོན་གཉེར་ལ་མགོ་བ་མ་ཡིན་ནོ། །ཞེས་བྱ་བའི་བདུད་ཚིག་ལ་ཤེས་ལྡན་དག་གིས་རྣ་བ་དགབ་པར་བྱོས་ཤིག །ཞེས་དང་། ཡང་དེ་ཉིད་ལས། རང་གཞན་ འཁོར་ བ་ ལས་ གྲོལ་ བ་ དོན་ དུ་ གཉེར་ བ་ དག་ གིས་ ནི། འཁོར་བའི་རྩ་བ་གཅོད་བྱེད་ཀྱི་ཐབས་ཕྱིན་ཅི་མ་ལོག་པ་སྟོན་པར་

བྱེད་པའི་བསྟན་བཅོས་འདི་དག་ལ་གཅེས་སྤྲས་སུ་བྱ་བར་རིགས་ཏེ། ཐ་ན་ལྟོ་བ་ཁེངས་པ་ཙམ་ཞིག་དོན་དུ་གཉེར་བ་དག་ཀྱང་། བཟའ་བཏུང་ཁོ་ན་གཅེས་སྤྲས་སུ་འཛིན་པར་མཐོང་ན། གོ་འཕང་མཆོག་དོན་དུ་གཉེར་བར་ཁས་འཆེ་ཞིང་། དབང་པོ་རྣོན་པོ་རྟོག་པ་སྔོན་དུ་གཏོང་བར་ཁས་འཆེ་བཞིན་དུ་མངོན་པར་འདོད་པའི་དོན་དུ་གཉེར་བྱ་མཆོག་ཐབས་དང་བཅས་པ་ནི་ཚད་མས་ངེས་པར་བྱེད་པའི་ཚུལ་གང་ལ་རག་ལས་པ་དེ་ཉིད་ལ་གཅེས་སྤྲས་སུ་འཛིན་པར་མི་བྱེད་པར། བསྟན་བཅོས་འདི་དག་རྩོད་པ་ལྷུར་ལེན་གྱི་གཞུང་ལུགས་ཤུན་ལྤགས་དང་འདྲ་བར་བཟུང་ནས། ལམ་དང་ལམ་མ་ཡིན་པའི་ཐ་སྙད་ཙམ་ཡང་རྣ་བའི་ལམ་དུ་སྔོན་ཆད་མ་ཞུགས་ན། དོན་ལ་མཁས་པ་ལྟ་སྨོས་ཀྱང་ཅི་དགོས་པའི་བླུན་པོ་རིའི་ཕྱུག་ཏུ་ཆེ་ཡོལ་བར་བྱས་པ་ཙམ་གྱི་ང་རྒྱལ་འབའ་ཞིག་ལ་རང་གི་ཡིད་སྙིང་ནས་རངས་པར་བྱས་པ་འགའ་ཞིག་གིས་ཚིག་འབྲུ་བྱུང་རྒྱལ་དུ་སྨྲས་པ་དག་ལ་བསམ་གཏན་པའི་མན་ངག་ཏུ་མིང་བཏགས་ནས་

སྙིང་པོར་ལྟ་བུར་འཛིན་པ་གང་ཡིན་པ་དེ་ནི། དབང་པོ་རྣོན་པོ་ལྟ་སྨོས་ཀྱང་ཅི་དགོས། དད་པའི་རྗེས་སུ་འབྲང་བ་ཙམ་ཡང་མ་ཡིན་ཏེ། དད་པར་བྱ་བའི་གནས་མ་ཡིན་པ་ལ་དད་པར་བྱེད་པའི་ཕྱིར་རོ། །དེའི་ཕྱིར་དེ་ལྟ་བུ་ནི་བསམ་པ་རང་བཞིན་དུ་མི་གནས་པ་ལྦུ་བའི་རྡོག་པོ་ལ་རྐང་པའི་སྐེགས་འཆའ་བ་དང་མཚུངས་སོ། །ཞེས་དང་། ཡང་དེ་ཉིད་ལས། བཅོམ་ལྡན་འདས་ཀྱིས། ལས་འདིས་འབྲས་བུ་འདི་ལྟ་བུ་དུས་འདི་ཙམ་ན་འབྱིན་ནོ། །ཞེས་གསུངས་པའི་ལུང་གི་བརྗོད་བྱ་ལྟ་བུ་གཞལ་བྱ་ཤིན་ཏུ་ལྐོག་གྱུར་གྱི་དོན་ལ་འཇུག་ལྡོག་བྱ་ཚུལ་ནི། རྟོག་པ་སྔོན་དུ་གཏོང་བའི་སྐྱེས་བུ་དག །ཤིན་ཏུ་ལྐོག་གྱུར་གྱི་དོན་ལ་འཇུག་སྡོག་བྱས་པས་ཕན་ཡོན་དང་ཉེས་དམིགས་ཆེན་པོ་བཤད་པའང་ཐོས་ལ། དེ་ལྟ་བུ་ལ་འཇུག་ལྡོག་མ་བྱས་ན་དོན་ཆེན་པོ་ལས་ཉམས་པར་འགྱུར་བ་ཡང་སྲིད་སྙམ་ཞིང་། ཐབས་གང་ལ་བརྟེན་ནས་འཇུག་སྡོག་བྱ་སྙམ་དུ་སེམས་སོ། །དེ་ལྟར་བསམས་པ་ན་ལུང་ལ་མ་བརྟེན་པར་ཚད་མ་

གཞན་ལ་བརྟེན་ནས་འཇུག་ལྡོག་བྱ་མི་ནུས་པར་ཤེས་ཤིང༌། ལུང་དེ་ཉིད་རང་གི་བསྟན་བྱའི་དོན་ལ་ནི་སླུ་བ་ཡིན་མིན་ཇི་ལྟ་བུ་ཞེས་དཔྱོད་པར་བྱེད་ལ། དཔྱད་པ་ན་ལུང་དེའི་བསྟན་བྱ་དེ་ལྟ་བུ་ཡིན་པ་ལ་མངོན་སུམ་དང༌། དངོས་པོ་སྟོབས་ཞུགས་ཀྱི་ཚད་མས་གནོད་པ་མེད་ཅིང༌། ལུང་དེ་ཉིད་ཀྱི་བརྗོད་བྱ་ཤིན་ལྐོག་སོན་བྱེད་ཀྱི་ཚིག་རང་ལ་ཡང༌། སྔ་ཕྱི་དང་དངོས་ཤུགས་འགལ་བ་སོགས་ཀྱིས་མི་གནོད་པ་སྟེ། དཔྱད་པ་གསུམ་གྱིས་དག་པར་མཐོང་ནས་དེའི་ཚེ་ལུང་དེ་ཉིད་རང་གི་བསྟན་བྱའི་དོན་ལ་མི་སླུ་བར་ངེས་ཏེ། ལུང་དེས་བསྟན་པ་དང་མཐུན་པར་འཇུག་ལྡོག་བྱེད་པར་འགྱུར་བ་འདི་ནི། ལུང་གི་བརྗོད་བྱ་ལ་ངེས་པར་ཇི་ལྟར་སྐྱེ་བའི་ཚུལ་ཡིན་ནོ། །ཞེས་དང༌། ཡང་དེ་ཉིད་ལས། ཚུལ་གསུམ་སྒྲུབ་བྱེད་ཀྱི་ཚད་མ་ཇི་ལྟ་བུ་ཞེ་ན། སྦྱིན་པས་ལོངས་སྤྱོད་ཁྲིམས་ཀྱིས་བདེ་ཞེས་པའི་ལུང་དེ་དཔྱད་པ་གསུམ་གྱིས་དག་པར་མངོན་སུམ་གྱིས་གྲུབ་ལ། དཔྱད་པ་གསུམ་གྱིས་དག་པ་ལ། རང་གི་

བརྗོད་བྱ་ལ་མི་སླུ་བའི་ཁྱབ་པ་རྟགས་ཀྱིས་འགྲུབ་སྟེ། བརྗོད་བྱའི་དོན་ལ་བསླུ་ན། ལུང་དེས་བསྟན་པ་ལྟར་མ་གྲུབ་དགོས་ལ། དེ་ལྟར་ན། ལུང་དེས་བསྟན་པ་ལྟར་བརྗོད་བྱའི་དོན་ལ་ཚད་མས་གནོད་པ་འབབ་དགོས་ལ། དཔྱད་པ་གསུམ་གྱིས་དག་ན། ཚད་མས་གནོད་པ་མེད་དགོས་པའི་ཕྱིར་རོ། །ཞེས་དང་། ཡང་དེ་ཉིད་ལས། རིགས་པའི་སྒོ་དུ་མའི་སྒོ་ནས་ཚུལ་བཞིན་དུ་ལེགས་པར་བསམས་པས། འཁོར་བ་སྡུག་བསྔལ་གྱི་རང་བཞིན་དུ་ཤེས། དེའི་རྒྱུ་བདག་ཏུ་འཛིན་པ་སྤང་བྱ་དང་སྤོང་ནུས་སུ་ངེས་ཤིང་། ཐར་པ་ཡོད་ངེས་དང་། ཐར་པ་ལ་ཐོབ་འདོད་ཀྱི་བློ་སྙིང་ཐག་པ་ནས་སྐྱེས་པ་ན། ཐར་པ་དོན་གཉེར་གྱི་བློ་མཚན་ཉིད་ཡོངས་སུ་རྫོགས་པ་ཡིན་ཅིང་། དེ་ལྟ་བུའི་ཐར་པ་དོན་གཉེར་གྱི་བློ་རིགས་པའི་ལམ་ནས་དྲངས་པའི་ངེས་པ་གཏིང་ཚུགས་པ་མ་རྙེད་ན། གཞན་གྱི་ཚིག་ཙམ་ལ་བརྟེན་པ་དང་། རང་ལ་སྡུག་བསྔལ་དྲག་པོ་ཐོག་ཏུ་བབ་པ་མ་བཟོད་པས་ཡིད་འབྱུང་ཐར་འདོད་དྲག་པོ་སྐྱེས

པ་ལྟར་སྣང་ཡང་། གཞན་གྱི་རིགས་པ་ལྟར་སྣང་དང་ཚིག
ཙམ་ལ་བརྟེན་ནས་ཟློག་པར་ནུས་ཤིང་། འཕྲུལ་གྱི་སྡུག་བསྡིལ
དྲག་པོ་དེ་ཙུང་ཟད་ལོག་ནས། ཚེ་འདིའི་བདེ་བ་འགའ་ཞིག་གིས
ཡིད་ཕྲིད་པ་ན། ཡིད་འབྱུང་དེ་འདྲ་སླར་ལོག་ནས་ཡིད་འབྱུང་དང
བྲལ་བའི་གནས་སྐབས་ལ་བརྟེན་པར་འགྱུར་ཏེ། ཇི་སྐད་དུ། དེ
ལོག་ན་ནི་རང་ཉིད་ཀྱི། །རང་བཞིན་ཉིད་ལ་སླར་བརྟེན་འགྱུར།
།ཞེས་གསུངས་པ་ལྟར་རོ། །ཡང་དངོས་སྟོབས་རིགས་པའི་དབང
ཕྱུགས་རྒྱལ་ཚབ་དར་མ་རིན་ཆེན་གྱི་ཞལ་ནས། དྲི་མེད་རིགས
ལམ་འབྱེད་པའི་མཐུ་མེད་ཅིང་། །གསུང་རབ་གདམས་པར
འཆར་བའི་མན་ངག་མེད། །རྒྱལ་བའི་དགོངས་པ་འགྲེལ་ལོ
ཞེས་སྨྲ་བ། །སངས་རྒྱས་བསྟན་ལ་བཏང་སྙོམས་བྱས་ན་མཛེས།
།ཞེས་དང་། ཡང་དེ་ཉིད་ཀྱི་ཕར་ཕྱིན་ཐེག་མཆོག་སྒོ་འབྱེད་ལས།
ཐོབ་བྱའི་འབྲས་བུ་རྣམ་པ་ཐམས་ཅད་མཁྱེན་པ་ཉིད་དེ་ནི་ཤེས་བྱ
ཐམས་ཅད་མངོན་སུམ་དུ་གཟིགས་པ་ཕལ་ཆེར་གྱིས་འདོད་ཀྱང་།

དེ་ཐོབ་པར་བྱེད་པའི་ལམ་ནི་སྟོང་པ་ཉིད་ཀྱི་དོན་གཅིག་པུ་བསྒོམས་པས་ཆོག་པར་འདོད་པ་དང་། རྒྱ་ནག་ཧྭ་ཤང་སོགས་དང་། ད་ལྟ་ཡང་ཕྱི་རོལ་པ་དང་ཐུན་མོང་བའི་ཞི་གནས་ཀྱི་ཕྱོགས་སུ་གཏོགས་པ་ཙམ་ལ་གནས་ལུགས་ཀྱི་དོན་བསྒོམ་པར་བཟུང་ནས། སྦྱིན་པ་རྒྱ་ཆེན་པོ་གཏོང་བ་དང་། ཚུལ་ཁྲིམས་རྒྱ་ཆེན་པོ་བསྲུང་བ་སོགས་སྦྱོར་བཅས་ཡིན་གྱི་སངས་རྒྱས་ཐོབ་པའི་ལམ་རྣལ་མ་མིན་པར་འདོད་པ་དག །རྒྱང་རིང་དུ་དོར་བར་བྱའོ། །ལུགས་ངན་པ་འདི་བརྟནཆགས་པས་གཞུང་ལུགས་ལ་སྦྱངས་པའི་སྡེ་སྣོད་འཛིན་པ་གཅིག་དང་། སྦྱངས་པ་ཡེ་མ་བྱས་པ་གཉིས་ཉམས་ལེན་ལ་མང་ཞུང་ཙུང་ཟད་ཀྱང་མི་འོང་བ་དང་། སྡེ་སྣོད་འཛིན་པ་རྣམས་ཀྱང་སྒྲུབ་པ་བྱེད་པར་མིང་བཏགས་པའི་ཅི་ཡང་མི་ཤེས་པ་རྣམས་ལ་སྐྱབས་སུ་འགྲོ་བ་དག་འབྱུང་བ་ཡིན་ནོ། །ཞེས་དང་། ཐམས་ཅད་མཁྱེན་པ་སྒྲུབ་ཚུལ་ནི། ཡང་དེ་ཉིད་ལས། རྣམ་མཁྱེན་མཚོན་པར་བྱེད་པའི་ཆོས་བཅུས་རྣམ་མཁྱེན་དེ་ཡུལ་གྱིས་

ཡུལ་ཅན་མཚོན་པའི་ཚུལ་གྱིས་གོ་བར་བྱེད་དེ། རྒྱུ་འབྲས་གཙོ་བོའི་དོན་གྱིས་རྣམ་པ་མཁྱེན་པའི་རྣམ་མཁྱེན་གྱིས་རྟོགས་པར་བྱ་བའི་ཡུལ་དེ་བསྟན་ན། ཐེག་པ་ཆེན་པོའི་ལམ་གྱི་ལུས་ཡོངས་སུ་རྫོགས་པ་གཅིག་གོ་བར་བྱ་བའི་ཆེད་དུ་ཡུལ་གྱིས་ཡུལ་ཅན་མཚོན་པ་ཡིན་ནོ། །ཆོས་བཅུ་པོ་དེ་ཡང་སྐབས་གསུམ་པར་བསྟན་པའི་སྐྱེས་བུ་འབྲིང་གི་བསམ་པ་སོགས་སྦྱངས་པ་སྔོན་དུ་བཏང་ནས་སེམས་ཅན་གྱི་དོན་དུ་སངས་རྒྱས་ཐོབ་པ་དམ་བཅའ་བ་དང་། དེའི་དོན་བསྒྲུབ་པ་གཉིས་སུ་འདུས་ལ་ཕྱི་མ་ལ་དམ་བཅའི་དོན་ཇི་ལྟར་སྒྲུབ་པའི་ཚུལ་བསྟན་པ་དང་། དོན་དེ་བསྒྲུབས་པས་སྒྲུབས་རྒྱུད་ལ་བསྐྱེད་ཚུལ་སྟོན་ཏོ། ཕྱི་མ་ལ་སྒོམ་བྱུང་གི་སྒྲུབ་པ་སྐྱེས་པའི་མཚན་གཞི་ངོས་བཟུང་བ་དང་། ཐེག་པ་ཆེན་པོའི་རིགས་དང་ལྡན་པའི་གང་ཟག་གིས་ཤེས་བྱའི་ཆོས་ཐམས་ཅད་ལ་དམིགས་ནས་ཆེད་དུ་བྱ་བ་ཆེན་པོ་གསུམ་གྱི་དོན་དུ་བསམ་པ་དང་།སྦྱོར་བ་རྒྱ་ཆེན་པོ་བསྒྲུབས་པས་ཚོགས་རྒྱ་ཆེན་པོ་བདེ་བླག་ཏུ་

རྫོགས་ཤིང་། རྣམ་མཁྱེན་དུ་གདོན་མི་ཟ་བར་ངེས་པར་འགྱུར་བའི་ལམ་གྱི་རིམ་པ་རྣམས་སྟོན་པ་ཡིན་ནོ། །ཞེས་དང་། རྗེ་བླ་མས་ཀྱང་། དང་པོར་རྒྱ་ཆེན་ཐོས་པ་མང་དུ་བཙལ། །བར་དུ་གཞུང་ལུགས་ཐམས་ཅད་གདམས་པར་ཤར། །ཐ་མར་ཉིན་མཚན་ཀུན་ཏུ་ཉམས་སུ་བླངས་ཀུན་ཀྱང་བསྟན་པ་རྒྱས་པའི་ཆེད་དུ་བསྔོ། གསུང་ཐོར་བུ་རྣམས་རྫོགས་སོ།།

།། ༈ ཐམས་ཅད་མཁྱེན་པ་སྒྲུབ་ཚུལ་བཞུགས་སོ།། །།ཚད་མའི་ལམ་ཁྲིད་ལས། ཐུབ་པ་བཅོམ་ལྡན་འདས་ཆོས་ཅན། གྲོལ་བ་དོན་གཉེར་གྱི་སྐྱོབ་ཡིན་ཏེ། གཞན་ལ་བདེན་བཞིའི་གནས་ལུགས་ཕྱིན་ཅི་མ་ལོག་པ་སྟོན་པར་མཛད་པའི་ཕྱིར། དེ་གང་ལས་བཞེས་ཞེ་ན། བརྗོད་བྱེད་རྒྱས་འབྲིང་བསྡུས་གསུམ་ཆོས་ཅན། མཁྱེན་པ་རྣམ་དག་སྔོན་དུ་སོང་སྟེ། བདེན་བཞིའི་གནས་ལུགས་ཕྱིན་ཅི་མ་ལོག་པར་སྟོན་པའི་རྗོད་བྱེད་རྣམ་དག་ཡིན་པའི་ཕྱིར།། །།སྐྱེ་བ་སྔ་ཕྱི་ཡོད་པའི་སྒྲུབ་བྱེད་བསམ་པ་ནི། སྐྱེས་བུ་འཆི་ཁ་མའི་ཡིད་བློ་

ཆོས་ཅན། རིག་པ་ཕྱི་མ་མཚམས་སྦྱོར་ཏེ། རིག་པ་ཡིན་པའི་ཕྱིར། དཔེར་ན། ད་ལྟར་གྱི་རིག་པ་བཞིན། སྐྱེས་མ་ཐག་པའི་རིག་ཆོས་ཅན། རིག་པ་སྔ་མ་སྔོན་དུ་སོང་སྟེ། རིག་པ་ཡིན་པའི་ཕྱིར། ད་ལྟར་གྱི་རིག་པ་བཞིན། དེ་ལྟ་མ་ཡིན་པར་འགྱུར་བའི་བདག་ཉིད་ཀྱི་ཉེར་ལེན་ནམ་བདག་རྐྱེན་བྱས་ན། འགྱུར་བ་ཀུན་སྒྲོག་ཆགས་སུ་ཐལ་བར་གྱུར་རོ། །མདོར་ན་ཡིད་བློ་རྒྱུ་མེད་བཀག་པས་རྒྱུ་བཅས་སུ་གྲུབ་ཅིང་། རྟག་པ་བཀག་པས་མི་རྟག་པའི་རྒྱུ་ཅན་དུ་གྲུབ་ལ། བེམ་པོ་ལྷོག་བྱེད་ཀྱི་རྒྱུ་ཡིན་པ་བཀག་པས་རིག་པ་ལས་སྐྱེ་བར་གྲུབ་ཅིང་། གཞན་གྱི་རིག་པ་ལས་སྐྱེ་བ་བགག་པས་རང་གི་རིག་པ་ལས་སྐྱེ་བར་གྲུབ་ལ། རྒྱུ་མེད་དང་མི་མཐུན་པའི་རྒྱུ་ལས་སྐྱེ་བ་བཀག་པས། སྐྱེས་མ་ཐག་པའི་རིག་པ་དེ་རིག་པ་སྔ་མ་སྔོན་དུ་སོང་བ་དང་། འཆི་ཁའི་རིག་པ་དེ་རིག་པ་ཕྱི་མ་མཚམས་སྦྱོར་བ་གྲུབ་པས། ཐབས་ཤེས་བརྟེན་པའི་རྟེན་རིག་པ་ཙམ་རྒྱུན་ནམ་ཡང་མི་ཆད་པའི་བརྟན་པར་གྲུབ་ཅིང་། གོམས་

ཟིན་འབད་པ་སྐྱུར་མ་ལ་མི་ལྟོས་བའང་གྲུབ་པས་བསམ་པ་ཕུན་ཚོགས་ལེགས་པར་གྲུབ་པ་ཡིན་ནོ། །ཞེས་སོ།། །།མཁས་གྲུབ་ཐམས་ཅད་མཁྱེན་པས་མཛད་པའི་ཚད་མའི་ལམ་ཁྲིད་ལས། དེས་ན་བདག་རང་བཞིན་གྱིས་གྲུབ་པ་ཁེགས། དེ་ཁེགས་ན་བདག་རང་བཞིན་གྱིས་ཡོད་པར་འཛིན་པའི་བློ་དེ་དངོས་པོའི་གནས་ལུགས་ལ་འཛིན་སྟངས་ཕྱིན་ཅི་ལོག་ཏུ་ཞུགས་པའི་བློར་གྲུབ། དེ་གྲུབ་ན་དེ་དང་འཛིན་སྟངས་དངོས་སུ་འགལ་བའི་གནོད་བྱེད་ཀྱི་གཉེན་པོ་སྟོབས་ལྡན་ཡོད་པར་གྲུབ་ཅིང་། དེ་ཉིད་ནི་བདག་མེད་རྟོགས་པའི་ཤེས་རབ་ལས་འོས་གཞན་མེད་པར་གྲུབ་པས། བདག་མེད་རྟོགས་པའི་ཤེས་རབ་གོམས་པས། བདག་འཛིན་མ་ལུས་པ་སྤངས་པར་རྟོགས་ནུས་སོ། །འོན་ཀྱང་བདག་མེད་རྟོགས་པའི་ཤེས་རབ་བསྒོམས་པ་ལས་གསལ་སྣང་རབ་ཀྱི་མཐར་ཕྱིན་ནས་བདག་འཛིན་མ་ལུས་པ་སྤངས་པ་མི་སྲིད་སྙམ་ན། དེ་བཤད་པ་ནི། བདག་རང་བཞིན་གྱིས་སྟོང་པར་རྟོགས་པའི་བློ་ཆོས་ཅན།

ཁྲོད་གོམས་བྱེད་ཀྱི་ཡན་ལག་ཞི་གནས་དང་ཚོགས་རྒྱ་ཆེན་པོ་གསོག་པ་དང་འབྲེལ་ཏེ་གོམས་པར་བྱས་ན་གོམས་ཡུལ་བདག་མེད་ཀྱི་དོན་ལ་གསལ་སྣང་རིམ་གྱིས་མཐར་ཐུག་པར་འགྲོར་རུང་སྟེ། ཁྲོད་རྟེན་བརྟན་འབད་རྩོལ་སྐྱུ་མ་ལ་མི་ལྟོས་པར་གོམས་པ་ལས་སེམས་ཀྱི་ཡོན་ཏན་དུ་འགྱུར་བའི་ཕྱིར། དཔེར་ན། འདོད་འཇིག་མྱ་ངན་གོམས་པ་བཞིན། འདིའི་ཁྱབ་པ་དཔེའི་སྟེང་དུ་གྲུབ་ལ། ཕྱོགས་ཆོས་བསྒྲུབ་པ་ནི། རྟེན་བརྟན་པ་མི་འཐད་དེ། རྒྱུའི་དྲོད་བཞིན། འབད་རྩོལ་སྐྱུར་མ་ལ་སྟོས་དགོས་ཏེ། དཔེར་ན་མཆོངས་པ་བཞིན། ཟེར་ན། མི་མཚུངས་ཏེ། རིག་པའི་ཡ་མཐའ་དང་མ་མཐའ་ཐུག་མེད་དུ་གྲུབ་པས་རྟེན་བརྟན་ཅིང་བདག་མེད་རྟོགས་པ་གོམས་ན་མཐའ་མེད་དུ་འཕེལ་ནུས་པས་འབད་རྩོལ་སྐྱུར་མ་ལ་མི་ལྟོས་པའི་ཕྱིར། སེམས་ཀྱི་ཡོན་ཏན་དུ་འགྱུར་ཚུལ་ནི། བདག་མེད་རྟོགས་པའི་ཤེས་རབ་ཡུན་རིང་དུ་གོམས་པའི་མཐར་རང་གི་སེམས་ཀྱི་བདག་ཉིད་དུ་འགྱུར་བ་ཡིན་ནོ།།

།ཆོས་ཀྱི་བདག་མེད་གོམས་པས་ཤེས་སྒྲིབ་ཙུང་ཟད་སྤོང་ནུས་ཀྱང་། གོམས་པ་ལས་གསལ་སྣང་རབ་ཀྱི་མཐར་ཕྱིན་ནས་ཤེས་སྒྲིབ་མ་ལུས་པར་སྤངས་པའི་སྒོ་ནས་ཐམས་ཅད་མཁྱེན་པ་ཐོབ་པར་འགྱུར་བ་དག་མེད་སྙམ་ན། ཆོས་ཀྱི་བདག་མེད་རྟོགས་པའི་བློ་ཆོས་ཅན། ཁྱོད་གོམས་བྱེད་ཀྱི་ཡན་ལག་བྱང་ཆུབ་ཀྱི་སེམས་དང་ཕ་རོལ་ཏུ་ཕྱིན་པ་དྲུག་དང་མ་བྲལ་བར་བྱས་ནས་གོམས་པ་ལས་གསལ་སྣང་རབ་ཀྱི་མཐར་ཕྱིན་པར་འགྱུར་ཏེ། ཁྱོད་རྟེན་བརྟན་འབད་རྩོལ་སྔར་མ་ལ་མི་ལྟོས་པར་གོམས་པ་ལས་སེམས་ཀྱི་ཡོན་ཏན་དུ་འགྱུར་བའི་ཕྱིར། ཕྱོགས་ཆོས་སྒྲུབ་པ་ནི་གོང་དུ་བརྗོད་ཟིན་ཏོ་ཞེས་སོ།། །།རྒྱལ་ཚབ་ལམ་ཁྲིད་ལས། བརྩེ་བ་སྙིང་རྗེ་ཆེན་པོ་ཆོས་ཅན། ཁྱོད་བསྒོམ་བྱའི་དོན་ལ་གསལ་བ་རབ་ཀྱི་མཐར་ཐུག་པར་འགྱུར་རུང་སྟེ། རྟེན་བརྟན་གོམས་ཟིན་འབད་པ་སྔར་མ་ལ་མི་ལྟོས་པར་འབད་པ་སྔ་མས་རིགས་འདྲ་ཕྱི་མ་ལ་ཕན་འདོགས་ནུས་པ་ཡིན་པའི་ཕྱིར། དཔེར་ན། འདོད་ཆགས་གོམས་པ་

བཞིན་ཞེས་དང་། གལ་ཏེ་སྤྱངས་པ་ཁྱད་པར་གསུམ་ལྡན་འབྱུང་དུ་མི་རུང་ན། དྲི་མ་རྟག་པའམ། མི་རྟག་ཀྱང་སྤྱོང་བའི་ཐབས་མེད་པའམ། ཐབས་ཡོད་ཀྱང་མི་ཤེས་པའམ། ཤེས་ཀྱང་འབད་པ་མི་བྱེད་པ་ཡིན་དགོས་ན་རྣམ་པ་བཞི་ག་མི་སྲིད་པས་སྤྱངས་པ་ལེགས་པར་གྲུབ་པ་ཡིན་ནོ་ཞེས་སོ།། ༈ །།མངོན་མཐོའི་རྒྱུ་འབྲས་སྒྲུབ་ཚུལ། ཐར་ལམ་གསལ་བྱེད་ལས། དཔྱད་གསུམ་གྱིས་དག་པའི་ལུང་ཡིན་པ་དེ་ནི་རང་གི་བསྟན་བྱ་ལ་མི་བསླུ་བས་ཁྱབ་སྟེ། དཔེར་ན་བདེན་བཞི་སྟོན་པའི་གསུང་བཞིན། ཚུལ་ཁྲིམས་བསྲུང་བས་ལྷར་སྐྱེ་བར་སྟོན་པའི་སངས་རྒྱས་ཀྱི་གསུང་ཡང་དཔྱད་གསུམ་གྱིས་དག་པའི་ལུང་ཡིན་ནོ། དེ་ཚད་མ་ཡིན་པའི་རྒྱུ་མཚན་ཅི་ཡིན་ཞེ་ན། དོན་དེ་དག་ཇི་ལྟར་བསྟན་པ་ལྟར་ཁས་བླངས་པ་ལ་མངོན་སུམ་ཚད་མས་གནོད་པ་མེད་པ། དངོས་པོ་སྟོབས་ཞུགས་ཀྱི་རྗེས་དཔག་གིས་གནོད་པ་མེད་པ། ལུང་ལ་བརྟེན་པའི་རྗེས་དཔག་གིས་ཀྱང་གནོད་པ་མེད་པ། རང་ཚིག་སྔ་ཕྱི་འགལ་

བ་དང་དངོས་ཤུགས་འགལ་བས་ཀྱང་གནོད་པ་མེད་པའོ། །དོན་བསྡུས་ནས། ཤིན་ཏུ་ཟློག་གྱུར་སྟོན་པའི་བཅོམ་ལྡན་འདས་ཀྱི་གསུང་ཆོས་ཅན། རང་གིབསྟན་བྱ་ལ་མི་བསླུ་བ་ཡིན་ཏེ། དཔྱད་པ་གསུམ་གྱིས་དག་པའི་ལུང་ཡིན་པའི་ཕྱིར། བཞི་བརྒྱ་པར་སྟོང་ཉིད་སྟོན་པའི་གསུང་དཔེར་མཛད་ཅེས་གསུངས་སོ།། །།རྟེན་འབྲེལ་བསྟོད་པ་ལས། དོན་བཞིན་གཟིགས་ནས་ལེགས་གསུང་པ། །ཁྱོད་ཀྱི་རྗེས་སུ་སློབ་པ་ལ། །རྒུད་པ་ཐམས་ཅད་རིང་དུ་གྱུར། །ཉེས་ཀུན་རྩ་བ་ལྡོག་ཕྱིར་རོ། ཁྱོད་ཀྱི་བསྟན་ལས་ཕྱིར་ཕྱོགས་པས། །ཡུན་རིང་ངལ་བ་བསྟེན་བྱས་ཀྱང་། །ཕྱི་ཕྱིར་སྐྱོན་རྣམས་བོས་པ་བཞིན། །བདག་ཏུ་ལྟ་བ་བརྟན་ཕྱིར་རོ། །ཨེ་མའོ་མཁས་པས་འདི་གཉིས་ཀྱི། །ཁྱད་པར་ཁོང་དུ་ཆུད་གྱུར་པ། །དེ་ཚེ་རྐང་གི་ཁོང་ནས་ནི། །ཁྱོད་ལ་ཅི་ཕྱིར་གུས་མི་འགྱུར། །ཞེས་དང་། བསྔགས་འོས་བསྔགས་བསྟོད་ལས། །བཅོམ་ལྡན་དུས་ཀུན་གཏོགས་པའི་ཆོས། །རྣམ་ཀུན་འབྱུང་གནས་ཐམས་ཅད་ནི། ལག་

མཐིལ་སྐྱུ་རུ་ར་ལྟ་བུ། །ཁྱོད་ཀྱི་ཐུགས་ཀྱི་སྤྱོད་ཡུལ་གྱུར། །ཞེས་གསུངས་སོ།།

-0

།།འདི་ནི་བློ་དམན་འགའ་རེ་ལ་ཕན་ཕྱིར་དུ། དགེ་བའི་བཤེས་གཉེན་ཆེན་པོ་སྐྱོར་དཔོན་རིན་པོ་ཆེ་ནས་རྗེ་ཡབ་སྲས་ཀྱི་གཞུང་རྣམས་ལས་བཏུས་ཏེ་ཕྱོགས་བསྒྲིགས་སུ་མཛད་པ་དགེ་ལེགས་འཕེལ།།

BIBLIOGRAPHY

Co ne bla ma grags pa bshad sgrub
bLo rtags 'dres ma : Mind and Reasoning
Sermey Library, Sera Monastic University, 1998

rTags rigs rgyas pa : Detailed Exposition of Reasoning
Sermey Library, Sera Monastic University, 1998

dGe 'dun grub
Tshad ma rnam 'grel legs par bshad pa : An Explication of the Commentary to "Valid Cognition"

rGyal tshab rje dhar ma rin chen
rNam 'grel thar lam gsal byed : Clearing the Path to Liberation
Varanasi, 1995–96

mKhas grub chen po dge 'dun bstan dar ba
Phar phyin mtha' spyod spyi don : Analysis of Perfection of Wisdom
Sermey Library, Sera Monastic University, 1998

mKhas grub dge legs dpal bzang
rGyas pa'i bstan bcos tshad ma rnam 'grel gyi rgya cher bshad pa rigs pa'i rgya mtsho : Great Commentary; Ocean of Reasoning
Sermey Library, Sera Monastic University, 2000

Pha bong kha pa byams pa bstan 'dzin 'phrin las rgya mtsh
Liberation in Our Hands: Part Three—The Ultimate Goals,
Translated by Sermey Khensur Lobsang Tharchin with Artemus B. Engle
Mahayana Sutra and Tantra Press, 2001

dPal chos kyi grags pa
rGyas pa'i bstan bcos tshad ma rnam 'grel
Pramāṇavārttikakārikā : Commentary to "Valid Cognition"
Drebung Loseling Library Society, 2002

Supplementary Texts for the Study of the Perfection of Wisdom at Sera Mey Tibetan Monastic University, vol. 2

Trehor skyor dpon blo bzang dar rgyas
Thar 'dod rnams la snying ltar gces pa'i nyer mkho 'ga' zhig

Sermey Khensur Rinpoche Lobsang Tharchin

Sermey Khensur Rinpoche Lobsang Tharchin (1921–2004) was born in Lhasa, Tibet. He entered the Mey College of Sera Monastery at an early age and proceeded through the rigorous twenty-three-year program of Buddhist monastic and philosophical studies. Upon successful completion of the public examination by the best scholars of the day, Rinpoche was awarded the highest degree of Hlarampa Geshe with honors.

In 1954, he entered Gyu-me Tantric College. In 1959, Rinpoche went into exile. While in India, he became actively involved in Tibetan resettlement and education by developing a series of textbooks for the Tibetan curriculum and teaching at several refugee schools, including those at Darjeeling, Simla, and Mussoorie.

In 1972, Khensur Rinpoche came to the United States to participate in the translation of various Buddhist scriptures. Upon completion of this project, he was invited to serve as Abbot of Rashi Gempil Ling, a Buddhist temple established by Kalmuk Mongolians, in Howell, New Jersey. Rinpoche also founded the Mahayana Sutra and Tantra Center, with branches in Washington, D.C. and New York. Over the years he offered a vast range of Buddhist teachings on both Sutra and Tantra. In particular, every spring he would impart Lam Rim teachings for several weeks to accompany the Highest Yoga Tantra initiations he gave in the summer, followed by extensive explanations in the fall.

In 1991, Rinpoche served as Abbot of Sera Mey Monastery in South India. After his appointment there, where he accomplished a monumental work to improve the lives of the monks, he returned to the United States to resume the teaching of Mahayana Dharma, while continuing to help Sera Mey Monastery from afar.

On December 1st, 2004, on the 20th day of the 10th month of the Wood Monkey year 2131, Rinpoche passed and remained in his final meditation for five days. His holy body was cremated on Je Tsong Khapa Day, December 7th, 2004, at Rashi Gempil Ling, First Kalmuk Buddhist Temple in Howell, New Jersey.

Note about
TREHOR SKYOR DPON RINPOCHE BLO BZANG DAR RGYAS

In an earlier work (*Offering of the Mandala*), Khensur Rinpoche makes brief mention of this holy lama with reference to achieving Buddhahood:

"Many great beings both in India and Tibet have been able to accomplish this [enlightenment]. I'm sure that most of you have heard of the saint Milarepa who, although he had accumulated great sins during the earlier years of his life, was still able to attain perfect enlightenment in the latter part. In more recent times, a Tibetan Lama named Trehor Kyorpon, who escaped Tibet in the same year as the Dalai Lama, was able to attain perfect enlightenment during his lifetime. This *geshe* from Drepung Monastery passed away only a few years ago in Dalhousie."

Other titles published by
MAHAYANA SUTRA AND TANTRA PRESS

- Achieving Bodhichitta
- A Commentary on Guru Yoga
- Esencia del Lojong del Mahayana
- Essence of Mahayana Lojong Practice
- Essence of Nectar
- Key to the Treasury of Shunyata
- King Udrayana and the Wheel of Life
- Liberation in Our Hands
  Part One: The Preliminaries
- Liberation in Our Hands
  Part Two: The Fundamentals
- Liberation in Our Hands
  Part Three: The Ultimate Goals
- La Liberación en Nuestras Manos
  Primera parte: Los preliminares
- La Liberación en Nuestras Manos
  Segunda parte: Los fundamentos
- Nagarjuna's Letter
- Offering of the Mandala
- Pointing the Way to Reasoning
- Preparing for Tantra
- Principal Teachings of Buddhism
- Six-Session Guru Yoga
- Sublime Path to Kechara Paradise

For more information, visit our website at
http://www.mstp.us/